THE LAST REVOLUTIONARIES

The Last Revolutionaries

The Conspiracy Trial of Gracchus Babeuf and the Equals

LAURA MASON

Yale

UNIVERSITY PRESS

NEW HAVEN AND LONDON

Published with assistance from the Annie Burr Lewis Fund and from the foundation
established in memory of Calvin Chapin of the Class of 1788, Yale College.

Yale University Press books may be purchased in quantity for educational, business,
or promotional use. For information, please email sales.press@yale.edu (U.S. office)
or sales@yaleup.co.uk (U.K. office).

Set in Electra LH type by IDS Infotech Ltd.
Printed in the United States of America.

Library of Congress Control Number: 2021945492
ISBN 978-0-300-25955-1 (hardcover : alk. paper)

A catalogue record for this book is available from the British Library.

This paper meets the requirements of ANSI/NISO Z39.48-1992
(Permanence of Paper).

10 9 8 7 6 5 4 3 2 1

For Wendy
and
Max & Isabel

The republican is not a figure of eternity but of his own time; his paradise is here on earth, where he wants to enjoy liberty and happiness without delay . . . [because] all time in which he is denied such enjoyment is lost forever.

François-Noel Babeuf, *Journal de la liberté de la presse* 5 (1794)

To make revolution . . . is to conspire against an unacceptable state of things. . . . So long as the worthless has not been abolished and the good is not yet guaranteed, I will not admit that we are done making revolution. Or, better yet, I will not admit that we are done making revolution for the people.

Gracchus Babeuf, *Tribune of the People* 36 (1795)

For Wendy
and
Max & Isabel

The republican is not a figure of eternity but of his own time; his paradise is here on earth, where he wants to enjoy liberty and happiness without delay . . . [because] all time in which he is denied such enjoyment is lost forever.

François-Noel Babeuf, *Journal de la liberté de la presse* 5 (1794)

To make revolution . . . is to conspire against an unacceptable state of things. . . . So long as the worthless has not been abolished and the good is not yet guaranteed, I will not admit that we are done making revolution. Or, better yet, I will not admit that we are done making revolution for the people.

Gracchus Babeuf, *Tribune of the People* 36 (1795)

CONTENTS

CONTENTS

ACKNOWLEDGMENTS

Gracchus Babeuf believed ideas are born of community. Although he highlighted how they depend on past knowledge, he might just as well have explained how ideas are nourished by friendship, collegiality, and assistance in the present. During the many years I have worked on this book, I have been fortunate beyond measure in finding all that.

The three people to whom I dedicate this book gave special inspiration. My sister, Wendy Stella, consistently amazes me with her determination, generosity, and resilience, but it was her request for something to read that drew me forward more times than I can say. I hope some of the following pages will speak to her. As children, Max and Isabel enticed me to leave my desk and root myself in daily life. I am as grateful for that as I am for the wry, principled adults they have become. Perhaps they will find echoes within this book of some of what I continue to learn from them.

I have benefitted enormously from the comments of generous readers who pushed me to argue more sharply and speak more clearly. Laura Wexler tackled an early version of the full manuscript, advising on personalities and structure with an energy that sped me forward when it was badly needed. Tim Tackett's welcoming but reliably rigorous reading reminded me that I might yet say more to historians of the French Revolution. Charles Walton, whose enthusiasm and shared commitments have long buoyed this work, deepened my thinking about economics and social justice in particular. Suzanne Desan shared her own and her graduate students' thoughts on a penultimate version of the manuscript, offering precise, enthusiastic suggestions that encouraged not by hinting that I had fallen short but by expressing conviction that I could go further still.

In Athens, Georgia, Jonathan Davis, Sheri Smith, and Adele White posed questions about early chapters that long guided me. In Baltimore, I could not have managed without the sociability and enthusiastic critique of Patricia Meisol, Rita Costa-Gomez, Barbara Morrison, John Bainbridge, and Stephanie Citron. In Paris, Janet Skeslien Charles guided some early formulations with her distinctive eye for good prose. Historians whose feedback, conversation, and encouragement inspired me include Elizabeth Amann, Jack Censer, John Clarke, Stephen Clay, Natalie Davis, Bernard Gainot, Jeff Freedman, Katie Jarvis, Mette Harder, Tom Kaiser, Peter McPhee, Jeremy Popkin, Tip Ragan, Stéphanie Roza, Pierre Serna, and Todd Shepard. Francesca Rose offered last-minute assistance on illustrations, and Max Kwass-Mason provided invaluable IT advice. Many thanks to all of you.

Scholarly collectives that gave my work generous attention include Steven Kaplan's Early Modern Group at Cornell, among the first to discuss this project, on a snowy afternoon that seems almost a lifetime ago. Steve's characteristically searching commentary raised questions that I chewed over for years. Participants at the St. Quentin Babeuf conference listened enthusiastically and offered a glimpse of the unique network of French scholar-activists and activist-scholars to whom Babeuf continues to speak. I am grateful, too, for opportunities to discuss versions of this project with members of the "Impossible Settlement" conference organized by Judith Miller and Howard Brown at Emory University; the Research Triangle French Cultural Studies Group; the New York Area Modern Europe Reading Group, so amiably organized at that time by Rosemary Wakeman and Tip Ragan; Pierre Serna's French Revolution Seminar at Paris I; the Washington, DC, Old Regime Group; and the European Seminar in the Johns Hopkins History Department. Members of the Société archéologique, scientifique et littéraire du Vendômois gave me access to the Trinity Abbey, enlarging my sense of the physical space in which the Equals' trial took place.

The University of Georgia and Johns Hopkins University have been my institutional homes, offering resources, funding, and community. In particular, the History Department and the Film & Media Studies Program at Johns Hopkins gave me new room for intellectual growth at a key moment. I am grateful to all of my colleagues there for their warm welcome. I thank Gabrielle Spiegel, in particular, for the visionary leadership that made my move possible, and Linda DeLibero, who collaborated in that vision and became a friend in the process.

My research was generously funded by the University of Georgia and the UGA Willson Center for the Arts and Humanities, a Franklin College Faculty Development Grant, and an American Council of Learned Societies grant. Sabbatical leave from Johns Hopkins University (2012–13) gave me valuable time to write. Finally, my year as a fellow at the Columbia University Institute for Scholars at Reid Hall (2006–7) enabled research and writing within a lively intellectual community. My thanks to Danielle Haase-Dubosc, director of the Institute, Naby Avcioglu, and Mihaela Bacou for all they did to make that year so warmly productive.

Finally, there are the friends and family members who have sustained me with love and excellent conversation throughout: my sister, Cheryl Brown, and my mother, Sylvia Twomey; the many members of the Kwass family; Jenn, Aaron, and Maggie Thompson; Sabrina Bouarour; Marybeth Hamilton; Bryant Simon and Ann Marie Reardon; Steve Soper and Susan Rosenbaum; Clarissa Rose; and Jean Friedman. A shout-out, as well, to Jean Johnston and my fellows in her Saturday morning group who sustain strength and sanity, and never more so than in recent years.

There are not enough words for all that Michael Kwass has contributed, so I will be brief. His conversation, willingness to read, and generous feedback enhanced this work at every stage. More importantly, his sound convictions, steady presence, and friendship enrich my life.

Introduction

Because the rue de la Grande Truanderie abuts the central market in Paris, it was already crowded when Jean-Baptiste Dossonville landed there with hundreds of troops on a May morning in 1796. The police inspector's target was Gracchus Babeuf, a radical journalist who publicly denied the legitimacy of the sitting government. For six months, Babeuf had been urging the people to rise up and reignite the French Revolution. They must restore their stolen democracy, he argued in the pages of his *People's Tribune*, and sweep away private property. Only then would they realize the revolution's true aim: a world of perfect equality.

A police agent had gone after Babeuf when he began publishing such things in the fall, but the journalist slipped away and continued to incite from a hiding place in the city. Now, with an address provided by a police informant, Dossonville believed he had cornered Babeuf. To prevent another escape, the inspector stationed cavalry at both ends of the block, filled the street with foot soldiers, and discouraged sympathizers by circulating a rumor that the troops were going after highway robbers. Then he climbed to the third floor of his targeted building and rushed an apartment, where he found Babeuf writing quietly in a back room with two men standing nearby. "A look of utter dejection crossed all three faces," Dossonville would later say, but the men made no move to defend themselves. "Babeuf stood from his chair and cried out: *It's all over. Tyranny has won!*"

The authorities declared victory that afternoon. "A horde of thieves and murderers was plotting to slaughter legislators, members of government, commanders of the army of the interior, and all constituted authorities in Paris." A general massacre and pillage of the capital were to follow. "But remain calm, good citizens, the government is vigilant. It knows the conspiracy's leaders and their plan of attack." Police had arrested several suspects in addition to Babeuf. All would feel the full weight of the law.

Citizens heaved a collective sigh of relief. Newspapers crowed that "crime conspires in vain" and praised the government for standing guard against threatening violence. It was a moment of triumph for a regime struggling to restore peace and prosperity in the wake of revolution and war.[1]

The evanescence of that triumph would take all of France by surprise.

The arrest and trial of Gracchus Babeuf and sixty-four others, known as the Equals, took place in the shadow of the French Revolution. That revolution began in 1789 with high hopes of swift change, but resistance and radicalization prolonged it for years. By 1795, the battered National Convention that had led France through war, terror, and reaction was determined to stabilize the republic by ending the revolution. Legislators abolished their democratic constitution and called into being a more conservative government, the Directory. Inaugurated that fall, the Directory promised to heal the nation's bitter polarization, renew order, and guarantee rule of law. The arrest and trial of the Equals would be its first real test.

The situation became fraught in the wake of Babeuf's arrest. As police went after hundreds of old revolutionary militants, the right claimed that the arrests proved how much radicalism continued to threaten France. Democrats, to the Directory's left, expressed fear that the government was rousing political hysteria and insisted that Babeuf was a harmless eccentric incapable of pulling off a plot like the one described. The regime charged that such expressions of doubt were themselves conspiratorial and arrested more democrats.

By the time the trial opened in the winter of 1797, the case against Gracchus Babeuf and the Equals had become a media event that cascaded through pamphlets, populated newspaper columns, and filled broadsides pasted on city walls. The defendants found themselves on the national stage called into being by this publicity. Seizing that stage, they declared their innocence. They were not vicious conspirators for absolute equality, as prosecutors alleged, but patriots framed by a hostile administration for protecting free speech and defending the sovereignty of the people. Speaking to the nation through sympathetic newspapers, they mocked the court that tried them and celebrated the French Revolution. When prosecutors argued that they had been organizing a terror like the one that had borne away thousands a few years earlier, they countered that they were advocates for liberty.

The trial lasted for months, far longer even than the proceedings that had condemned the king of France. Standing before a high court in a remote provincial town, prosecutors and defendants looked beyond questions of guilt or innocence to interrogate the state of the nation. Was democracy possible without social equality? Could the republic guarantee the dignity of all citizens? And, in the dying light of revolution, they asked how to end years of upheaval without resorting to the coercion and tyranny the French Revolution was meant to abolish.

By the time verdicts were delivered, a full year after the first arrests, the trial had sapped the Directory's credibility, transformed the once marginalized journalist Babeuf into a national icon, and propelled the nation toward Napoleon Bonaparte. The latter would, in a few years, sweep away the last vestiges of the great republican experiment initiated by the French Revolution.

Why is all of this not better known?

The import of this trial was obscured by three men who wrote about the conspiracy that prompted it. The first was, ironically, the activist who immortalized Gracchus Babeuf: his former ally and co-defendant, Filippo Buonarroti. In an 1828 bombshell, *Babeuf's Conspiracy for Equality*, Buonarroti promised to tell all about the shadowy plot. Dismissing the Equals' courtroom plea of innocence decades before, Buonarroti affirmed the Directory's charges. He and Babeuf had organized with thousands to excite a new revolution that was about to explode when the Equals were denounced and arrested. Had it not been for their betrayal, the conspirators would have built a society of perfect equality whose every detail they had imagined. He revealed all of this now, Buonarroti explained, because most of his accomplices were dead and he wanted to preserve their aims for future generations.

It was a triumphant story of powerful, far-seeing militants who played a pivotal role in the French Revolution and missed their mark by a fraction. Much of it was invented. Buonarroti attributed his own ideas about perfect equality to Babeuf and inflated the small, disorderly scheme in which they shared to a national offensive that almost toppled the government. Arrests and trial became a pale epilogue to the formidable conspiracy.

A generation later, Karl Marx and Friedrich Engels built on Buonarroti's heroic narrative by naming Babeuf the first modern communist. The man who called himself a tribune tried to organize a nascent proletariat against private property, they argued, and in so doing transformed communism from utopian ideal to worldly aim. Interested in that innovation alone, and believing the conspiracy doomed to failure because it was historically premature, Marx and Engels had even less reason than Buonarroti to dwell on the trial.[2]

Activists, political theorists, and historians followed in their footsteps, excavating the origins of Babeuf's thought, exploring how he developed the communist idea, and debating whether he promised universal liberation or dictatorial horror. Taking Buonarroti's *Conspiracy* as gospel, they accepted the old plotter's words as true even when that demanded intellectual contortion to accommodate contradictory evidence. For these descendants, too, the trial was an afterthought.[3]

And yet, it was through their trial that Gracchus Babeuf and the Equals became part of the public record Buonarroti would later embroider. Without that cause célèbre, the Equals might well have faded away, actively hounded into silence or simply driven to retreat by a hostile and increasingly exclusive political world. Instead, they blazed brightly on a stage prepared by the government, and their memory lived on.

The trial of Gracchus Babeuf and the Equals offers far more, however, than the origin story of Buonarroti's book. It illuminates the world that excited the conspiracy and the government that pursued it. In particular, it explains why a regime meant to end the French Revolution perpetuated it instead, and how it destroyed the republic it was meant to preserve.

Sandwiched between the revolutionary Terror of 1793–94 that was associated with Maximilien Robespierre, and Napoleon Bonaparte's Empire in the next century, the Directory has long been the poor cousin of the revolutionary age. Generations of historians followed Napoleon's publicists in dismissing it as decadent and dysfunctional. Those who redeemed it in the late twentieth century did so less through correction than by celebration. The champions of the Directory claimed that it revitalized civil society, fostered commercialism, even nourished democracy. On the contrary, as the trial of the Equals suggests, the Directory tried to put the genie of revolution back in the bottle by dispelling political activism and minimizing aspirations to social equity. Believing it could whittle the republic's popular foundation to a splinter, the regime roused conspiracy, produced a trial that inflated the plot's importance, and helped drive the republic to ruin.[4]

If this appears too bitter a conclusion for the brilliant hopes excited in 1789, the history of the Equals' trial is not exclusively one of defeat. Their spirited opposition, democratic allies' imaginative defense, and activists' reformulation of civic commitments that the Equals came to embrace all underscore the resilience of resistance. Babeuf and the Equals may not have founded what they called "common good" and "perfect equality," but they bequeathed new aspirations for liberty and equality to contemporaries and generations that followed. Intellectuals and activists would appropriate, reformulate, and celebrate their ideas across the centuries.

This is a history of the French Revolution for the twenty-first century. The century before our own witnessed worldwide revolutionary struggle for liberation that brought down governments and whole empires, founded new regimes, and excited bitter resistance, inspiring historians of the French Revolution to see that event from the vantage point of their time. They asked about revolutionary origins, the nature of popular mobilization, how radicalization and resistance produced terror. By contrast, this century is dominated by rising authoritarianism that challenges representative government, equal justice, and social welfare across the globe as ordinary people fight tooth and nail for fundamental rights and basic necessities.[5]

The time has come to turn away from origins and mobilization to examine the end of the French Revolution. The Directory's assault on revolutionary promises of liberty, equality, and fraternity and its fatal attack on representative government are potent reminders that France did not just produce one of the modern world's first democratic republics. It generated, as well, a precocious example of how a republic destroys itself from within, underscoring the delicate nature of democracy. Seeing the Directory through the prism of the Equals' trial illuminates the unworthy collapse of France's first republic to a general on horseback just ten years after the astonishing popular defeat of the Bastille prison.

As the trial of the Equals illuminates the end of the French Revolution, it reframes the man who stood at its center: Gracchus Babeuf. It does so by setting aside Marxist claims that Babeuf's thought and activism were significant only in retrospect, to focus on his experience as a poor man in a revolutionary age.

As a commoner born "in the mud," Babeuf was both singular and exemplary. This ambitious autodidact confronted the rigid hierarchies of an old regime and was liberated, like millions of others, by the French Revolution. He became an activist, journalist, elected official, and bureaucrat, seizing opportunities produced by the times to improve his own, his family's, and his fellow citizens' condition. The extraordinary change he witnessed fed his hope for more. When the revolution reversed course, his hope encouraged resistance and continued radicalization. The repudiation of private property for which Babeuf would be remembered came late in life, produced by a private alchemy of deprivation, philosophical study, and revolutionary activism.

Babeuf's self-reflection, his ability to compose thousands of pages about what he witnessed, and his determination to preserve that record set him apart. But those practices tell us about more than just one man. They illuminate the suffering and commitment, high hopes and bitter disappointment he shared with fellow citizens across the revolutionary decade. Like the snapshot of the Directory offered by the Equals' trial, so the image Babeuf crafted of himself and his contemporaries speaks across centuries to our moment of political polarization and profound inequality.

Babeuf's experience underscores the terrible cost of poverty and disenfranchisement, and the dangerous game elites play when they accrue wealth, power, and privilege with little thought for their fellows. He warned even before 1789 that "terrible disparity between the fortunate above and the unfortunate below" fosters revolt. He would later add that the more egregious the inequity, the more radical the solution. Such pronouncements attested to the determination of the poor and disenfranchised, but they also counseled the wealthy and powerful on the wisdom of making concessions rather than driving a desperate people to revolt. The Equals reminded rich and poor alike that, in the words of one of their reluctant allies, "there is no possibility of true and enduring liberty without equality of rights."[6]

The trial of Gracchus Babeuf and the Equals suggests what we may yet learn from the French Revolution.

ONE

Must There Be Distinctions among Men?
(1760–92)

The region of Picardy lies in northern France, where it touches the English Channel in the west, between Calais and the river Somme, before swinging eastward to trace a broad crescent between Paris and Flanders, and finally bump up against the province of Champagne. The landscape changes from coast to hinterland as shoreline cliffs give way to gently undulating plains traversed by slow-moving rivers. The climate is mild and the soil rich. Such natural resources had, by the eighteenth century, been improved by centuries of intensive labor. Picardy's fertile ground bore wheat, oats, and rye to feed hungry Parisians to the south. Its towns housed textile works that turned out luxurious tapestries, popular linens, and homely workers' caps for all of Europe.[1]

Environmental advantage and human industry produced significant wealth. Affluent farmers lived in comfortably furnished houses, ate from pewter dishes, and wore sturdy woolen jackets to church. They owned draft animals; set aside grain, beans, and salt pork for lean winter months; and could even make loans to their less fortunate neighbors. In Picard towns, shopkeepers owned their places of business, and many merchants were wealthy enough to build elegant villas with private courtyards, like those that lined the rue Saint-Gilles in Abbéville.[2]

As riches accumulated at the upper reaches of Picard society, ordinary folk suffered. Many who helped create the region's wealth by planting and threshing or spinning and weaving were excluded from its benefits because they were unable to buy or rent the land, the price of which had risen steadily over the course of the eighteenth century. Those who had lost the smallholdings their parents or grandparents once sharecropped were reduced to working as hired hands on large estates. And yet, almost all were subject to the dues and taxes that weighed on commoners throughout France. Peasants paid rent on meager scraps of land, fees for its transfer, and a portion of their harvest in exchange for planting. Like landless laborers and hardworking artisans, they were liable to heavy taxes that funded the crown's costly wars and serviced its rising debt. On top of that, the government piled onerous consumption taxes on food, drink, salt, and tobacco. The church got its share in the form of a tithe taken annually from their gross harvest.

Taxes, dues, and tithes did not just weigh on ordinary working people but were baldly regressive, funneling money from society's base to its summit. The tithe more often enriched comfortable bishops in far-flung cities than local priests who lived in a state of poverty like that of the parishioners they tended. Nobles were fattened by rights to require tenants to use their commercial mills and bread ovens, and to exclude neighbors from wastelands rich with the firewood, nuts, and rough pasture that could make a world of difference to a family struggling to get by. Even the market for bread shifted resources upward, as rising prices for rough loaves emptied the pockets of working people while enriching large landholders who had surplus grain to sell. So it was that, among the abundant wheat fields, busy workshops, and opulent chateaux of Picardy, "high prices [and] shortages ravaged the . . . masses until they were completely exhausted."[3]

This was the world into which François-Noel Babeuf was born in 1760, "in the mud," he would later say. His mother, Marie-Catherine, was an illiterate village woman who married in her twenties, bore thirteen children, and saw nine of them die before reaching adulthood. His father, Claude, was a proud, earthy man several decades Marie-Catherine's senior, who tried to escape the difficult circumstances of his own youth by joining the army. He had deserted abroad and spent twenty years on the lam until an amnesty brought him home to a modest inheritance. When that money was gone, the retired soldier became a guard for a private tax agency. By the time their first child,

G . BABEUF

Agé de 34 ans .

François Bonneville, "Portrait of Gracchus Babeuf,"
1794(?). Source: BnF.

François-Noel, was born, Claude and Marie-Catherine were living in the
northern city of Saint-Quentin.[4]

Claude hoped to see his son rise in the world but had precious few resources to realize that dream. With a puny salary stretched thin by too many
mouths to feed, he had no money for proper schooling and no gift for culti-
vating patrons. So he joined his modest reserves of knowledge with a wellspring of brutality to bully an education into his boy. It was from his father,
François-Noel would recall, that he acquired literacy and a first taste of tyranny and resistance. "I keenly remember the martial tone and brutal ges-

tures with which he . . . persecuted my childhood, pushing me several times
to . . . curse his unhappy existence . . . And yet, my distaste was compensated by the satisfaction of passing for an eight-year-old prodigy. My small
pride was already so great that I sacrificed everything to the gratification of
earning acclaim from a public that did not know what it cost me."[5]

When the boy's willingness to sacrifice gave way to the adolescent's rebellion, Claude sent him to dig ditches. The "terrible hardship" of five years'
back-breaking labor persuaded the younger Babeuf "to seek a less exhausting way to earn a living," so he recovered his pen and apprenticed to a feudal notary.[6]

It was an odd professional debut for a youth who would become the most
radical egalitarian of his time, because the feudal notary's principal task was
to help nobles wring additional profit from their tenants by recovering
lapsed dues. It was work Babeuf would find difficult to justify, as if a poor
man pulling himself up in a hard world could freely choose how he did so.
He could, however, readily explain its impact on his thinking. "I found the
terrible mysteries of noble usurpation in the dust of the feudal archives,
which is why I became feudalism's most terrible opponent under the new
regime."[7]

However odd the beginning, it was successful. Bright and ambitious,
Babeuf established his own practice in just three years and won an important commission to investigate the records of the chateau Damery. As he
lodged there to complete the work in 1781, he began to read philosophy in
the well-stocked library — "Voltaire and Plato, Aristotle and Jean-Jacques
[Rousseau]" — and met a serving woman named Marie-Anne Lenglet. Babeuf was rising quickly in the world and handsome, with deep-set blue eyes,
a fine straight nose, and thick brown hair that the chateau women fussed
over. Perhaps Marie-Anne liked his looks or his way with words or his tena-
cious determination. He may have been drawn to her grit, which he thought
characteristic of country women, or her steady resourcefulness. They became lovers and married a month before the birth of their daughter, Sofie.
He was twenty-two and she was twenty-six when they formalized a partner-
ship that would be exceptional in any age for its mutual respect and profound loyalty.[8]

The little family settled in the town of Roye sometime in 1782 or 1783. Babeuf was soon earning enough to rent an office and support them all, including a second child named Robert, as he tried to put himself on more equal footing with the local elites. Roye was a small town dominated by families who served its law court, a tight-knit group that socialized and intermarried, and did not welcome upstarts. Babeuf applied twice to join them in Roye's Masonic lodge, where nobles played at egalitarianism by mingling with distinguished commoners, and he was twice refused. When he asked a local count for whom he was working if they could share meals, he got a frosty reply. "If it does not suit you, Sir, to eat with my servants, and you cannot find any place in town to take a meal, do not think you can make some arrangement with me."[9]

Relief from such small-town pretension came in the form of a corresponding membership in the provincial academy of Arras. Located about fifty miles north of Roye, Arras hosted one of dozens of academies that encouraged reform by publicizing the novel ideas of the Enlightenment. Regular members, most of whom belonged to the same narrow elite that dominated Roye, used its library, heard lectures, and participated in essay competitions that posed questions practical "Is it useful to reduce the number of roads surrounding the villages in the province of Artois?" and abstract, like the one Jean-Jacques Rousseau so famously answered in Dijon: "Has the restoration of the sciences and arts tended to purify morals?"[10]

Corresponding memberships in the Academy permitted less affluent people to borrow reading materials by mail and to exchange ideas with its presiding secretary, an energetic noble named Ferdinand Dubois de Fosseux. Babeuf was awarded one such membership in 1785, which allowed him to read more widely and sharpen his critical skills in letters to Dubois that trace his deepening thought on subjects that would dominate his life: the causes, consequences, and remedy of poverty.

Babeuf was not alone in reflecting on poverty, for it was a subject that was coming to be understood in new ways in the eighteenth century. Although France no longer suffered famine or plague, the land could not support its growing population. Rising prices and stagnant wages subjected a growing number of families to perpetual fear of hunger and permanent threat of ruin by illness, accident, or a few bad harvests.

The working poor of Picardy responded to their decline by committing small acts of resistance, helping themselves to the bounty of forests or threatening wealthy families whose enrichment they understood to come at their expense. Philosophers and government administrators wrote books that treated misery not as the inevitable curse Christians traditionally imagined, but as a social failing subject to rational solution. Depending on their inclinations, these reformers denounced the laziness of the poor and endorsed beggars' prisons or decried the greed of the rich to advocate for more work and better wages. The variety of solutions multiplied across the century.[11]

Babeuf tackled the issue in an early letter to Dubois, written in the summer of 1786, which fused the intimate experience of hardship with his growing knowledge of philosophy. Gesturing to philosopher Jean-Jacques Rousseau's essay on the origins of inequality, Babeuf argued that humans have a natural right to subsistence which entitles them to more than the "privation from cradle to grave" he witnessed in Picardy. But respect for that right had been smothered by a hunger for property that created monopolies on the land and deprived many households of essential goods. "There is such terrible disparity between the fortunate above and the unfortunate below . . . that the victims of this monstrous inequality cannot help but complain." Concluding with what might seem clairvoyant were it not so firmly rooted in local resistance, Babeuf warned that ideas of "reform or revolt" take root "in the minds of those who resent or fear the state of things."[12]

A permanent solution was necessary, Babeuf argued. He did not, however, imitate ancient advocates of agrarian law by proposing that large estates be seized and redistributed. Such radical change would excite war, and, in any case, farming large parcels of land was more efficient. But the alternative he imagined showed him moving away from the notions of private property and paid labor he would ultimately reject.

Babeuf argued that property-holders should create cooperatives to share costs, labor, and wealth to everyone's benefit. Members "would make more enlightened improvements because there is more [knowledge] in twenty heads than in one, and all would be more energetic because no one would want to be accused of being a weakling . . . On a collective farm, everything is done on time because there are always plenty of people ready and willing to work." Such a system would improve the condition of whole families. "We would no longer see poor old women, frighteningly thin and dirty, herding a few scabby cows from which they hoped for a bit of milk . . . [or] malnourished mothers destroying their health . . . [by] prostituting their breasts to the town's babies."[13]

The last dig in that letter targeted a social order that benefited men like the noble Dubois, which may be why Babeuf did not send it. Instead, he engaged in tentative dialogue about literary points of grammar, edging toward more direct criticism of inequality as his confidence grew. In the spring of 1787, he sent Dubois a pamphlet on military organization whose judgments the latter thought too sharp to publish, and he proposed a question for the academy's annual essay competition that asked whether the abolition of property would foster social equilibrium. Then, in the fall of that year, Dubois shared word of a prospectus entitled *The Herald of Worldwide Change*.[14]

Penned by a lawyer named Nicolas Collignon, the prospectus promised a book with gloriously utopian remedies for poverty. Collignon did not just advocate for sufficient food to keep poor bodies alive but dreamed of satisfying meals that provided meat, vegetables, fine wines, and tasty desserts. He did not envision spartan shelter for the unhoused but imagined warm, clean, spacious dwellings. Publicly celebrating the right to subsistence that Babeuf reflected on privately, Collignon concluded that it could be realized through the equal division of labor, goods, and knowledge. "Whoever does not work, does not deserve to eat." Such a system would simplify laws and eliminate the need for policing because crime would vanish when "everyone is fed, lodged, clothed, and raised properly."[15]

Dubois laughed at the ideas as he described them, but Babeuf found cause for serious reflection. Giving voice to his mounting determination to address inequality, he compared Collignon's prospectus to a proposal for uniform laws of succession that Dubois had also shared. The latter was far less compelling, Babeuf argued, because inheritance was a source of inequality. Any standardization of it would be a "puny remedy" for a significant ill, which would not "prevent my children from being born penniless and in need while the children of my millionaire neighbor open their eyes on a world overflowing with things."

Collignon, Babeuf continued, saw the more significant disparities that plagued their world. Alluding to the philosopher Rousseau, Babeuf demanded: "Why give greater consideration to the [man] who carries a sword than to the one who forged it? Did nature, in giving wing to our species, impose laws different from those that guide other creatures? Is one individual meant to be less well nourished, less well dressed, less well housed than another?" That the author of the *Herald* did not think so was visible in his proposal for equal enjoyment of goods. "Hurrah!" Babeuf concluded. "I will be among the first to populate this new republic."[16]

Dubois replied with polite condescension. "I appreciate your reflection on the different projects I sent you. Sadly, the one that pleases you most is not practical, and the closer one looks, the more clear it becomes that this is a dream." The secretary might have thought Babeuf a dreamer, too, because, no matter how well informed by his own experience of poverty, the latter did not offer practical solutions either.[17]

He would do so shortly. Remembering Collignon's promise of food that fills the belly and satisfies the senses, Babeuf would keep pace with a world whose means and expectations for change were undergoing dramatic transformation.

The French monarchy was mired in debt, thanks to decades of military adventuring and expensive borrowing, and a cruelly inequitable system of taxation that sheltered the wealthy from the regime's heaviest taxes. When the crown tried to address its deficits by demanding that nobles renounce their tax exemptions, the latter replied that they alone could not authorize such fundamental reform. The king must consult the nation. Having exhausted all other possibilities by 1789, Louis XVI convoked the Estates General, a representative body that had not met for almost two centuries. He commanded his subjects to elect deputies and draft grievance lists to guide their labor, allowing censorship to lapse. Proposals for reform poured forth.

Twelve hundred men representing the traditional orders of clergy, nobility, and commoner descended on Versailles in May with a historic sense of mission. Within a few weeks, the Estates encountered the first of many challenges that would radicalize and divide its members. Negotiations stalled over how delegates of each order were to vote, and the commoners found themselves shut out of their meeting hall. Rightly describing themselves as representatives of "ninety-six one-hundredths" of the nation, they refused to disperse, renamed themselves a National Assembly, and invited the other estates to unite with them. The king capitulated after several tense days, ordering nobles and clergy to join the iconoclasts. The new Assembly went to work, its labors publicized by pamphlets, newspapers, and engravings that were pouring across France.

Political negotiation stalled again in July. Because the crown had been amassing troops near Versailles for weeks, the dismissal of popular reform minister Jacques Necker excited fears that a royal coup was imminent. Parisians mobilized, pillaging weapons from local arms depots before marching on the fortress-like Bastille prison to demand its gunpowder. When bargaining degenerated to battle, the crowd defeated the king's soldiers. The astonishing victory, on the afternoon of 14 July 1789, forced the mortified crown to withdraw its troops and recall Necker. The Assembly returned to work.

Babeuf arrived in Paris a few days later. As he watched an explosive combination of popular activism and elite legislation transform reform into revolution, he entered a world that would change his life and galvanize his thinking.

It was an abrupt departure from the private sorrow and disappointment that had crowded the preceding years. Babeuf's beloved daughter Sofie, his little "masterpiece of nature," died suddenly in 1787, leaving him hobbled by grief. His professional life began to spiral downward not long afterward, when a local marquis named Soyecourt canceled work he had commissioned from Babeuf and refused even to reimburse expenses already incurred with a claim that the latter was incompetent. Babeuf ceded to outrage by suing for breach of contract. It was a reckless decision, because the court was peopled with Soyecourt's cronies, who ruled in the marquis's favor. As word spread of the case, other clients reneged on their bills.[18]

The entire family tumbled into the poverty Babeuf believed they had escaped, felled by privileged impunity. By the spring of 1789, they were living in Roye's working-class district. As Babeuf cast about for new ways to support them, he took up a pamphlet he had drafted a year earlier and added an introduction that linked the land survey reforms he proposed to current debates over taxation.[19]

The new introduction returns to the unequal distribution of resources Babeuf had discussed with Dubois a couple of years earlier, replacing the utopian solutions he had championed then with practical reform. The state ought to abolish dues imposed by nobles and clergy, he argued, to make itself the sole custodian of taxation. Then it should simplify and equalize, levying one proportional tax on land and another on persons. Finally, it ought to redistribute wealth downward by investing the monies it accumulated in public works that would benefit ordinary folk. The new methods of land survey he described, Babeuf promised, would make such change possible.[20]

Babeuf arrived in Paris in July 1789 to negotiate publication of this pamphlet, which he called *The Permanent Land Register*. When not consulting with printers, he traveled to nearby Versailles to watch the Assembly deliberate and to marvel at its assault on the stark injustice of the Old Regime. "People say out loud that they no longer want nobles or feudal titles or chateaux or high clergy," he wrote to Marie-Anne. "They are right many times over and I applaud it." Understanding that his career as a feudal notary would be swept away with the old order it served, Babeuf was no less enthusiastic. "I am even ready to lend a hand to something that would overturn my own stew pot. The selfish will call me crazy, but no matter."[21]

As was true of many men in the Assembly, however, Babeuf's passion for change was tinged with uneasiness about the crowds that helped make it possible. The victors of the Bastille, believing its commander had ordered his troops to fire on them, decapitated the man and paraded his bloody head through the streets. During Babeuf's stay, another crowd beheaded conservative minister Joseph Foulon and stuffed straw into the dead mouth, to avenge the man's alleged jeer that the hungry could eat hay. It was a ferocity rooted in fear and suffering, Babeuf explained to Marie-Anne. "I understand that the people take justice into their own hands, which I approve so long as that justice is satisfied by punishing the guilty. But must it be so cruel? Punishments of every sort—quartering, torture, the wheel, the stake, the whip, the post, executioners everywhere—have corrupted us! Instead of policing us, our masters turned us into barbarians because that is what they are themselves."[22]

Legislators would reflect on such issues in coming years with less acumen and far less charity, debating how to deal with crowds whose force they required but whose violence they could not control. Babeuf would return to such issues as well, asking with growing urgency how to channel the popular desire for justice into enduring rights for all.

An opportunity to tackle these issues awaited on Babeuf's return to Roye in the fall of 1789. He found the town up in arms over commercial duties long hated for inflating the price of necessities like salt and soap, and perceived necessities like tobacco, wine, and beer. The duties were inequitably distributed, their levy humiliating, and punishment for evading them cruel and violent. All of that had long deepened Picard resentment, encouraging electors in the region to demand in 1789 that the Estates General abolish the duties. When word came in July that Parisians had sacked their customs barriers, Picard crowds attacked their own customs houses and local administrators ceased assessing goods. The National Assembly pushed back, insisting that indirect taxes remain in force until the new order was organized. When authorities in Roye tried to resume assessments, they met with fierce resistance from brewers, tavern hosts, and innkeepers.[23]

Babeuf saw in all of this twinned opportunities to improve the popular condition and to support his own family by working as an activist. He may have been drawn to the conflict, as well, by knowledge that the municipal authorities under fire included the very men who had almost ruined him by dismissing his case against the marquis de Soyecourt a few years earlier. So, with the same talent for linking immediate reform to broader political principle advertised in his *Permanent Land Register*, Babeuf drafted a petition to the National Assembly pointing out that excises contradicted the equitable taxation deputies claimed to defend.

The argument was not meant just to win legislative acquiescence but also to educate fellow citizens. Babeuf traveled from town to town for months, collecting signatures for his petition and encouraging activism with passionate public speeches until violence broke out in the spring of 1790. By then, he had become so closely associated with the opposition that he was accused of inciting the violence and imprisoned.

The Roye municipal authorities resumed assessments by force at about the same time, but the dispute was not over. When agitation intensified in Picardy and elsewhere, the National Assembly backed down, and Babeuf was freed in midsummer after Parisian militants threatened to demonstrate on his behalf. He returned to Roye and leapt once more into the fray, this time taking the side of Picard peasants who challenged monopolies on the land, like those he had long criticized, by demanding access to vacant properties and freedom from lingering feudal dues.[24]

The activism was contentious and occasionally dangerous, but also exciting and informative. It enhanced Babeuf's appreciation of what ordinary people could accomplish and raised his hopes for what they might yet do. It was not, however, lucrative. Babeuf's status as a militant frightened off clients for whom he might have advocated as sales of his *Permanent Land Register* languished and other sources of income proved hard to come by.

Poverty dogged the family. Another daughter had been born in 1788, named Sophie after her dead sister, and a second son in 1790. Babeuf and Marie-Anne cherished the children but could barely meet their needs. She took odd jobs, borrowed when able, and ducked creditors. He traveled to rally activists and look for work, writing letters home punctuated with worry. "I cannot tell you how much it pains me to leave you in such a state," he told Marie-Anne at an especially difficult moment. "We can only hope this will be the last obstacle we face."[25]

Despite this hardship, Babeuf's thinking about politics was maturing quickly. Musing in a neatly penned notebook, he asked to whom political power belonged and how it was to be exercised. Such questions would haunt revolutionaries to the very end of the decade.

With the Declaration of the Rights of Man and Citizen of 1789, legislators had announced that sovereignty "resides essentially in the nation," adding that "no body nor individual may exercise authority that does not expressly emanate from it." How exactly was that statement of principle to be realized? Who was considered a member of the nation? Did all have the same right to share in governance? How were they to "confer authority"? As the National Assembly debated all this, deputies heard speeches for and against extending political rights to those who were not wealthy, white, male, or Christian.

Babeuf weighed in, quietly, in his notebook, making a case for popular democracy informed by the activism around him and, quite probably, by the writings of Gabriel Bonnot de Mably. That philosopher, who died almost forgotten in 1785, had found a new audience in 1789 among readers excited by his radical reflection on popular will and political change. Decades before the taking of the Bastille, Mably had argued that government can only be legitimated by popular consent. And because popular rights are perpetually threatened by the powerful, he added, foresight and determination to safeguard them remain forever necessary.[26]

Babeuf echoed Mably by defining popular sovereignty as something wrested from a universal "penchant for domination" that requires a "machine" to protect it from the perpetual "state of war between the governed and the governors." Believing the National Assembly such a machine, Babeuf thought all citizens should choose its members and was outraged when legislators rejected universal suffrage. "Liberty, that most precious of rights," he objected, "consists of nothing other than obeying laws formulated by oneself or one's chosen representatives. Where there are no rights, there are no duties."[27]

Even had universal suffrage been granted, Babeuf is unlikely to have thought that a sufficient guarantee of popular participation. Recalling the activism he witnessed in Paris in 1789 and had encouraged in Picardy in 1790, he aspired to a democracy founded on more comprehensive engagement. All citizens—and Babeuf seems to have included women—must be able to attend Assembly meetings and weigh in on legislators' debates, for "who can say where the best counsel will be found?" They should be able to veto laws, suggest improvement of the Constitution that shaped their lives, and be guaranteed the free speech necessary to express their will and expose plots against it.[28]

Like his embrace of democracy, Babeuf's evolving thought about improving social welfare and enhancing social equality was informed by his reading of philosophy and galvanized by the impact of revolutionary events. For, shortly after initiating the political transformation of France, the National Assembly proceeded to reconfigure its social order, too.

As word of the Bastille's defeat spread through the countryside in the summer of 1789, rural panic led to the looting of chateaux and destruction of feudal records. The Assembly, determined to cut short what it believed was popular expropriation, took the initiative on the night of 4 August by declaring "the feudal regime ... abolished in its entirety." With that, it launched a sweeping reconstitution of property.

The Assembly shattered the foundations of the nobility by annulling dues and privileges on which the latter's wealth and status had long been founded. Nobles could no longer restrict access to forests and waterways they did not own or require locals to use their commercial mills and ovens or exact unpaid labor from tenants. They lost judicial and administrative offices from which they and their forebears had drawn power and income. Many were promised indemnities for what was so abruptly abolished, but payment was often ignored, and those who emigrated suffered still greater loss when their properties were confiscated as spoils of war.

The Catholic church was subject to even more comprehensive expropriation. The Assembly suppressed the tithe and nationalized the church, seizing and selling its vast landholdings to fill government coffers and increase France's population of small property owners. If the latter projects were not entirely successful, the vast reconfiguration of ownership was no less thoroughgoing.[29]

These events were accompanied by heated debate that suggested just how arbitrary the Assembly's activity had rendered the idea of property. How it was to be defined and how it was to be distributed seemed suddenly up for grabs as legislators insisted on the inviolability of some forms and swept away others. Radicals advocated for still more comprehensive redistribution by calling for the agrarian law of ancients. According to Tiberius and Caius Gracchus in second-century BCE Rome, agrarian law could ameliorate inequality by making vacant wastelands available to the poor for farming. A more radical variant associated with Lycurgus of Sparta was intended to abolish inequality entirely by confiscating and redistributing all land. Both forms were debated and frequently confused prior to the Revolution. The subject became more bitterly contentious after the Assembly struck down privilege, conservatives insisting that any distribution of wasteland was but a first step to expropriation. Tensions mounted steadily until the mere mention of agrarian law was enough to earn hisses and denunciation.[30]

Babeuf knew of agrarian law, had even reflected on and rejected it in his unsent letter to Dubois of 1786. Now, as the Assembly redefined property, his thinking radicalized. Revisiting the natural right to subsistence that Rousseau had elaborated and Mably affirmed, Babeuf argued that "every individual has a natural right to what he requires to survive. Survival is inseparable from food, therefore the individual has a right to livelihood. [It] also depends on liberty, because whatever keeps the unfree in a state of dependence obstructs their ability to preserve themselves." Since no one might legitimately deprive his fellows of subsistence, the landholding minority must offer food and work to the landless majority. Any who found such a duty inconvenient, Babeuf added, might keep in mind that gross inequality rendered property vulnerable to those "whose astonishing force is capable of the worst excesses if deprived of labor and income."[31]

The argument, in substance and fiery conclusion, was much like that of Babeuf's unsent letter to Dubois in 1786. This time, however, he did not imagine that the good faith of large landholders would be sufficient. Instead, he proposed a modest form of agrarian law. "One could declare by civil law that all [abandoned land] would become the inviolable property of any person . . . prepared to occupy it and invest the labor necessary to make nature's gifts bloom."[32]

Babeuf went still further in a letter to Picard legislator J. M. Coupé, in fall 1791. Abandoning all notion of private property in land, he encouraged Coupé to embrace the radical variant of agrarian law. "At birth, every person should receive a portion sufficient [for survival], like air and water, which he does not bequeath to his heirs at death but returns to society." Such a world, Babeuf added, echoing Collignon's heady promises, would render law obsolete by sweeping away the discord of inequality. Was not the purpose of revolution, after all, to improve everyone's condition? "What is society's aim . . . [if] not to insure its members' greatest well-being?"[33]

That Babeuf understood his ideas to be controversial is suggested by his discussing them sotto voce with Coupé. But he was optimistic about the future. Looking to the rising political star Maximilien Robespierre, he badly misread that deputy's political convictions by insisting that he, too, was "a great agrarian" who only hedged on the issue because he understood that "the time is not yet come." Soon, Babeuf concluded confidently, all would speak openly of such things.[34]

Throughout the revolution's astonishing early years, citizens assumed the king was on their side. That changed on the night of 21 June 1791, when the royal family slipped away from the Tuileries Palace, leaving a letter that disavowed all Louis XVI had claimed to support. "The king does not think it possible to govern a kingdom . . . by the means established by the National Assembly." When servants discovered the royals' absence, the news swept the city with an audible roar. The municipal council sat for days without break, the National Assembly governed alone, and citizens abandoned the respectful terms they once used for their king to call him, instead, a "liar," a "coward," and a "traitor."[35]

Louis and Marie-Antoinette were stopped almost twenty-four hours later, more than a hundred miles east of the capital and apparently headed for Austrian lands. The man who frustrated their flight was a sharp-eyed stableman named Jean-Baptiste Drouet, who recognized the king from images printed on paper money and rallied local forces to detain him. Louis XVI and Marie-Antoinette were returned to Paris under armed guard. Drouet became a national hero, acquiring status that would unexpectedly shape Babeuf's fate years later.

In the summer of 1791, it was the king's fate that concerned the nation. Legislators fearful of abolishing a thousand-year-old monarchy and unwilling to abandon the constitution they had labored over for almost two years agreed at last to the fiction that Louis XVI had been kidnapped. Rather than deposing him, they organized an elaborate ceremony in which they formally adopted France's first written constitution and the king swore to protect it. The event, in the fall of 1791, rang hollow.

The revolution's way forward became narrower still in the spring of 1792, when France declared war on a hostile Austria. The effort did not begin well. Military defeats accumulated, seasoned officers defected, and fear mounted that Louis XVI and Marie-Antoinette sided with the enemy. Unwilling to be ruled by a man they considered a traitor, ordinary Parisians joined with recently mobilized soldiers and members of the National Guard

to storm the Tuileries palace on 10 August 1792. The National Assembly ratified the uprising by arresting the king and queen, and organizing Europe's
first popular democratic elections. All free male citizens over the age
of twenty-five would be eligible to vote. When representatives to the new
National Convention gathered in September, they affirmed France's second revolution in three years by abolishing the monarchy and declaring a
republic.

From the calling of the Estates General early in 1789, public activism galvanized Babeuf's thinking. Having reflected on the causes and consequences
of poverty, he was inspired to translate philosophical critique into modest
suggestions for reform. As he became an activist, battling alongside Picard
brewers and peasants in 1789 and 1790, he came to appreciate the power of
direct action. As he witnessed the abolition of Old Regime privilege and the
seizure of church lands, Babeuf saw a dramatic and inspiring realization of
the philosophical claim that property might be reorganized for society's
greater good. He would continue to reflect on the relationship between
popular democracy and social welfare as the revolution expanded and contracted in years to come.

In the fall of 1792, the revolution was expanding. Elections and the declaration of a republic had thrown open the doors of power to millions of new
men, Babeuf among them. He was elected to local office in Picardy, testimony to his renown among newly enfranchised citizens and his capacity to
propose reform that was progressive but not too radical. He campaigned for
universal education, guaranteed employment, and public assistance, but
breathed not a word of agrarian law.[36]

In the months that followed, Babeuf gained valuable experience of formal politics. Picardy was deeply divided between eager militants like him
and conservative elites like those he had so long challenged, men with
whom Babeuf collaborated and against whom he argued while helping to
mobilize troops and organize public welfare. He accused opponents of royalism when tensions ran high and, impatient with centuries of injustice,
tried to hasten change. He criticized a local theatrical troupe for staging a
farce that did not encourage the right political principles, and he publicly

burned old tapestries and portraits he considered "symbols of despotism." That such activity did not always win locals' affection is suggested by "the jeers and threats" of the hostile crowd that greeted his bonfire of luxuries. Then, more dangerous antagonists swung into view.[37]

Sometime in the fall of 1792, Babeuf had notarized a fraudulent bill of sale. Whether he did so out of genuine ignorance or in an effort to block a purchase by land speculators is impossible to know. His adversaries assumed the worst and capitalized on it, seizing this opportunity to be rid of an abrasive rival. A local council investigated the charges and strained all credibility by exonerating every party to the phony transaction except for the man who notarized it. Early in 1793, a local court condemned Babeuf to twenty years in irons.

By then he was on the run.[38]

TWO

Hope and Despair (1793–95)

Babeuf's flight took him to Paris, where the French Revolution was expanding at breakneck speed. Speakers appealed to passersby in public squares, singers roared out the *Marseillaise* from street corners, and radical journalist Jean-Paul Marat promised to lay bare "the very souls" of the nation's enemies while his counterpart Jacques-René Hébert demanded cheap bread, "for fuck's sake." Politics had become integral to daily life as revolutionaries competed to set the nation's agenda.[1]

In Paris, the most numerous activists were sans-culottes. If their name, which signaled the absence of upper-class breeches, and their depiction in newspapers, speeches, and popular engravings suggested that they were working people, sans-culottes were in practice a more varied group. They included artisans and tradespeople, but also radical journalists like Marat and Hébert, local politicians, and militants known as Enragés, all united in the fight for affordable food, adequate work, and fair wages.

Sans-culottes were also proponents of direct democracy. Like Babeuf, they did not think voting was a sufficient expression of sovereignty, so they petitioned, marched, and insisted that they be able to veto legislation and recall deputies from a National Convention they defined as "composed of men paid to make the laws . . . we ask for." Sans-culottes were able to realize some of the democratic practices they aspired to thanks to the capital's forty-eight sectional assemblies, former administrative districts that had become vital nodes of Parisian political life by 1793. In times of calm, sectional

Jean-Baptiste Lesueur, "Republican Meal in Paris," 1794. Source: Musée Carnavalet, Paris.

assemblies offered places where neighbors could read and talk together, fostering the community they galvanized when crises of rising prices or "counter-revolution" struck.[2]

Sectional assemblies were not the only centers of political life. There were also clubs organized by age, like the Young Friends of the Republic, or by sex, such as the well-known Society of Revolutionary Republican Women, or, most commonly, by political opinion. The most powerful club was, by 1793, that of the Jacobins. Although its well-educated, well-connected, and relatively well-to-do members did not mingle regularly with sans-culottes, as the Enragés did, or make membership readily accessible to them, like the Cordeliers, the Jacobin Club welcomed working people as audiences for its meetings, advocated noisily for their interests, and was able to follow through on its promises thanks to the many members who sat on the Paris Municipal Council or were deputies to the National Convention.

Jacobins were not, however, without political challengers in the winter of 1793. They were locked in what would prove deadly rivalry for leadership of the National Convention with Girondin colleagues. Opposition between these factions had simmered for more than a year, fed by policy differences and personal animosity. If Jacobins were unfair in caricaturing Girondins as enemies of the people and the republic, Girondins won no advantage in Paris by accusing sans-culottes of being unruly radicals.[3]

This was the world into which Babeuf plunged at the beginning of 1793. All that he would witness there in the next two years—the most ambitious, tumultuous, and divisive of the decade—would accelerate his reflection on democracy, subsistence, and popular activism. First, however, he had to find some means of support. Babeuf arrived with uncanny speed at the door of one of the capital's most volatile figures, Enragé ally Claude Fournier, "the American," and was soon employed as the man's secretary. It was an excellent perch from which to follow the bitter contest over food that was convulsing Paris.[4]

Feeding France was a long-standing concern of the Old Regime that acquired new dimension at mid-century with rising debate about freeing the grain trade. Grain was crucial to the nation as a primary source of calories and powerful economic force. The crown regulated its trade by controlling prices when shortage struck and ensuring that the restive capital had sufficient flour, measures royal administrators considered essential for public order but which the king's subjects believed were among his duties to his people.[5]

Because the production, sale, and purchase of grain were so important, reformers hoping to encourage economic growth looked to that market first. The most iconoclastic of them were the Physiocrats, who wanted landholders to manage their properties without state interference and hoped for unfettered negotiation between buyers and sellers of grain. Liberalizing that trade, Physiocrats insisted, would allow the economy to flourish naturally. Admittedly, the poor could suffer as free trade drove prices upward, but, they promised, everyone would benefit over the long term.

These ideas were put to the test when royal administrators in the 1760s abolished long-standing regulation. Prices shot upward in a movement intensified by poor harvests, creating scarcity that, in turn, excited unrest. The crown backed down, but not for long. In 1774, royal minister Jacques Turgot provoked the Flour War when he took his own stab at freeing the grain trade. Once more, soaring prices roused hungry crowds. When consumers blocked transports to sell the grain at what they considered a fair price, authorities charged them with being irrational and deployed armed guards. Disdain and violence intensified the conflict, which finally forced the crown to abandon its project and restore market controls that lasted until 1789.[6]

As crowds protested the effects of freeing the grain trade, philosophers criticized the thinking behind it. Many of the latter shared Physiocrats' aspiration to foster economic growth but thought the crown should encourage more equitable change by creating jobs and raising wages to protect consumers as they entered a newly freed market in subsistence goods. In this way, the Physiocrats' critics argued, the king could reconcile liberty with protection, public good with private interest.[7]

The philosopher Mably, who would become Babeuf's intellectual lodestar, was particularly outraged. He charged that the Physiocrats preferred abstraction to real-world conditions and so failed to appreciate that the poor could not buy grain when prices rose. They could only starve. The Physiocrats' plan was impractical because it depressed a market they claimed to encourage. Worse yet, it was immoral because it violated a natural right to subsistence that philosophers like Jean-Jacques Rousseau rightly defended. "If the poor are as much citizens as the rich," Mably argued, "who would be foolish enough to pretend that a healthy politics ought not to dictate how the rich enjoy their fortunes to prevent them from oppressing the poor?"[8]

These issues were taken up again when the French Revolution disrupted the nation's already faltering economy. Rural unrest, disordered systems of transport, and the complexities of wartime mobilization weakened trade in meat and grain. Inflation and shortage of coin hindered buying and selling. By the fall of 1792, the fight for liberty by enslaved people in France's Caribbean colonies had cut into supplies of sugar and coffee. As shortages and prices rose, sans-culottes protested, broadening the debates about property that had been roiling France since the abolition of privilege in 1789. Like Rousseau and Mably, sans-culottes prioritized rights to self and subsistence over rights to private property, making arguments that would enhance Babeuf's thinking about need, equity, and common good.[9]

Parisian crowds responded to their deteriorating condition in 1792 as hungry crowds had done a generation before, by forcing shopkeepers to sell goods at what they considered "just" prices. When shortages re-emerged in spring 1793, these city people—who had no chickens, no gardens, no bounty of rivers and forests to supplement their diets when prices rose and who believed France had enough land to produce for everyone—insisted on their right to subsistence. Hoarders and speculators profited from their suffering, sans-culottes charged, violating the natural law that "the productions of the earth belong to all men." Such activity and such people must be punished. Enragé Jacques Roux summed up much as Rousseau and Mably and Babeuf had done: "liberty is but a vain phantom when one class of men can starve another with impunity."[10]

The Convention did not rally at first. Girondins led the opposition to sans-culottes' proposals, objecting that market regulation would deny citizens "free enjoyment of what they acquire by their own labor." Better to even the scales with measures like progressive taxation and universal education. Although the Jacobins were not especially eager for price controls either, they hoped to strengthen their alliance with the sans-culottes by distinguishing themselves from the Girondins. Accordingly, they walked a finer line between resisting intervention and defending popular interests, which was visible in Robespierre's flip-flopping on these issues. In fall 1792, he argued that subsistence is a fundamental right, but the following winter dismissed popular demands for affordable sugar as petty.[11]

When sans-culottes renewed their agitation for affordable food in spring 1793, the Jacobins finally took a firm stand. Robespierre exhorted the National Convention to guarantee popular well-being, recalling that in 1789 legislators had not been afraid to sweep away privileges that nobles considered property, nor had they accepted the king's claim of a "hereditary right . . . to oppress, degrade, and squeeze" the nation's citizens. Why then, he asked, was the Convention so respectful now of monopolists and speculators? Property in land or commerce was created by social convention and it could be limited by social convention too. Let the deputies acknowledge that the right to property is limited, like all others, "by the obligation to respect others' rights." Surely the most fundamental right was "the preservation of . . . existence and liberty," so prices that put essentials beyond reach were criminal. Ten days later, the Convention imposed a maximum price on grain.[12]

Babeuf was thrilled to hear such bold public affirmation of his private conviction of a right to subsistence and delighted that the National Convention had addressed sans-culottes' need. "How amazing . . . the times!" he wrote to the Jacobin attorney general for Paris, Anaxagoris Chaumette. "The world's fate hangs on them!" But the necessary work was not yet done, he warned, because inflation still put too many goods out of reach. Chaumette and his allies must continue agitating until every legislator acknowledged, with Robespierre, "that the right to property may not encroach on our fellows' existence."[13]

The letter must have impressed Chaumette, because he offered Babeuf a job in the Paris Food Administration helping to provide a million pounds of bread to the capital daily. That position served as a springboard to more demanding work in fall 1793, when Babeuf moved to the National Provisioning Commission to assist in supplying the army. It was illuminating experience for the man who would soon propose that citizens deliver all that they produced to a common storehouse for redistribution.[14]

The political landscape was dominated by the struggle between Jacobins and Girondins throughout much of the spring of 1793. Had the times been less troubled, the legislators might have negotiated a truce founded on their shared commitments to democracy and a more equitable economy. Amid deepening polarization, however, and under the mounting pressures of war, inflation, and popular activism, each side indulged in desperate mudslinging. Robespierre's enraged claim that the Girondins were counter-revolutionaries found fertile ground among sans-culottes seething at the deputies' resistance to price controls. In late May, thousands descended on the Convention to demand that it expel the Girondins. Legislators bowed reluctantly to what Parisian militants considered an expression of direct democracy, but which provincial constituents saw as the tyranny of the capital, by forcing out twenty-nine deputies and freeing the Jacobins of their vocal opposition.[15]

Babeuf believed the purge brought France closer to "saintly equality" by destroying opponents he hyperbolically labeled as "aristocrats." "I think things are going better and better," he told Marie-Anne, "and that the conclusion will come quickly, before the enemies of common good can even see what is going on." Able at last to support the family, he begged her to bring everyone to Paris. "I swear, I cannot live here alone any longer." Marie-Anne arrived that summer with little ones in tow, dressed in rags but bearing outsize republican names. Sophie recalled the girl in Rousseau's famous treatise on education, as well as her vanished sister, and her brother Robert had been rechristened to honor the true subject of that book: Émile. The baby bore the simple antique moniker Camille.[16]

This was a common practice among citizens eager to represent their sense of being reborn by adopting ancient names like Socrates or Brutus, or giving revolutionary titles to their children, like the parents of Jasmine Patriote Républicain and Nicolas Égalité. More ambitiously, the National Convention reordered time by creating a calendar whose year I was the first of the republic and whose months celebrated seasons rather than Roman gods and emperors. Ongoing social upheaval was visible in engravings that exalted working people rather than princes or nobles, and popular plays that pitted virtuous sans-culottes against scheming aristocrats. In public conversation, "citizen" and "citizenness" (*citoyen/citoyenne*) replaced the traditional honorifics of "monsieur" and "madame."[17]

Cultural change is an empty gesture if not accompanied by institutional reform, and the Convention came through. Under Jacobin leadership, it adopted a new Declaration of Rights in 1793 that announced: "society's aim is common good." That the republican deputies defined "common good" more generously than had their predecessors in 1789 was visible in their inclusion of equality among "natural and inalienable rights." They gave further substance to the phrase by enhancing social equality with promises of universal education, employment, and public assistance, and they strengthened political equality by ratifying the democratic practices initiated in 1792.[18]

Legislators continued to reinforce equity by mandating more progressive taxation and equal inheritance within families, planning for public hospitals, encouraging minimum wages, and providing for public employment. Jacobin delegates to the provinces fostered social good by organizing community granaries to collect surplus for redistribution when shortages struck. Some citizens denounced the last measure as forced leveling, but others described it as fraternal sharing like the "loaves of equality" that mingled fine grains normally reserved for the wealthy with lesser takings abandoned to the poor, to ensure enough bread for all.[19]

Critics complained, discreetly in 1793–94 and more vociferously later, that such measures encroached on private wealth. But, contrary to the conclusion many of them drew, the Jacobins were not enemies of private property. Robespierre and his fellow club members aspired to a world of rough equivalence, not absolute equality, one populated by modest landowners whose holdings ensured their independence. They believed they encouraged that by attacking privilege and dismantling monopoly, arguing, as Babeuf had done years before, that modest redistribution protected property against the desire for radical leveling excited by gross inequality.[20]

Robespierre traced the boundary between improvement and rupture when he told the Convention that "extreme inequality" was "the source of many ills and crimes," only to add, "I am no less convinced that equality of goods is a fantasy." His readiness to redistribute some wealth through progressive taxation and market regulation was driven, as well, by his conviction that possession of self took priority over property in land or things. The government must protect the citizen's self by guaranteeing food and labor. It was an equation Babeuf would eventually take in a direction Robespierre never intended, by arguing that possession of self and a right to subsistence foreclosed all right to private property.[21]

Sans-culottes marched again in September 1793, this time with Babeuf's benefactor Chaumette at their head. As thousands crowded into the Convention's hall to demand affordable food, legislators set maximum prices on a broad range of consumer goods and decreed a revolutionary army to requisition supplies from the countryside. The deputies promised to amplify these practical measures by more comprehensively pursuing counter-revolution, adopting a Law on Suspects that permitted indictment of anyone whose "conduct, associations, remarks or writings show them . . . to be . . . enemies of liberty" and enlarging the Revolutionary Tribunal to speed prosecution of those ensnared by the law. The September demonstration brought Parisian sans-culottes to new heights of influence. It also marked a fatal turning point, for the decrees won that day would subvert the popular power that elicited them.[22]

Babeuf did not see the danger. Like many sans-culottes, he believed he had witnessed the dawn of a new age in which government would truly serve the people. He must have thought he would play an important part as well. But that dream was cut short when news reached the capital of the fraud conviction that had driven him from Picardy almost a year earlier. Authorities learned of it in November 1793, plucked Babeuf from the revolutionary ferment, and hustled him off to prison. He would not forget the flame of activism he had seen burn so brightly in 1793. Indeed, he would spend the rest of his life trying to reignite it.

Babeuf's family renewed their bitter intimacy with poverty as a new year began. The children went hungry and contracted smallpox. Marie-Anne stretched herself thin by nursing them, scouting for food, and setting aside what she could to supplement her husband's spartan prison diet, until she became so sick that she almost died. "I barely escaped," she told Babeuf, "you cannot imagine how weak I am." But, she added passionately, "I will never abandon you."[23]

Her letter landed in the airless cell from which Babeuf battled the civil charges against him by writing petitions that described his pursuers as counter-revolutionaries. An appeals court overturned his conviction on a technicality and remanded him to Picardy for a new trial, where a sympathetic prosecutor demanded further investigation and persuaded political allies to post bail for the indigent prisoner in the interim. The moment he was freed, Babeuf headed back to Paris. By then, it was midsummer 1794, a season whose heat the revolutionary calendar noted by calling this the month of Thermidor.[24]

As Babeuf wrestled with his undying fraud case, the nation suffered losses foreshadowed in the sans-culottes' victory of September 1793. Legislators had been struggling well before the Parisians marched, trying to secure the nation against armies that pressed in on every side, dissident republicans rising in the southwest, and royalists waging civil war in the west. When sans-

culottes added to the turmoil by making new demands for food, the deputies prepared their demobilization. Legislators created a revolutionary army as the crowd demanded, which enrolled activists and took them from the capital. The Convention offered stipends to attend sectional assembly meetings, promising that they would ease the condition of working people, but the stipends also brought in hungry newcomers who diluted militants' influence. Those stipends gave legislators ready excuse, as well, to reduce assembly meetings from once daily to once every five days and so make the sections less responsive to the flow of events. Finally, deputies adopted the Law on Suspects saying that it would protect the people, then turned that law against many of them.[25]

In following months, the Convention restored order to France with growing efficiency and often terrible cruelty. Critics of the regime, whom the Law on Suspects named as "enemies of liberty," were condemned as traitors and imprisoned or executed. Foreign armies were repulsed, domestic resistance savagely repressed, insurrectionary cities devastated. One deputy, dispatched to repress counter-revolution in the west, reported seeing "republican soldiers rape rebel women on the stones piled by the side of the road." Another, fighting insurgents in the southwest, ordered that hundreds of presumed rebels be mowed down by firing squad.[26]

Jacobin encouragement of a more egalitarian republic continued throughout. Legislators had hoped that the sale of church property and parceling out of wastelands would make France a nation of smallholders, but wealthy proprietors were too often the successful purchasers. Robespierre's most radical colleague, Louis Antoine Saint-Just, responded by proposing to seize land from citizens only suspected of counter-revolution and selling that, too. His decree was of dubious legality and not widely executed, but its memory would linger, intensifying opponents' resentment and deepening their conviction that the Jacobins were enemies of property.[27]

By late winter 1794, the republic's crises were ebbing. Foreign armies had been driven back, rebellious cities pacified, domestic guerrillas subdued. But rather than abandoning the terror with which it restored order, the Convention intensified the repression. It demobilized sans-culottes and drove Enragés into silence, then narrowed orthodoxy to a razor's edge by going after new critics. When the radical journalist Hébert encouraged Parisians to turn out once more because food was still scarce and expensive, he was accused of plotting against the revolution, hauled before the Tribunal, and executed. The moderate deputy Danton and his allies were next, charged as well with conspiracy. Tried quickly by the Revolutionary Tribunal, they were guillotined. The Convention's infuriated search for traitors extended even to the widows of these men, some of whom were executed together in mid-April.

In June, legislators mounted a new assault on due process by denying counsel to defendants who appeared before the Revolutionary Tribunal and permitting hearsay to be used against them. Executions soared. By the summer of 1794, hundreds of people died on the guillotine each month in Paris. An eerie conformity settled over public life, forcing even the radical Saint-Just to admit that "the revolution is frozen."[28]

Babeuf arrived in Paris as the crackdown reached its zenith to find the once vibrant city stilled, newspapers silenced, militants cowed. In the National Convention, however, a peculiar alliance was forming among legislators eager to repeal exceptional measures, legislators determined to extend them further, and legislators agitating for change to hide their own corruption. What all could agree on was that Robespierre had to go. On a late July morning, they rallied colleagues by shouting, "Down with the tyrant!" and took Robespierre into custody, purged the Committee of Public Safety, and went after those Jacobins' allies. Over the next three days, the Convention sent more than one hundred men to the guillotine without hearing or trial.[29]

These events would be remembered by the revolutionary date on which they began, 9 Thermidor year II (27 July 1794), and later spoken of as if they marked a decisive break between tyranny and liberty. That is not how it was experienced at the time. Citizens were uncertain about what direction the revolution should take and had no clear guidance from the Convention, where deputies briefly joined by animus against Robespierre soon fell out. Some insisted that civil liberties and rule of law be restored immediately. Others countered that extending exceptional measures was the only way to save the republic. Debating one another in the Convention and the Jacobin Club, they appealed to the public in hope of winning some advantage.[30]

The newly freed Babeuf had a very clear sense of how France ought to proceed: the Convention should resume the revolution's expansion by restoring civil liberties and democratic practices. He was given a platform to make his case by Stanislas Fréron and Jean-Lambert Tallien, deputies who helped bring down Robespierre and quickly mobilized for reform. They hired Babeuf as an ally and gave him a newspaper of his own.

Babeuf rallied his family to produce the new *Journal of the Free Press*. Marie-Anne and nine-year-old Émile folded and distributed the pages he wrote, while the little ones stayed quietly at home, "so devoted [do] they seem already to the homeland." With no time to cook, everyone lived on nuts, raisins, and bread.[31]

Babeuf explained the paper's title to readers by expanding on the political necessity of free expression. "The writer who is a friend of the people and champion of its rights . . . requires absolute liberty . . . to evaluate legislation . . . and offer a healthy ballast against politicians' ambitions." Legislators must guarantee the free speech that Fréron and Tallien also promoted and, he added, continue to build on Robespierre's defeat by activating the suspended constitution and scheduling long-delayed elections. By so doing, they would restore "justice, fraternity, trust, domestic security, happiness [and] republican morals," to rescue France from "ceaseless, chilling, repressive terror."[32]

To revitalize popular activism, Babeuf allied himself with sans-culottes and Enragés in the new Electoral Club, which also demanded activation of the constitution and prompt elections. Using methods that had served citizens well in 1792 and 1793, club members drafted a petition for the Convention and appealed to the Paris sections, as Babeuf publicized their efforts in his newspaper. In the waning months of 1794, however, such practices no longer worked. Paris sections, disorganized by the repression of terror and divided after Thermidor, did not sign on. Jacobins objected, as they had long done, that elections were impossible because "counter-revolutionaries" might still corrupt them. Deputies in the National Convention refused to receive the Electoral Club's petition, reformers and hardliners finding brief comity in their resistance to renewed sans-culotte activism.[33]

If calls to restore democracy fell on deaf ears, demands to settle the political scores that had accumulated over the preceding year did not. Newspapers and pamphlets, tight-lipped since autumn 1793, became effusive with tales of greed, wrongful imprisonment, and high crimes. Many such accounts revealed genuine violations but were no less entangled with the bitter disputes in the Convention. Articles fusing stories of violence with criticism of government encroachment on private wealth proliferated at the same moment legislators debated whether to restore property seized from émigrés. The authors, neglecting difficult wartime conditions, concluded that the Jacobins had wanted only to fleece the rich. Such charges gained potency as they circulated through culture high and low, from the literary journal that named the guillotine a "gold mine" for "coin[ing] money" in the center of Paris to the popular play that cast sans-culottes as swindlers who used political denunciation to enrich themselves.[34]

At the forefront of this mounting crusade against Jacobin government were Babeuf's patrons, Stanislas Fréron and Jean-Lambert Tallien. Themselves guilty of extortion, embezzlement, and excesses of violence in the preceding year, these men founded careers after Thermidor on obscuring their own crimes by calling out others'. Tallien popularized the naming of Robespierre's government as the Terror, and Fréron's newspaper, *The People's Orator*, set a standard for mingling accounts of genuine transgression with invented tales of depravity.[35]

The distance between these legislators and Babeuf became clear to the latter in early October, when Fréron condemned political clubs. Although he took aim at the Jacobins, Fréron implicitly challenged all associations that Babeuf might characterize as institutions of direct democracy by calling them illegitimate competitors with the National Convention. "Two sovereign powers may produce contradictory systems" that have discordant effects, he argued. The people had confided sovereign power to their legislators and could only end the nation's turmoil by allowing the latter to govern without interference. On the day after Fréron's editorial appeared, municipal workers barreled into the meeting hall of the Electoral Club and gutted it.[36]

Babeuf struggled to keep up. He had believed he was enrolled in a fight against tyranny that would allow the revolution to continue expanding and better serve the people. Seeing that fight turn against the very democracy he defended, Babeuf fashioned the identity that would define the rest of his life.

With the next issue of his paper, he declared the crusade for a free press victorious and doubled down on his defense of what he called the rights of man. "I must take a stand against usurpers of those rights and their allies by adopting titles consistent with [my] part . . . in an on-going struggle." He re-named his paper *The People's Tribune*, to celebrate ancient Roman advocates for the plebeians, and renamed himself in honor of those tribunes' contemporaries: agrarian law champions Caius and Tiberius Gracchus. As Gracchus Babeuf, he promised, he would fight for the people as his chosen forebears had done. "I will even say that I would be happy to be martyred like them for my devotion."[37]

Turning on Fréron and Tallien, Babeuf condemned their hypocrisy. They claimed to be "devoted friends of the people" but brazenly insisted that "the violation of [popular] rights . . . [is] the best and only means to guarantee liberty." Ordinary folk might be taken in by their lies, but "devotees of popular rights," like Babeuf, would set them straight. As Mably had said, "when a free people does not recognize its danger, honest men must . . . come to liberty's aid."[38]

This was the same Babeuf who had so unsuccessfully sued the marquis de Soyecourt in 1788: passionate, principled, and reckless when angry. Just as in Picardy, he challenged men with more money, more power, and fewer scruples. Fréron and Tallien persuaded Babeuf's publisher to cut ties with him and denounced the journalist to police. He spent the next three months in hiding.[39]

The cards were on the table. What Babeuf had believed was a sincere effort to restore democracy appeared only to empower new tyrants. The revolution he had hoped to see expand anew and give still greater power to the people was threatening to contract instead.

Babeuf's search for a new publisher silenced the *Tribune* at the very moment when public opinion turned decisively against the Jacobins. The shift was hastened by the notorious trial of a Jacobin deputy named Jean-Baptiste

Carrier, charged with committing atrocities in the port city of Nantes in fall 1793. As witnesses testified about torture and mass murder, public revulsion spread from Carrier to his fellow club members. In late October 1794, crowds of reactionary youth attacked the Paris Jacobin Club and brawled with members until the Convention shuttered the hall, dissolving the nation's most powerful civic association.

Carrier's trial offered new opportunity to associate revolutionary violence with Jacobin efforts to tap private wealth. One pamphlet claimed that he arbitrarily imprisoned "almost all . . . who had money," and even the official indictment accused Carrier of "knowingly perpetrat[ing] all kinds of extortion . . . under the mask of patriotism." A former Jacobin named Joachim Vilate went still further. Hoping to save himself by tarring others, Vilate claimed that the Jacobins were proponents of agrarian law who believed France had too many mouths to feed. So, he continued, they tried to reduce the population with slaughter in the counter-revolutionary Vendée. It was an outrageous lie and a wild misrepresentation of Jacobin activity, ideology, and political aims. Still, amid the heat of guilt, regret, recrimination, and revenge that followed Thermidor, it caught fire.[40]

Babeuf was among those who believed Vilate. Unlike most of his fellows, he did not use the man's tale as an excuse to repudiate democracy and social welfare but took it as occasion to reflect on tyranny and public good. Brushing aside claims that Carrier had an unusual propensity for cruelty, Babeuf focused on the government that empowered him. The deputy was a cog in a badly conceived machine, he argued, which centralized power by subjecting France to the whims of a few. A truly democratic government would have denied limitless power to its deputies and worked from the bottom up, coordinating private citizens to share in the renewal of their republic.

As for Vilate's claim that the Jacobins were advocates of agrarian law, Babeuf agreed that "a state's soil should insure the existence of all members." Failure to do so was not because there were too many people, but because too few people had access to the land. Returning to the subjects of poverty, subsistence, and justice that had so long occupied his mind, Babeuf argued that good government would ensure "that all have enough, and none too much," by sharing out the earth's bounty. If there were still not enough to go around, such a government would resort not to slaughter but to common sacrifice. "The simple laws of nature demand the partial and equal privation of each to satisfy the needs of all."[41]

Writing six months after Robespierre's defeat, Babeuf saw no sign of common sacrifice. On the contrary, the Convention turned its back more firmly on the people as winter set in, enlarging on its resistance to popular democracy by repealing social welfare policies. In late December 1794, legislators abolished the wage and price controls adopted under sans-culotte pressure in September 1793. Prices soared, and shortages deepened.[42]

Having at last found a new publisher, Babeuf resurrected his *Tribune* to advertise regret for his unwitting part in mobilizing reaction. "When I thundered passionately to bring down the monstrous edifice of Robespierre's system, I did not imagine I was helping to create a new structure that . . . would prove equally disastrous to the people. I did not foresee that my demands for leniency; for the abolition of slavery, despotism, and barbarism; for the greatest freedom of written and spoken opinion, would be used to sap the Republic to its very foundation." The Convention had not dismantled the system that silenced the people in the preceding year, only supplanted its architects. By continuing to resist "public censure, . . . calls to order, . . . surveillance of governors by the governed, . . . challenge of abuses and offenses of power," it silenced the very citizens it was meant to serve.[43]

In his next issue, Babeuf joined his critique of vanishing political rights to a defense of public welfare. "I see fundamentally opposed parties . . . The first wants a republic of patricians and plebeians . . . the second wants not just equality of rights but . . . the legal guarantee of an honest living and essential social benefits in fair exchange for the labor each contributes to the common good." Although the plebeian party represented the greatest number of citizens, it lost significant advantage by allowing itself to be painted as naïve and preferring peace to equal rights and justice. Their moment was slipping away. "Plebeian representatives," Babeuf called out, "wake up!"[44]

Remarkably, given the steady rightward drift of public opinion, the *Tribune* was successful. Babeuf's paper had debuted in the summer of 1794 with about eight hundred subscribers, and not only survived his enforced silence in the fall but flourished. By early 1795, press runs were climbing to two thousand copies, which may have reached five times as many people because issues were so often read aloud and shared from hand to hand. These were smaller numbers, to be sure, than the fifteen thousand subscribers who buoyed Fréron's reactionary *People's Orator*, but they were significant for troubled times that had sent most democratic papers into free fall. Enthusiasm for Babeuf's words did not, however, move his readers to action.[45]

When Babeuf arrived in Paris in January 1793, he had seen a better world being forged. As he watched sans-culottes demand that the National Convention address their need, and listened to popular activists and Jacobins extend the re-imagination of property from abolishing privilege and seizing land to regulating trade and commerce, Babeuf's thinking about need and equity continued to evolve. Meanwhile, his work in the Paris Food Administration and National Provisioning Commission suggested just how much a state could do to ensure provisioning. All of it made a powerful impression, raising Babeuf's hopes for what the nation might yet achieve.

By the beginning of 1795, the promise of a better world was slipping away. The sectional assemblies and political clubs that had galvanized popular activism were withering, citizens cowed by repression and weak with hunger were in retreat, legislators were increasingly hostile to popular democracy and public welfare. Fearful that a vital political moment was vanishing, Babeuf vented his anxiety in the content of his writing and the very form of his *Tribune*. As issues grew from eight to sixteen to thirty pages, with numbering that continued from one to the next, they began to suggest installments of a political pamphlet rather than issues of a newspaper. Argument became harangue as he lectured, warned, and exhorted, trying to preserve his own faith in the revolution as much as that of his readers. "No one governs for long if despised by the people," he said hopefully. The Convention might disperse the Electoral Club and shut down the Jacobins, but citizens would find new ways to organize themselves. "Each hovel, every granary" would become a tiny political association. "Take your inquisition into these countless sanctuaries," he taunted police, "you will never have enough spies [to watch them all]."

"Should the people rise up?" he asked at last. "Absolutely, if it does not want to lose liberty forever and see its rights stolen." Could the people rise up? "What is to stop it? . . . A people before whom crowned heads bowed is not made to be subjugated by a handful of wretched tyrants!"[46]

That was the last straw. In early February 1795, police arrested the man his neighbors called "one of our finest patriots" and attacked the press freedom he had so recently declared secure, confiscating every issue of the *Tribune* they could lay hands on. Seven months after the supposed liberation of Thermidor, Babeuf was silenced, and the revolution was visibly contracting.[47]

THREE

Re-imagining Revolution

Public misery, deepening before Babeuf's arrest, became catastrophic as the hard winter of 1794–95 dragged on. Despite a steady decline in the value of paper money, the Convention abolished price controls on consumer goods in late December. The consequences of that decision were intensified by an unprecedented freezing of the Seine, which halted the transport of grain and fuel. Shortages worsened and inflation soared, the price of butter and meat doubled and then tripled. Municipal administrators distributed potatoes to compensate for the dearth of bread, but few Parisians had enough firewood to cook them because the capital's merchants were charging such extortionate prices. People fainted in the streets or starved or took poison to escape their desperation. When the Seine thawed, the bloated bodies of suicides washed up on the riverbanks.[1]

The agony of famine was compounded by the gross inequity of suffering as the starving poor watched wealthy Parisians indulge their every appetite. Hungry children cried as rich customers crowded into bakeries for fine rolls in the morning and into exclusive restaurants for oysters at night. Working families shivered at home while elegant women in diaphanous gowns drifted through well-heated villas. Shabbily dressed laborers were eclipsed by stylish men draped in showy scarves. Through it all, gilded thugs ruled over the city's public spaces, bullying sans-culottes, smashing busts of republican heroes, and roaring out an anthem whose cheery tune stood in bizarre contrast to savage lyrics that called the Jacobins "drinkers of blood" and urged listeners to "hound them to death!"[2]

Jean-Baptiste Lesueur, "Poverty and Need in Paris," 1796. Source: Musée Carnavalet, Paris.

As the cold, drawn, hungry poor watched wealthy reactionaries enjoy fine meals, warm dwellings, and glittering entertainments while denouncing the "Jacobin Terror," they began to recall Robespierre's reign as one that had offered them work, bread, and respect. In the spring of 1795 their mounting anger exploded in popular insurrections whose ferocity would galvanize legislators to finish off the popular movement they had so uneasily negotiated with since 1789.

The first uprising came in early April. Working people descended on the Convention to demand cheap bread and the democratic constitution, but many old militants were dead or gone from the capital. Without leaders to formulate demands or sympathetic deputies to translate the crowd's energy into legislation, insurgents milled around until troops arrived to clear them from the assembly hall. Angry deputies followed by purging radical colleagues they thought likely to sympathize with the activists and, almost as an afterthought, promised to supplement bread rations with biscuits and rice. Popular anger simmered.[3]

Thousands rose up again in late May, during the republican month of Prairial. Mothers with hungry children demanded that men leave their workplaces to march on the Convention with them, and activists ransacked weapons depots as they had done in 1789. This time, however, they sought arms to use against the assembly rather than in defense of it.

As insurgents entered the National Convention, they killed a deputy try-ing to block their way, cut off his head, and paraded it among his colleagues. Still lacking leaders, they seemed uncertain about what to do next. A noisy standoff ensued as demonstrators dizzy with hunger and drunk on cheap wine from barrels tapped in the courtyard threatened the well-dressed legis-lators who had too long ignored their need. When a few deputies tried to calm the crowd by proposing to activate the democratic constitution of 1793 and to improve provisioning, their colleagues grudgingly accepted the mo-tions. After hours of tense uncertainty, troops arrived to expel the intruders.[4]

The May events, remembered as the Prairial insurrection, marked a turning point. Legislators determined to be done with Parisian militants, who had pressed at them so insistently since 1789, sealed the political reac-tion by redefining those revolutionaries as thugs and criminals. They re-pealed motions accepted under pressure from the crowd, arrested the colleagues who proposed them, and sent soldiers and gilded youth into working-class neighborhoods to detain suspects and seize weapons. Then they convened a military tribunal, which judged 149 people in ten weeks and sentenced 36 to death. When the purged legislators—including Jean-Marie Goujon, who had advocated for "bread of equality"—learned that they had been condemned, they emulated their ancient Roman heroes by stabbing themselves as a final expression of freedom.[5]

When news of the Paris insurrections spread to the provinces, sporadic assaults on old militants hardened into systematic reprisal. Jacobins were massacred in prisons as authorities stood by, retired activists were lynched outside their homes, and broken bodies were left at crossroads in bloody warning. When survivors tried to bring charges, they found police uncoop-erative and judges indifferent. Humiliated, purged, starved, murdered. Jac-obins and sans-culottes would long remember the violence they suffered in this bitter third year of the republic.[6]

Babeuf learned of these events from the provincial city of Arras, where he had been sent after his February arrest. Prisons in that small city were being emptied of the Terror's "counter-revolutionaries" and filled with the Reac-tion's "terrorists." Babeuf was considered one of the latter. Conditions were

Charles Monnet and Isidore-Stanislas Helman, "Insurrection of 1 Prairial Year III," 1797. Source: BnF.

grim, the prisons becoming noxious and disease-ridden as the number of detainees rose well beyond what any of those prisons were meant to house. Babeuf was given bread and water to eat and "a handful of straw" to sleep on in a place called Les Baudets.[7]

The austerity did not so much demoralize detainees as deepen their commitment. They built a vibrant community through conversations shouted across narrow streets and broad courtyards, and by writing letters that were smuggled from cell to cell and prison to prison, permitting militants to introduce themselves, explain what they had done for the Revolution, and debate what remained. Those with resources supplemented private letters with newspapers they read aloud and passed along to others. A journalist named René Lebois produced handwritten editions of his paper, named after Jean-Paul Marat's famous *People's Friend*, to keep fellow prisoners up to date. Such communication was all the more important to men like Babeuf, who were isolated by the authorities' confiscation of their letters from the outside.[8]

In Arras, Babeuf met Charles Germain. Younger than the tribune by about a decade, Germain had enjoyed a more privileged youth. He was born to a comfortable Protestant family in the southern city of Narbonne in 1770 and spent several years studying in Paris. When the family fell on hard times, he joined the army and marched through southern France and northern Italy before facing a rupture of his own making. Germain gave a controversial political speech at the Terror's height for which he was discharged and imprisoned. Liberated after Thermidor, he was arrested once more for brawling with a reactionary in the galleries of the National Convention and was imprisoned in Arras.[9]

Upheaval was not uncommon in these years. Men and women moved between towns, changed occupations, got in trouble for unpopular opinions. But Germain's temperament undoubtedly complicated his circumstances. At the best of times, he was good company, ready with a joke and fond of teasing. It is not difficult to imagine his wide face and heavy features—his "broad turned-up nose, full mouth, and round chin"—creased with laughter. But he also suffered paralyzing bouts of depression and had a hot temper, which probably explains his unfortunate speech during the Terror and the fight after Thermidor. His temper would excite bitter quarrels in years to come, but, for the moment, Germain was in the flush of new friendship with a like-minded soul.[10]

Germain was enclosed at the Dominicans, not far from the Baudets prison where Babeuf was housed. After introducing himself by letter in the spring of 1795, he and Babeuf began to correspond. The bond that grew up between them was unlike anything Babeuf had known. Until then, the tribune had been the supplicant, whether as an autodidact seeking guidance from a cultivated academician, the rough provincial in need of a Parisian patron, or the eager journalist subsidized by duplicitous reactionaries. In Germain, Babeuf found an acolyte who admired him as a celebrated elder.

The two shared a passion for politics that Germain leavened with boisterous playfulness, surely a tonic to Babeuf's sober intensity. In return, Babeuf offered conversation about practical matters when Germain became depressed, inviting the younger man to rejoin the living. Germain was generous with the fruits of his education, sharing what he had learned in school, offering up riches gleaned from his prison study of history and philosophy, and passing along issues of the democratic *Journal of Free Men* that he received in prison. Thanks to that paper, the men could discuss current events with enviable knowledge.[11]

Both of them understood France to be at a crossroads. "It is imperative to save the republic, restore the people to its rights, once more root liberty and democracy in our soil," Germain swore. "By what means can we accomplish such a fine project?" Babeuf answered by proposing something like agrarian law. When he had last made that recommendation, to the deputy Coupé in 1791, it had fallen flat. This time, it landed.

"Your plan is one the Gracchi themselves would have instituted," Germain enthused. Admittedly, some would accuse Babeuf of "destroying commerce, ruining industry, exalting laziness," but Germain had a counter-argument. Drawing on years of classical education and, quite probably, familiarity with Rousseau, he challenged the imagined critics by recalling Lycurgus's warning to Sparta against a "disastrous taste for luxury" and the extravagance that destroyed ancient Carthage from within.[12]

This was familiar republican moralizing, which associated the virtuous republic with modest, simple lives. Babeuf answered with a more sophisticated analysis, making clear just how much he had learned from the century's debates about economic growth and Mably's critique of the Physiocrats. "Can we add something a little more convincing?" he asked Germain. The example of the ancients would not answer the partisans of growth who dismissed republican moralizing by arguing that commerce "should invigorate everything . . . nourish everyone, from the first worker, who grows . . . essential goods, to the manufacturer who directs large enterprises, to the merchant who insures the circulation of manufactured goods."

Commerce might be invigorating in theory, Babeuf admitted, but they both knew that, in practice, wealth was distributed with cruel inequality. A privileged few monopolized the land and all the wealth it produced, forcing the rest to "work a lot and eat very little." Recalling the hoarders and speculators damned by sans-culottes for starving the nation, Babeuf argued that commercial middlemen raised prices and lowered wages to enrich themselves and leave "the many hands from which everything comes" empty. He and Germain must found a new sort of exchange that would provide equal benefit to everyone.

Now, Babeuf reached far beyond an agrarian law that would redistribute land and sans-culottes' proposals to regulate commercial trade. They must abolish private property entirely. Leave each person "to the trade he exercises honestly, by which he lives happily," and require them to deliver what they produce to a common storehouse. There, agents, "[who] work not for themselves but for the great family [of man], will return . . . to each . . . his equal share of goods in exchange for what he contributes." Only then could commerce "invigorat[e] everything . . . nourish all associates equally."

Such a system would not just perfect commerce, Babeuf promised, but improve every dimension of republican life. Accidents would no longer leave families unsheltered and starving. The aged and infirm would be saved from begging. Workers would not suffer from an absence of competition, as critics claimed, but be liberated from having to lie about their skills in order to get ahead. Shopkeepers would cease hoarding, and merchants would no longer cheat. No one would be judged by how much they possessed. "There will be neither high or low, first or last, the efforts and objectives of all associates . . . will converge on the great fraternal aim of common prosperity, a limitless source of individual well-being."[13]

It was a remarkable vision. But it was not unprecedented. Babeuf clearly drew on utopian treatises he had encountered in recent years. Collignon's influence was visible, as was Mably's description of a "charming dream" about a republic in which redistribution of goods permitted citizens to live in virtuous happiness. Babeuf had clearly read, as well, Étienne-Gabriel Morelly, who complemented Mably's dream of redistribution with proposals for a paternalist government to supervise.

Although Babeuf said nothing of his revolutionary experience in the letter that described this project to Germain, it must have shaped his reading of the utopians because, unlike Mably and Morelly, he believed a world without property could be established in the here and now. The philosophers had described such places as irretrievable ideals of the past or impossible dreams for the future. Babeuf, a revolutionary who had seen the abolition of once sacred institutions, thought it could be realized in the present. This, he had come to believe, was the French Revolution's true purpose.[14]

As the prisoners talked about how to bring this new world into being, Germain suggested an uprising "in a single night, at a given hour, under the guidance of trusted agents." Babeuf, arrested for publicly advocating far less, disagreed. "What you propose could [be realized] if it were possible to freely instruct and indoctrinate . . . But it is all too clear that, were you to undertake such education, you would most certainly be arrested at the very outset by those in power." Worse still, what if they tried to raise an insurrection, only to find that they did not have enough followers?

With uncanny prescience, Babeuf imagined the outcome. "What an awful impression that would make on people unprepared for such a forceful, unexpected act! They would condemn your followers as crooks, incendiaries, certified thieves. It would be useless to advertise our sacred manifesto amidst such generalized horror . . . That powerful minority of cheats who trick the masses and monopolize information to obscure the truth with falsehood, would use lies and slander to excite public anger. From every side, they would damn the apostles who light the way, insuring that the manifesto endorsing true social organization would be destroyed the moment it appeared. The ignorant crowd would . . . rage blindly against us. Our stillborn project . . . would be remembered as a hateful idea that joined the most extravagant eccentricity with a criminal plan to overturn all proper order."

They must advance cautiously, he counseled. "We should . . . settle in a heavily populated area where opinions are favorable to us. Once in place, we can easily advertise our doctrine. There are many passionate disciples . . . ready to welcome our first efforts. Their enthusiasm . . . will encourage their neighbors to join us." Babeuf must have been thinking of Paris, with its unique collection of radicals, as an ideal base from which to win over France.[15]

Shut up in the prisons of Arras, Babeuf did not just imagine radical equality but began organizing to bring it into being. His leap from utopian dream to revolutionary project would inspire Karl Marx and Friedrich Engels, fifty years on, to anoint him the first modern communist. For the moment, it was Charles Germain who signed on.

He advised Babeuf on winning over soldiers. "Family, friends, fellow citizens will show them the promised land and they will soon understand that the true enemy is the oppressor who would have commanded them to run us down like thieves." He encouraged his friend to hold tight to their common dream when the latter became discouraged. "The homeland must be saved and the people restored to abiding happiness . . . all of these evils and all anxieties will bear fruit, strengthening me to realize the sublime project you inspire." And he relieved the tedium of prison life by looking to the future. "Let's talk a little about our glorious project," he pleaded playfully. "What [ruling] did you issue? Did you hear from our good [acquaintances from Lille], to whom you wrote? Can we count on their bravery, their enthusiasm? Did they passionately embrace the saintliest of causes?" The next day he wrote, "I carried out your orders, my tribune. Gouillart [a fellow prisoner] is a knight of the order of equals, he took his vows with the [devotion] and piety appropriate to our mission for justice and reason." As summer progressed, Germain abandoned the familiar republican "good wishes and fraternity" for the salutation, "greetings in saintly equality," expressing their new aspirations. "We are equals and equality will be our homeland."[16]

Charles Germain publicized the new doctrine among men whose militant credentials he knew, but neither he nor Babeuf was ready to take it to a wider public. They were, for the moment, caught up in a struggle to preserve democracy. Success in that fight was essential to defeat social hierarchy, they thought, because popular democracy empowered ordinary folk to elect deputies who would serve their interests by enhancing equality. The constitution of 1793 must be preserved at all costs.[17]

It was, at that moment, under attack.

After the springtime insurrections of 1795, the National Convention had created a Commission of Eleven to prepare the suspended constitution for activation. The Eleven unilaterally reformulated the charge by abandoning the democratic constitution and drafting a replacement. In June of that year, they presented the new code to their colleagues and joined them in debating its final form.[18]

The chair of the Eleven, François Boissy d'Anglas, promised that the new constitution would end the revolution because it had been purged of what

he considered its predecessor's most disastrous promise: a right to insurrection. It had been purged as well of a great many other promises, giving
weight to Babeuf's charge that a class war was in progress by abolishing universal male suffrage and guarantees of rights to education, work, fair wages,
and public assistance. What would become the constitution of 1795 lacked
even an endorsement of "common good," like those that graced the pream-
ble to the glorious Declaration of the Rights of Man of 1789 and introduced
the first article of the Declaration of 1793. Legislators feared now that such
a statement could be used to justify insurrection.[19]

When Charles Germain learned of the new constitution, he brushed it off.
Even if republicans in the Convention were inclined to adopt, royalists
would surely block it, understanding that "no matter how much it counters
liberty and equality," it would not serve their purposes. His confidence was
badly misplaced.[20]

Legislators adopted the constitution of 1795 and submitted it to the nation for approval in a late-summer referendum. The prisoners organized as
best they could. Germain asked allies to read his objections to electoral assemblies. Babeuf wrote a pamphlet explaining that the new constitution's
disregard for public instruction would return them to the France of his
youth, in which "those who cannot pay teachers learn nothing, know nothing." The code would also destroy the popular sovereignty republicans believed they had secured in 1792, by making suffrage dependent on income
and education. It would further erode democracy by creating an upper legislative chamber with veto power. Under its conditions, revolutionaries
would find themselves telling their children: "I risked my life a hundred
times over for the triumph of liberty and equality, . . . but, in dying, I leave
you neither property, education, nor even civil liberties; reduced to slavery,
you are once more subservient to the rich and educated. We destroyed nobility and privileges for ourselves but restored them to you." Babeuf and
Germain must have felt themselves crying in the wilderness when voters accepted the constitution of 1795.[21]

For the moment, change closer to home demanded the men's attention.
As the prisons of Arras filled steadily with former activists, they had become

hotbeds of radicalism. Babeuf and Germain encountered provincial sans-culottes there, including old subscribers to the *Tribune* and a postman arrested for organizing workers. They debated an alliance with the radical journalist Lebois and encountered an activist from the west named Nayez whom Germain dismissed as "a gossip, a sycophant, a nobody with nothing and no inclination for good." When authorities realized what militancy they were fostering in that small northern town, they dispersed the prisoners in late summer 1795.[22]

Babeuf and Germain were flung from the frying pan of revolutionary enthusiasm into the fire of revolutionary experience when transferred to the Paris Plessis prison, where they met seasoned political veterans. The genial Italian exile Filippo Buonarroti was a former lawyer who had served as a revolutionary administrator in Corsica, Sardinia, and the Piedmont. Augustin Darthé, a tight-lipped northerner, had assisted the provincial administrator Joseph Lebon, who was disparaged as a second Carrier. Buonarroti and Darthé knew far more about organizing people in service to revolution than either Babeuf or Germain. Both would soon become Equals.[23]

The prisoners in Plessis talked politics as eagerly as their compatriots had done in Arras. Loyal to Robespierre's memory, they celebrated him as a defender of popular rights and lamented his defeat, admitting that the Terror's violence was awful but defending it as essential. Jacobin revolutionary government had preserved the republic from assaults on democracy and social welfare like those they had witnessed since Thermidor.

As happened in Arras, the prisoners' fellowship was deepened by imprisonment. "Those caged by aristocracy lived frugally in the closest fraternity," Buonarroti would recall of his time in Plessis, his intensity of feeling not lessened by the passage of three decades. "Honored by chains and poverty born of their loyalty, devoted to work and study, they thought only of the nation's ills and possible remedies. The patriotic songs they sang each night brought crowds of citizens to the place of their unhappy confinement, drawn by curiosity or sympathy."[24]

It was after arriving in Plessis that Babeuf saw his family for the first time in almost seven months. Marie-Anne had tried to hide the worst of their situation in one of her rare letters to reach Arras, but Émile managed to share news that his poor sister Sophie was gone. She was only four when famine pressed in the preceding winter and, left at home alone, had gobbled down a whole pot of cooked potatoes. The food overwhelmed her hungry little body. "We found her almost suffocated," Émile reported. "[Mama] gave her tea, bullion, enemas. Nothing [worked] . . . The surgeon said she would never recover. She lingered for two months with terrible convulsions." Then she died.

Émile followed this terrible news with a promise that "my little brother and I are well." Babeuf found otherwise when he laid eyes on them. "[The boys] were so exhausted that I hardly recognized them." Here was intimate evidence of a whole city's suffering. "I soon found my family's appearance reproduced a thousand times over in those around them. I saw clearly the unmistakable signs of general exhaustion that touched most Parisians, withering their faces and leaving their bodies unsteady."[25]

Government indifference starved his children, and official malice kept him ignorant of it. As he traded ideas with an eager acolyte and dreamed of a world to come, Babeuf's little ones had suffered and died. Although he rarely spoke publicly of this experience, it is difficult to read his anguished words about poverty or consider his rage at the indifference of the wealthy without believing that his children's hardship weighed heavily on his mind. His fury at power and privilege was driven by a sense of justice and equity but perhaps, also, by his guilt at having thrived while hunger wasted his family. Shamed by his inability to protect them from a society that put so little value on the lives of the poor, Babeuf found his determination mounting to sweep away such corruption.

The Reaction continued. Gilded youth, who served the National Convention by disarming and humiliating sans-culottes, became arrogant in their victory, intensifying their threats on political rivals as reactionary journalists praised royalist atrocities in the provinces. When an émigré army attempted to invade France from the west, the Convention acknowledged that it could no longer contain the right. Legislators, fearful that proponents of the Old Order would swamp the new government, manipulated the electoral system to retain power. They announced that two-thirds of the incoming legislative councils would be drawn from their ranks. It was a badly judged effort to define the nation's course by men who believed they could do so without negotiation or compromise. The Two-Thirds Decree frustrated reactionary hopes and excited fearful memories of Jacobin opposition to open elections during the era of revolutionary government.[26]

Insurrection exploded in October 1795, the revolutionary month of Vendémiaire year IV. For the first time since 1789, a Paris uprising was excited by right-wing middling sorts rather than radical working people. They raised barricades and fought government forces until troops commanded by the young general Napoleon Bonaparte flushed them from the city.

Although the Vendémiaire insurgents defended legitimate political interests by demanding free and open elections, their opponents dismissed them as royalists. Once having defeated them militarily, the National Convention parried politically by making overtures to the left. Its last act was to amnesty the democratic militants it had imprisoned in the preceding year. Babeuf and his new allies walked free from the Plessis prison, ready to restore democracy and renew equality.[27]

FOUR

The Plot against the Government

In a gesture long unthinkable, the former Jacobin P.-F. Réal publicly commiserated with a reactionary. "We are both tired of revolution," he admitted from the pages of his newspaper, "horrified by the bloody, wicked scenes that darkened it. Both of us hope liberty will spring forth, pure and dazzling, from this chaos of passion, revenge, reaction, and anarchy; that the sad days and clouded, gloomy skies of this long political winter will give way to the peaceful, happy era promised by stable government and the constitution we accepted." By "stable government" Réal meant the Directory. Inaugurated in October 1795, it was designed by men who believed the only way to end the revolution was by foreclosing further "tyranny" and "anarchy," for which they blamed the democratic constitution of 1793.[1]

In the summer of 1795, a Committee of Eleven named by the National Convention had drafted a new constitution. To root out institutional "tyranny," the Eleven replaced their all-powerful Convention with an Assembly divided between a lower Council of 500, which proposed legislation, and an upper Council of Ancients, which could veto laws but not amend them. To root out the personal power they had accused Robespierre of exercising, the Eleven refused to install a king, president, or prime minister but instead shared power among five men, who would constitute the Executive Directory from which the regime drew its name. To further restrict personal power, the Eleven mandated that one-third of each council and one member of the executive would be reelected annually. What they did not foresee was how such elections would destabilize a government that was already struggling to heal political polarization, restore domestic peace, and stabilize the economy after years of war and revolution.

The Eleven were even more troubled by the "anarchy" they recalled from the Terror, and for which they blamed popular democracy. Committee chairman Boissy d'Anglas argued that democracy rendered the law "powerless" by giving authority to "lazy, uncontrollable men." Sound government demanded "the best," by which he meant landholders who were "attached to the country that contains their property, the laws that protect it, [and] the peace that preserves it," and who possessed "the education that renders them fit to discuss, wisely and prudently, the benefits and disadvantages of laws that determine their country's fate."[2]

Boissy and his colleagues did not, however, believe that elevating "the best" would be sufficient. Determined to contain a populace they considered ignorant, disorderly, and grasping, they abolished universal male suffrage, setting a minimum tax threshold for voting to take effect immediately and a literacy requirement within ten years. They moved further from democratic practices by restoring the second round of voting, first established in 1791, and reducing the number of eligible electors by half. It was a stunning reversal of the broad franchise of 1793. And still, the Eleven did not stop. They made the looming literacy requirement more onerous by renouncing all promise of universal education. They limited other avenues of political expression by authorizing suspension of a free press and permitting breaches of free association. Citizens were henceforth forbidden to petition collectively. Any public gathering, armed or peaceful, might be dispersed by force. For those who could not see the writing on the wall, the constitution's intent was neatly summarized in article 363: "citizens may only exercise their political rights in [electoral] assemblies."

This was the code against which Babeuf and Germain warned in vain during the summer of 1795. Founded on an oxymoronic association of "tyranny" and "anarchy," it created a government with a profoundly ambivalent relationship to the nation's recent revolutionary past. For, having promised a fresh start with the Directory, the National Convention adopted the Two-

Thirds Decree that required the majority of the new councils to be drawn from its ranks. As the Vendémiaire insurgents rightly charged, that decree guaranteed the continued influence of the old.

The Vendémiaire insurgents were not the only ones to see flaws in the new regime. Other right-wing critics were dismayed by preservation of the republic. Democrats, to the left, were troubled by the constitution's purposeful marginalization of "the people." But however great its failings, the new constitution was delivered to a nation exhausted by war, devastated by domestic turmoil, wracked by economic dysfunction, and eager to recover. Disenchanted democrats joined weary monarchists in accepting the new regime of the Directory.

Many who acquiesced could justify themselves by pointing to the resurrection of Parisian public life in the fall of 1795. Democrats freed from the pressures of reaction crowded into the capital's popular cafes and mobbed its newly formed Pantheon Club to listen to newspapers being read aloud and to join in conversation about current affairs. Returned émigrés mingled in more exclusive salons, quietly mocking the "nonsensical dialect and vulgar reminiscences" of reactionary parvenus whose alliance they required to reinsert themselves into French politics and society. Fashionable reactionaries who had become notorious after Thermidor for their public scorn of republican austerity continued their familiar rounds of entertainment as they moved between restaurants, parties, and dance halls where "perfumed goddesses" locked eyes with dandies sporting outrageous pompadours.[3]

The press was equally vibrant, newspapers expressing such a variety of opinion that they recalled the ebullience of the revolution's early years. The radical dogmatism that had prevailed just two years before gave way to more fluid democratic opinions. P.-F. Réal and his co-editor at the *Journal of the Patriots of '89*, Méhée de la Touche, hoped to broaden suffrage but they endorsed the Directory and negotiated with right-wing editors far more energetically than did the *Journal of Free Men*, which was inclined to criticize the present regime and advocate for redemption of old Jacobins. These papers, and smaller ones like them, were doing better than democratic dailies of the preceding year but were still outsold four, five, even ten to one by right-wing sheets. The latter gave evidence, too, of a greater diversity of opinion, which ranged from the reluctant republicanism of the former monarchist Dupont de Nemours, at the *Historian,* to the crypto-royalism of the *Anti-Terrorist.*[4]

Whether reactionary, moderately republican, or enthusiastically democratic, journalists across the political spectrum shared P.-F. Réal's weariness with revolution and tried to heal old rifts by reaching out. Democrats sought common ground with moderate republicans, who attempted conversation with reactionaries. Whether to the left or right of the center the Directory defined, all were chastened by recent experiences of ostracism and inclined to accept Réal's advice to "embrace one another in good faith, vanquish memory, abolish the threat of division . . . [and] find in [the Directory] . . . the will and the means to save the nation."[5]

As democrats reeled from the loss of the 1793 constitution and debated how to accommodate the new regime, Réal took a vocal lead. He had promoted the peaceful resolution of political difference since Thermidor and continued to do so now. Although no friend of the sans-culottes, as was visible in his staunch resistance to Babeuf's call for new elections in the fall of 1794, and negotiating most publicly with men on his right, Réal made discreet alliances with radical democrats to his left. When the time came, he would defend their right to dissent.[6]

Among the most prominent democrats to Réal's left was Pierre-Antoine Antonelle, a former Jacobin imprisoned, like him, after opposing Robespierre during the Terror. A more vigorous advocate of popular democracy than Réal, Antonelle insisted that the abandonment of the democratic constitution was illegal—"the people freely sanctioned and solemnly accepted [it]"—and wrongheaded. Democracy did not weaken the republic, he argued, but strengthened it by enlightening the people and disarming rule by brute force. Like the British radical Thomas Paine, Antonelle believed democracy gave the masses reason to enroll in the nation's armies by proving that the republic they defended was their own. Political stability depended not on silence and exclusion, he concluded, but on freedoms of speech, assembly, and suffrage for all, because "there is no possibility of true and enduring liberty without equality of rights."[7]

And still, Antonelle welcomed the Directory with a supple pragmatism he would find lacking in the regime. He embraced the new constitution as "for the moment, our only means of order and strength," but reserved the right to encourage liberalization. What he and many like him understood was that the constitution's promise of order and its relatively firm guarantee of free speech could encourage loyal opposition by facilitating the return to public life of democrats tarred as "anarchists" after Thermidor. Perhaps, Antonelle and Réal intimated, the bitter charge of "factionalism" that had so long been used to foreclose debate might give way to more fluid notions of dissent.[8]

This was the world to which the democratic *Journal of Free Men* welcomed Babeuf upon his release from prison. "A republic requires a tribune . . . an honorable trade that Babeuf practiced before his persecution. He resumes it now, animated by the hardship that demoralizes too many. Just as the legislative assembly reinvigorates patriots, so Babeuf reinvigorates his trusty pen . . . We encourage patriots to . . . flock to their tribune and support the labors he resumes with newfound vigor."[9]

If editors at the *Free Men* hoped Babeuf would join them in publicizing measured critique of loyal critics, he quickly disabused them. He did not answer the welcome by exulting in recovered liberties, preaching compromise, and encouraging patience for reform. He remembered the ordinary citizens who had crowded sectional assemblies and thronged assembly halls until purged, hounded, and disarmed. He knew that many who survived the bitter winter of the previous year had lost children, jobs, homes. He saw families like his own devastated by need, peasants foraging for nettles to fill their bellies, veterans abandoned by the republic they had risked their lives to defend, women prostituting their bodies to get by, and suicides multiplying.[10]

Believing this much-vaunted civil peace more deadly than the revolutionary violence so loudly condemned, Babeuf roared out against democrats' willingness to compromise. "Who are these optimists, these phony patriots who . . . shout at the tops of their lungs *Everything is for the best in the best of all possible worlds?* What do you mean *everything is fine?* . . . I see not the slightest evidence that this is so . . . Doesn't a pound of bread still cost sixteen francs? A pound of meat, twenty? . . . Is there any sign that the institutions that rob and strangle ordinary people will soon change?" And all because their beloved constitution of 1793, "inspired by the muse of liberty herself," had been deceitfully replaced by one that opposed its every principle. This was not a revolution triumphant, as the Directory's proponents claimed, but one in its death throes. The people must rise up to restore all they had fought for: "ease, education, equality, and liberty for all, the common good."[11]

Babeuf's targets recoiled. The *Free Men* retracted its friendly endorsement, saying that "like all true friends of the republic, we denounce these reckless pages, which threaten to renew hostilities . . . and ruin the nation." Réal accused Babeuf of dangerous provocation. "If I were a royalist, I would . . . say: look, the terrorists are back . . . see them getting ready to destroy your constitution [by calling] . . . for the constitution of 1793."[12]

Babeuf countered that they were cowards and fools, blind to the precariousness of their situation. "If we let this moment slip through our fingers, we have no hope of restoring the liberty and happiness for which we sacrificed so much." Challenging Réal's claim that "the revolution is over and anyone who complains so bitterly is just an anarchist," he issued a declaration of his own. "To make revolution . . . is to conspire against an unacceptable state of things . . . So long as the worthless has not been abolished and the good is not yet guaranteed, I will not admit that we are done making revolution."[13]

Then Babeuf made clear just how all-encompassing his notion of revolution had become by going public with his opposition to private property. In a new issue of *The People's Tribune*, he mourned popular suffering. "The poor man dies next to an abundance that eludes him, which he may not, dare not touch," while "the rich hoarder, glutted on delicacies, rests peacefully atop sacks of flour heaped up by his own greed . . . Terrible famine, generated by the deadly system of counter-revolution, sends this generation and the next to the grave. The value of [paper money] is reduced to almost nothing . . . the cost of necessities is multiplied a hundredfold."[14]

The people, Babeuf continued, must defend their rights. "Let [them] proclaim [their] manifesto. Let them define the democracy they will . . . and should have. Let them explain that this democracy is the obligation of those who have too much to satisfy the needs of those who do not have enough, that the deprivation of the latter is to be found in the fortunes stolen from them by the former." Comparing himself to Moses, Babeuf volunteered to lead the people to a promised land by helping them realize society's highest aim: *common good.*[15]

Common good, he explained, repudiated the system of private property which permitted accumulation of land and goods that properly belonged to all people. It affirmed that taking more than one needed was "social theft," buying and selling was an assault on one's fellows, bequeathing what one accumulated was a plot against the collective.

Founding his argument on the right to existence that Rousseau and Mably had elaborated before 1789 and which Jacobins, Enragés, and sans-culottes defended in 1793, Babeuf went well beyond all of them. He exceeded even advocates of agrarian law who wanted to redistribute land. Any system that preserves the merest scrap of private property, he warned, contains the seeds of future misery because inequality inevitably metastasizes from ownership. There should be no property in material goods, no ownership of ideas, no claim that some skills be better compensated than others. No sort of industry or inventiveness would be prized more highly than another because all achievements are interconnected. Every citizen requires knowledge from the past and the help of others in the present to realize a project, so all should share in the rewards.

"Talk all you want about the best form of government," Babeuf quoted from the utopian Morelly, "you will not achieve anything unless you destroy the germs of greed and ambition." The people must create institutions to prevent anyone from becoming too rich or too poor, too powerful or too distinguished, they must create institutions that would improve everyone's condition by ensuring that each had enough. Just as he had said to Charles Germain in Arras, so Babeuf told the readers of his *Tribune* to "abolish private property; employ each man according to his skills; require everyone to deliver the fruits of his labor to a common storehouse; and create a simple administration to distribute it." This was the only way to guarantee "common good."[16]

Babeuf made his case by alluding to Enlightenment thinkers like Morelly and Jean-Jacques Rousseau, but he believed his most important predecessors were the Jacobins. The Declaration of Rights adopted under their leadership in 1793 opened with the affirmation that graced the *Tribune*'s masthead: "society's aim is common good." The Jacobin Saint-Just, he pointed out, had advocated for equality when he urged the poor to "speak as masters to their governors" and promised to redistribute counter-revolutionaries' property. Even the turncoat Joseph Fouché insisted that "all citizens have an equal right to society's advantages." Babeuf promised to bring to fruition what he believed these men had imagined.[17]

It was an astonishingly radical argument that suggests the extent of Babeuf's desperation to end poverty and his limited understanding of markets and social welfare. Believing, like the sans-culottes, that the land produced enough for everyone—even if it was only "just enough"—he was determined to bridge the growing chasm he saw between rich and poor. Having worked briefly in the Paris food administration, he seems to have had an exalted idea of how effectively a government might take in and share out goods.

The tribune's allusions to his intellectual and political forebears suggest, as well, the limits of his own education. He had come astonishingly far in life, reached well beyond the simple acquisition of literacy by schooling himself in philosophy and joining contemporary political debate. But he remained an autodidact and a relatively isolated thinker with limited opportunity to refine his ideas through dialogue. Even his prerevolutionary correspondence with Dubois, the most sustained intellectual relationship he had prior to meeting Charles Germain, was characterized less by critique and growth, advance and retreat, concession and considered resistance than by the simple opposition of competing opinions.

All of this was visible in a discussion founded on nuggets lifted from arguments whose broader intent Babeuf ignored. Deaf to nuance and blind to the political and intellectual ambitions of those he quoted, he mounted a rhetorical assault on property that credited the Jacobins as his predecessors. In so doing, he gave credence to the heated reactionary charge that Jacobin restrictions on the disposition of private wealth constituted a first step toward abolishing private property.

Seeing Babeuf endorse the charge that they were levelers, old Jacobins objected. The retired deputy Marc-Guillaume Vadier, who sat on the Committee of General Security during the Terror, plastered his protest on the walls of the city. "I too would like true equality . . . I have no property, or almost none. I have six children, all too young to work. I have the misfortune of not possessing a trade . . . [H]ow many pressing reasons to wish for real equality! But alas, is it possible? What good is it to show me that bliss on a horizon so far that I despair of achieving it?" Everyone knew, Vadier continued, that the comprehensive sharing of goods Babeuf imagined would sow chaos by demanding sophisticated calculation, sturdy contracts, and leaders to enforce them, rousing angry reaction, and killing off "taste, inspiration and the passion for beauty." After subjecting the nation to "years of anarchy," he concluded, Babeuf's plan would leave them all "worse off than we are now."

Antonelle spoke up, too. The institution of property was born of "greed and envy," he admitted, and gave rise to "vices that gnaw at us, desires that consume us, passions that divide us." Its abolition would improve the human condition, but "the roots of that fatal institution are too deep and too strong." The best they could hope for, he said, echoing other Jacobins and the much-admired Rousseau, was "a [more] tolerable degree of inequality."

Réal, a less enthusiastic proponent of popular democracy and social welfare, was simply enraged. "Let Gracchus Babeuf blather on about anarchy, bloodshed and redistribution of land; let fanatics justify him, those of us who want the republic and honest democracy, the constitution or death . . . will rally to the government."[18]

Repudiated by old Jacobins and fellow journalists, Babeuf found his audience in private homes and government offices, small shops and working-class cafés, even the army. Recovering the readership he had enjoyed before arrest, his paper matched or outstripped every democratic sheet but the *Free Men*. With more than six hundred subscribers and two thousand copies sold on the street, the *Tribune* reached further as issues were read aloud and passed from hand to hand.[19]

Readers took different things from its pages. "I am the only one in this column who receives your paper," a soldier wrote loyally, "but I circulate it as widely as I can. At least those near me can profit from your labors; they are friends of liberty and equality, virtuous plebeians who savor bold and dazzling principles; like me, they appreciate your frank understanding." Some wanted only to inform themselves, like the deputies who kept an eye on every shade of opinion and the watchmaker who paired the *Tribune's* radical preaching with a reactionary's editorializing, "because reliable values lie somewhere between." Others appreciated Babeuf's moving denunciation of their suffering or thought their political opinions validated by his defense of the democratic constitution. Some believed his condemnation of property was hyperbole, meant to defend measures of public welfare imposed in 1793 and 1794. Some saw the condemnation for the radical notion that it was and applauded. Others demurred, albeit more gently than Vadier or Réal. "True equality cannot exist. Renounce such fantastic ideas, the French could not adopt or try to live by them without creating a chaos more dangerous than that of the schemers, status seekers, royalists, and friends of tyranny who creep among us."[20]

If some readers misinterpreted Babeuf's condemnation of property, others probably missed it among the hundreds of pages he published between November 1795 and April 1796. The *Tribune* had become something like a running series of political pamphlets before Babeuf's arrest the preceding spring, and it continued to evolve now. Issues stretched to as many as fifty-five pages, sometimes suggesting a mind unraveling as they mingled tightly reasoned argument and eloquent demands for popular rights with inflated promises of relief, fiery expressions of mounting rage, and sheer paranoia. The democratic editors with whom he quarreled, Babeuf charged several times, rallied together to poison opinion against him.[21]

Just as admirers took what they wanted from the *Tribune*, so too did opponents. Jacobin hostility to the jeremiad against property was exceeded by the Directory's mounting anxiety about Babeuf's defense of the democratic constitution.

Despite bold promises of recovery, the Directory was vulnerable. Its coffers had been emptied by war and revolution, its ability to administer was disrupted by repeated changes in personnel, its capacity to police was sapped by the destruction of old social hierarchies. The poverty that plagued city and countryside alike was especially threatening in Paris, where crowds had taken to the streets even before 1789 and the memory of revolution weighed heavily.

It had been only three years since angry women requisitioned goods from shopkeepers and crowds marched on the Convention to demand price controls. Less than a year before, hungry insurgents had killed a deputy on the very floor of the assembly and dumped his severed head at his colleagues' feet.

There was, too, the intimate link between the regime's promise of renewal and its disavowal of democracy. Boissy d'Anglas had, after all, damned the democratic constitution of 1793 as "conceived by the ambitious, written by schemers, dictated by tyranny, and accepted by terror . . . [an] institutionalization of disorder [and an] instrument designed to serve the greedy, the interests of agitators, the pride of the ignorant, and the ambitions of tyrants." Having cast democracy as "the foundation of anarchy," he offered the Directory as an antidote.[22]

Babeuf's adamant refusal to bow to the new order was especially threatening because he not only demanded that popular democracy be restored but encouraged the very activism its critics feared. One police spy gave voice to common conservative concerns when he complained that the *Tribune* "excite[s] poor against rich and workers against shopkeepers, making people long for the reign of Terror and reversal of the Revolution's course since 9 Thermidor." Another warned that such messages were finding their intended audience: "last night, people's faces lit up as they listened to someone read an issue by Babeuf that enthused over Robespierre."[23]

Unwilling to make concessions to popular democracy or improve social welfare to win over a suffering population, the regime preferred to kill the messenger. A warrant was issued for Babeuf's arrest in early December 1795. He put up a fight against the police agent who came after him, scrambling into the street and wrestling with the man until sympathetic neighbors came to the rescue. Babeuf got away, but frustrated police seized every copy of his paper that they could lay hands on.

Once safely in hiding, the tribune reproached the government. "I truly believed the phrase in the constitution that says, *No one may be prevented from speaking, writing, printing, or publishing his thoughts*; and this one, *Those who commit arbitrary acts are guilty.* I thought such guarantees promised me safety in my own home. Now I know this is not so." The Directory, Babeuf charged, disdained its own constitution.[24]

Enraged police continued their hunt, turning against Babeuf's allies. They arrested René Lebois, editor of *The People's Friend*, after he advertised their humiliating failure to bring in the tribune, and they forced Marie-Anne to leave the children with a neighbor before tossing her in jail. Having locked her up, they deprived her of food to force her to reveal her husband's hiding place. But they had underestimated their prey. The tribune's wife was as resolute as the tribune himself and gave up nothing.

Marie-Anne's detention was not only illegal but also ill judged, because it rallied the very democrats Babeuf antagonized when left to his own devices. "Who ordered the arrest of Babeuf's wife?" the *Free Men* demanded. "The authorities did, because she distributed her husband's writings." Penalizing a journalist for what he wrote, the paper concluded, was a gross abuse of power.[25]

As Babeuf continued to publish his *Tribune* from a Paris hideaway, he set his sights on the Pantheon Club. Organized at the time of the Directory's inauguration to rally support for the new regime, the club attracted hundreds of old militants and disillusioned workers who proceeded to challenge its moderate founders. Babeuf insinuated himself into the rising tensions through his paper, using it to taunt moderates as government stooges and celebrate their opponents as visionary democrats. Charles Germain, Filippo Buonarroti, and Augustin Darthé joined the fray on the floor of the club. Germain detailed Marie-Anne's arrest to fellow members, exhorting them to contribute funds for the family's support. Buonarroti took the president's chair and allowed Darthé to read out an issue of the *Tribune* that regretted the notorious September Massacres of 1792, not for slaughtering some twelve hundred prisoners but for failing to eliminate all counter-revolutionaries. Some members of the audience were said to have cheered.[26]

The directors answered by citing the constitution's prohibition of "associations contrary to public order," and decreed the closure of the Pantheon Club. There was a break in the battle as police claimed that most Parisians, "who just want peace and tranquility, applauded." Even normally outspoken democrats were reserved, Antonelle suggesting that the government probably had good reason to act. The muted response may have seemed encouraging, but the authorities had made a dangerous move. By shuttering such an important public arena for dissent, they denied themselves an opportunity to keep an eye on their critics.[27]

The first pamphlet appeared a few days later. Several more appeared within weeks, and handbills blossomed on city walls. All of them, published anonymously, charged the Directory with corruption and demanded that the constitution of 1793 be restored. *Soldier, Stop and Read* described the government as "insidious" and "perverse," calling its excesses "an insult" to popular suffering. *An Opinion on Our Two Constitutions* compared the "freely, peacefully, unanimously, [and] publicly . . . accepted" constitution of 1793 with the one foisted on the people in 1795 to destroy them "as civic and political beings." The *Statement of Babeuf's Doctrine* embedded a demand for community of goods in another celebration of the constitution of '93 as "the one true law of the French."[28]

Official anxiety mounted. Police warned that "the most ridiculous rumors, the most despicable accusations against the government harden and heighten popular exasperation, causing unrest. The unemployed worker who has nothing to live on does not miss a chance to vent his anger at the state of things. He calls the constitution 'the code of the gilded million' and reviles its authors." Officers seized pamphlets and tore down posters, but new ones appeared, often to rousing effect.[29]

"Most people who read the *Statement of Babeuf's Doctrine* applauded it, especially workers . . . People in cafés and cabarets, and groups on the street hear that if the constitution of 1793 were still in effect, they would have meat and bread as they did two years ago . . . At nine o'clock last night, agitators in a large group on the pont au Change called the authorities blood suckers who grow fat on republicans. They asked good patriots to join them in destroying the so-called tyrants who govern, claiming that this is the only way to save the republic." A legislator received a letter from Toulouse, in the southwest, that reviled him and his colleagues as "assassins of the people" who "stole everything" and "were more power-hungry than despots." Word came from Châlons, in the north, that someone had posted a sign there calling for insurrection.[30]

Journalists across the political spectrum shared in the growing alarm. An editorial from Marseille warned against the deteriorating situation in the capital. In Paris, the democrat Réal and a reactionary editor shared their common conviction that the anonymous tracts threatened insurrection.[31]

And yet, however much political opponents might agree that the nation was in danger, they deferred remedy by blaming one another for it. Democrats insisted that the pamphlets' anonymous authors were crypto-royalists, trying to win support for a restored monarchy by sowing chaos. Royalists and reactionaries said the calls to restore the democratic constitution were part of an effort to reignite the Terror. Commentators across the political spectrum could agree on one thing only: "if the Directory does not confront these schemes and make some effort to frustrate them, it is lost and all of France with it."[32]

Unable to identify pamphlet authors or poster hangers, legislators resorted to threat. In mid-April, they decreed it a capital offense to promote "royalism, the constitution of 1793, . . . any government other than the one established by the constitution of [1795]," or to challenge the institution of property. Riding roughshod over cherished revolutionary liberties, just as the directors had done in closing the Pantheon Club, the deputies had little impact. Pamphlets continued to rain down, and public order deteriorated.[33]

In late April 1796, the Paris police legion mutinied. The legion had been created to keep order in the capital after the Prairial insurrection of spring 1795, but its political composition changed when right-wing men were purged after the reactionary Vendémiaire insurrection the following fall. Radicals flowed in to take the reactionaries' place but quickly called their own reliability into question by mingling with workers they might someday be called to discipline.

An unsettled government finally decided to rid the capital of the whole lot by dismantling the legion and enrolling its members in armed forces fighting in Italy or policing the counter-revolutionary Vendée. When the soldiers learned in late April that they were to be deployed, they mutinied, closing down their barracks, commandeering a wagon filled with arms, and casting about for alliances with local workers and soldiers stationed nearby. Everything hung in the balance until the executive director Lazare Carnot divided the legion against itself by ordering the arrest of the mutiny's leaders and sending the others home.[34]

His gamble paid off. The revolt melted away in a matter of hours. But the city was left badly shaken. "There are rumors that conspiracy is afoot; something is brewing behind closed doors."[35]

Relief came in the form of a letter that landed on Lazare Carnot's desk in early May 1796. Its author confirmed the lingering rumors by confessing that, "for more than a month, I have . . . been part of a conspiracy against the government." He was an army captain named Georges Grisel, who explained that he put off denouncing the plot until he could identify its leaders. Now he knew those men to include the fugitive Babeuf, two former generals, and perhaps even a sitting deputy. He was ready to tell all.[36]

Grisel met first with Carnot and then with the rest of the Executive Directory, and finally handed over two addresses. Several hundred troops were dispatched to a house in northern Paris, where soldiers found a half-dozen men sitting down to lunch. Among them were Charles Germain, Augustin Darthé, two former deputies to the National Convention, and the sitting deputy Grisel had alluded to. That legislator was none other than Jean-Baptiste Drouet, the sharp-eyed former postmaster who had so famously stopped the king's flight at Varennes in 1791 and become a hero for it.[37]

Meanwhile, police commissioner Jean-Baptiste Dossonville and his men closed in on a second lodging in central Paris. Knowing that crowds gathered quickly in this densely populated neighborhood and determined to prevent his prey from escaping, Dossonville cordoned off the street and spread word that the police were going after highway bandits. Then he climbed to the third floor of a nearby building and charged an apartment.

He found Babeuf writing quietly inside, in the company of Filippo Buonarroti and another man. "A look of utter dejection crossed all three faces," Dossonville would later say, but the men made no move to defend themselves. "Babeuf stood from his chair and cried out: *It's all over. Tyranny has won!*" Dossonville swept up a poster that demanded "the constitution of '93 or death" and a written order to assassinate members of the government, then sealed more than a dozen cartons of papers stacked up around the suspects. When he took the prisoners downstairs, a crowd shouted insults at men they believed to be common thieves. Babeuf looked surprised.[38]

The Directory declared victory that afternoon and described the conspiracy it said police had frustrated. "A horde of thieves and murderers was plotting to slaughter legislators, members of government, commanders of the army of the interior, and all constituted authorities in Paris . . . But remain calm, good citizens, the government is vigilant. It knows the conspiracy's leaders and their plan of attack."[39]

Despite the troubles the nation faced—foreign war, domestic chaos, empty coffers, a flailing economy—the Directory was greeted with hope and good will after its inauguration in fall 1795. If monarchists were disappointed by preservation of the republic and democrats discouraged by exclusion of the people, all were equally exhausted. The delicate possibility of reconciliation beckoned to citizens across the political spectrum who asked how to construct a loyal opposition and advance the reform they hoped for. Then Babeuf arrived on the scene.

And yet, however explosive Babeuf's language, he was not alone in threatening the nation's fragile compromise. He was singularly radical but, for just that reason, he was also isolated, quarreling with the very democrats whose alliance he needed to realize change. Directors and legislators did not see it that way. Determined to close the door on popular democracy, they raged at its most ardent advocate and steam-rolled revolutionary rights in order to silence him. In so doing, the Executive Directory and the legislative councils disturbed the equilibrium they had been called to foster. It was a foolish choice because, as Babeuf's own radicalization suggests, repression often strengthens an opponent's resolve. But the regime gave no sign of having the will or the strength to make concessions.

The arrest of Babeuf and almost a dozen others, on a May morning in 1796, appeared to put everything to rest. The troublemaker and his allies had been exposed. For a moment, it seemed that the project of ending the revolution by consolidating a conservative republic might continue. The directors believed the arrest of almost a dozen reputed conspirators proved their determination to restore order. They pledged to demonstrate their respect for rule of law by cautiously pursuing the case and organizing a rigorously fair trial. It was a moment of triumph rich with hope for equilibrium restored.

The moment was fleeting. This case would spiral into a polarizing debate, to weaken the Directory and forge an enduring reputation for a man who had, until then, fought for every scrap of notoriety he possessed.

FIVE

Fear and Polarization

The suspects were isolated and questioned separately. Charles Germain, Augustin Darthé, and Jean-Baptist Drouet, arrested in northern Paris, insisted on their innocence. Filippo Buonarroti, detained in the rue de la Grande Truanderie with Babeuf, said that he knew nothing about a plot, did not even know he was sitting on a poster calling for insurrection when Dossonville rushed in.[1]

It was Babeuf who breached the wall of silence. "Convinced, as I am, that the present government is oppressive," he told his interrogator, "I would have done everything in my power to overturn it. I was allied with every democrat in the republic." When the interrogator asked what date had been set for an uprising, Babeuf repeated that he was part of a collective. "It was not up to me alone to decide when insurrection would explode . . . the first favorable moment was to be seized to overthrow tyranny and deliver the people from their monstrous slavery and foul misery."[2]

Two days later, Babeuf took his defiance to the directors. "Do you consider it beneath you to negotiate with me as one power to another?" he asked in a long, needling letter. "You have seen the vast federation of which I am the center, you see that my party equals yours, you understand the terrible consequences. I am sure all of it makes you tremble." The directors could not win this battle, Babeuf warned. If they prosecuted him, he would defend the conspiracy as necessary to preserve eternal rights. If they condemned him, the memory of his martyrdom would endure. Rather than rouse a vast opposition they could not defeat, Babeuf counseled the directors to admit that they had abused their power, embrace the people's cause, and resurrect republican principle. "You know what influence I have over that class of men known as patriots. I will use it to convince them to take your side if you take theirs."[3]

It was a startling letter, delusional in its conviction that one man could shape the course of events from the depths of a prison cell. But Babeuf was determined to define himself at a critical moment and shape the battle for democracy he had come to believe could only be won on his terms. He could not yet know how or by whom his efforts would be frustrated, but someone more calculating might have guessed what the directors would do.

The arrests rallied support for the Directory across the political spectrum. From the affirmation of the reactionary *Critic of the Press* that the regime had earned the nation's gratitude to a cheer that "crime conspires in vain" from the democratic *Friend of the Laws*, newspapers of all stripes celebrated. On Paris streets, among the men and women Babeuf thought most likely to embrace his doctrine of *common good*, police claimed that "people read in the plan of massacre—*We must keep the people from thinking, they must commit acts that will make retreat impossible*—and become angry, understanding that these crooks wanted to force them to commit terrible crimes in order to make them victims of them too."[4]

But the directors were acutely aware of their own weakness. The economy was in shambles. Unemployment was rising and wages falling, paper money almost worthless, goods scarce. The government, sapped by debt, could not build up or restore order to a countryside teeming with bandits. Memory of the many insurrections that had shaken Paris, including the police legion mutiny less than a month before, created perpetual anxiety about security there. And, in the very week of Babeuf's arrest, the regime suffered humiliating defeats in two separate trials meant to demonstrate its ascendancy over extremism.[5]

Desperate for a victory, the directors summoned all the force they could muster. Understanding the plot as an effort to restore the democratic constitution and resurrect the National Convention, they asked the Council of

500 to require all demobilized soldiers, former civil servants, and retired deputies associated with the previous regime to leave the capital within seventy-two hours. The Council of Ancients broadened the order to exile such men from the entire Paris region. Minister of Police Charles Cochon hastily drafted a list of suspects targeting men he mistrusted for past activism and subscribers to the *People's Tribune*. Using that information, director Lazare Carnot issued 172 arrest warrants against old militants, former deputies to the National Convention, retired administrators and bureaucrats, and even the Jacobin prosecutor who had helped Babeuf with his fraud case in 1794.[6]

Just as Babeuf had predicted the year before, when explaining to Charles Germain what might happen if they tried and failed to raise an insurrection, the directors launched a publicity campaign. "Although it has not yet been possible to examine completely the papers found at Babeuf's lodging . . . what we have seen makes clear the horrors of the conspirators' crimes." They said that Babeuf and his allies had created a committee of insurgency to lead an assault on the capital, describing posters, manifestos, and detailed plans for their "bloody project."[7]

The directors affirmed their case in the days and weeks that followed by distributing pages from Babeuf's archive to the press and publishing them on broadsides for passersby to study in the street. There was a chilling command to "kill the Five," presumably the five directors, and all of their ministers, followed by orders to "seize the halls of both legislative houses . . . take the city gates . . . [and] send the shrewdest, most trustworthy men . . . to excite rebellion [elsewhere]." One note swore, "never was a plot as holy as ours." Another sketched a plan to restore the National Convention and revive revolutionary committees like those that had policed Paris neighborhoods during the Terror. A stamp that Babeuf acknowledged as his own was engraved with the words "Public Safety." His brazen letter to the directors made the rounds as well.[8]

The plot became a regular fixture in newspapers that had, since 1789, brought word of every facet of the revolution to the farthest reaches of France. Conservative and reactionary sheets were more popular than they had been at the beginning of the decade, but all papers loomed larger now. Having once been one means among many to share news and opinion, they

CONJURATION DE BABOEUF L'AN IV.

La France sous la forme d'une Mère nourice, jeune et vigoureuse admire l'harmonie de sa Constitution, des Authorités établies, et des Départemens. L'Anarchie furieuse et jalouse), conseillée par un Serpent astutieux va plonger ses poignards dans le sein de la Patrie. Mais le Génie deffenseur de la République, l'arrête dans ses fureurs.

Anon., "Babeuf's Conspiracy of Year IV," 1796. The caption explains: "France, in the shape of a young, healthy nursing mother, admires the harmony of her constitution, established authorities, and departments. Jealous, enraged Anarchy, guided by a crafty serpent, is about to plunge its knives into the Motherland's breast. But the brilliant defender of the republic stops it in its tracks." Source: BnF.

stood alone as political clubs and sectional assemblies vanished. They would play an outsized role in advertising competing opinions about conspiracy, arrests, and the trial to come but, for the moment, expressed common relief at the plot's frustration. That unity quickly faded.[9]

Reactionaries remembered "rumors of popular unrest" overheard in recent weeks, insinuating that legislators who were former Jacobins had always been in on the plot. "Did you notice how arrogantly [they] shouted, threatened, and tried to monopolize debate . . . ? Now we know it's because they were counting on imminent victory." Surely the Directory had known what was going on as well, they continued, for why else take so long to act? And once having acted, why do so with such fanfare? "Cannon and cavalry to arrest a man like Babeuf! . . . does [him] too great an honor, gives [him] too much importance."[10]

Babeuf's claim of a secret army deepened the uneasiness. "News throughout the republic confirms the conspirators' ties to provincial confederates," editors of the conservative *Evening Messenger* warned, publishing a byzantine account of rebel recruitment across France. "Our situation becomes more frightening each day," reactionary allies at *Critic of the Press* added hopelessly, "the conspiracy we think revealed continues within and beyond the city's walls."[11]

Private citizens and public officials joined the chorus of fear with denunciations of their own. Police in Lille pulled down posters infused with "Babeuf's language," by which they meant "incitement to overturn the constitution of 1795, and praise for the constitution of 1793 and Robespierre's regime." Conservatives in Metz accused a local journalist of abetting the conspiracy, and someone from Drouet's home town of Sainte-Ménéhould claimed that the deputy had been heard to say France ought to restore the guillotine. In Paris, a sitting legislator accused a colleague as a likely accessory.[12]

Authorities made a more lasting impression by purging democrats from bureaucratic offices and harassing old militants. Police in the provinces shut down a café, charging that it attracted "ferocious anarchists," and arrested a man, known in his small town for sporting a "Jacobin cap," after he questioned official accounts of the conspiracy. Administrators in the Marne declared that anyone suspected of loyalty to the constitution of 1793 would be excluded from the National Guard.[13]

Democrats, surveying the denunciations, purges, mounting violence, and widespread arrests, saw less careful investigation than political hysteria. They responded accordingly. Few of these newspaper editors shed tears for Babeuf, whom the moderate Réal had already dismissed as a "delinquent" and "con artist." "Babeuf acquiring fame, a place in history!" he snorted about the letter to the directors. The *Free Men* and *People's Friend*, to Réal's left, were more charitable, highlighting the truths of Babeuf's tirades and depicting him as "deeply embittered by the spectacle of extraordinary and lingering misery." But they made light of his "conspiratorial ambitions" by claiming they had long been visible to everyone and were "almost impossible to realize." The Directory gave far too much importance to a hothead's bravado, they cautioned, dismissing the case by dismissing the man.[14]

Whether moderates like Réal or radicals like the *Free Men*, democrats were uneasy about what news of the plot meant for them. Remembering the violence that followed Thermidor, they urged the Directory to proceed carefully. Even those who celebrated the frustration of a "ghastly conspiracy" worried that fear would excite reaction. Some went so far as to suggest that the true authors of the plot were royalists who hoped to discredit the nation's "true friends" by posing as anarchists. "The corruption of the wicked . . . is infinite . . . and the recklessness of the ambitious as great as their passion to rule!"[15]

Democrats shared common concerns, too, about Jean-Baptiste Drouet. Arrested in the rue Papillon with Charles Germain and Augustin Darthé, Drouet was not just an outspoken ally and sitting legislator. As the sharp-eyed stableman who had stopped the king's flight at Varennes in 1791 and a war hero famed for trying to escape from an Austrian mountain fortress with a crudely fashioned parachute, he was a living legend. Returned to France months before by an exchange of prisoners, he had arrived with hands unsoiled by Terror and a reputation unscathed by Reaction. When he learned that he had been elected to the Council of 500 in his absence, Drouet took the seat and settled in Paris. Now, he was a prisoner once more.

He appealed almost immediately to his colleagues in the Council of 500, explaining that he had been seeking advice on a letter to the directors when police stormed in to arrest everyone. "If public calm demands my confinement, I love my country too much to complain of what might be useful to it." But he wanted to explain himself.

A lifelong disciple of liberty and equality, Drouet said, he had always been forthright about his convictions. "I became a prisoner of war [at a time] when I had the pleasure of seeing my homeland realize ideas once considered fantastic. I had witnessed at last a great, sovereign, and free people in our corner of the world, crafting the laws necessary for its security. Even amidst revolutionary crisis, I saw that people resist ambitious neighbors and shed the prejudice of pride and superstition in the face of impotent rage. It consoled me in my hardship."

Imagine his shock, then, to find a conservative order upon returning to France. The legislative assembly had been divided between upper and lower houses, like the English parliament, and the new constitution was admired in Austria. "I could never stand agreeing with my homeland's enemies." However, because allies welcomed the regime and insisted that it was doing its best for the nation, Drouet joined in. All did not go as he hoped. "Most of the government's agents resisted the directors' professed intentions. Its offices were peopled by petty upstarts in whose mouths the word *citizen* turned to dust . . . [as they] ostentatiously snubbed those who had nothing to recommend them but civic virtue or heroic wounds."

The disheartened deputy was about to resign when he was arrested. "I do not pretend that I never spoke out against the government. On the contrary, each time . . . I saw it oppose public liberty, I attacked its efforts. Nor did I restrict myself to speaking up. I wrote still more . . . and am proud to have done so, because a representative of the people must be forever conscious of his constituents' interests, glory, and liberty." He was a loyal opponent working to improve the regime, Drouet insisted, not a conspirator trying to take it down.[16]

Other democrats raised their voices, worrying that Drouet was targeted as much for frustrating the king's flight in 1791 as for criticizing the Directory now. "France is indebted to his patriotic courage for the arrest of the crowned conspirator," Réal reminded readers, "his hands still bear the honorable marks of Austrian chains. I must have firm proof to overcome such worthy distinctions." *The People's Friend* and *Free Men* pointed to Babeuf's antagonistic tone in his letters to Drouet and noted that the men were arrested more than a mile apart. Finally, both stressed Drouet's status as a sitting deputy. If the Directory could not prove he was arrested in the act of committing a crime, it had breached his legislative immunity. That was an offense they knew all too well from the Terror.[17]

Reactionaries responded irritably at first. "A few people who call themselves *republicans* . . . believe or, at least, claim to believe . . . that if the conspirators . . . are pursued too energetically and their plans exposed, a reaction may follow. This implies that the quarrel is between republicans and royalists. On the contrary, it is between the constitution's friends . . . and France's enemies, whoever they may be."[18]

Then irritation became anger. "I have, citizens, heard several residents of this town deny the conspiracy whose discovery we owe to the Directory's vigilance and tireless efforts. I have seen them persist in treating it as a fantasy despite the evidence before their eyes and the formal declarations of key plotters." The author of these words joined other reactionaries in charging that democrats who continued to doubt the guilt of Babeuf and Drouet were clearly "among the first to know of [the conspiracy] and ready to join in."[19]

Describing political dissent as a form of treason had been a dangerously common political move during Terror and Reaction, as Réal's co-editor at the *Patriots of '89*, Méhée de la Touche, recalled in taking up the gauntlet. "I might blame Drouet for associating with Babeuf, a wretch with whom he ought to have nothing in common . . . But I say to those who want me to believe that he knew the latter's plans, shared in them, and anticipated slaughtering the Directory, the two councils, and the army's general staff, NO, and I will continue to say NO until I see proof of such wickedness." The *Free Men* refused the intimidation with similar energy. Editor P.-A. Antonelle, who had challenged Babeuf's condemnation of property months before, now challenged the rush to judge him. "Who cannot see . . . that there were no available means to realize or even initiate [this project], while . . . every means . . . to crush the conspirators . . . were always in place, easily organized and readily mobilized?"[20]

Seeing a familiar chasm yawn anew between left and right, moderates might have resisted the polarization. Réal had authority to do so, having appealed for compromise at the Directory's inauguration and engaged in friendly dialogue with conservatives. He might have found an ally on the right in Pierre Samuel Dupont de Nemours, a constitutional monarchist who shared his conviction that the constitution of 1795 was the republic's last, best hope. Both men had long insisted that the only way to save the nation was by giving priority to rule of law and public good over particular political loyalties.

Dupont, admittedly, imitated fellow reactionaries by publishing harrowing details of "a deadly project that might have been invented by Satan himself." But he alone praised the Directory's response without reserve. As debate intensified, however, he retreated from insisting that the case did not

pit right against left, by encouraging the government to replace its democratic administrators with conservatives, whom he thought better guardians
of order. Then Dupont joined in reactionary mudslinging by publishing a
letter that equated skepticism about the plot with plotting itself. "People ask
do you believe in the conspiracy? in much the same way they once asked, *do
you believe in magic?* That very question, those affected doubts . . . expose
the government's opponents." Democrats were using the old "Robespier-
rist" trick of manipulating public opinion to empower themselves, the writer
concluded. In so doing, they threatened to reignite the Terror.[21]

Other reactionaries published more outrageous editorials, claiming that
old Jacobins were raising armies or that the Directory delayed exposing the
plot because it was itself infested with "terrorists." But Dupont's erstwhile
moderation made his endorsement of this letter especially troubling. With
that gesture, he joined the rush to judgment that refused dialogue in order
to paint all democrats as dangerously unreconstructed Jacobins.[22]

Ultimately, it was up to the directors to overcome the polarization and safeguard the center they had sworn to protect. They might have done so by extending olive branches to both sides, disputing the claims of renascent
Jacobinism that terrified reactionaries and containing the purges that renewed democrats' sense of vulnerability. They might have refused to vilify
skepticism and discouraged the tendency, at both ends of the political spectrum, to treat the alleged plot as the tip of an iceberg of extremism. These
were, admittedly, tall orders, which required cautious diplomacy and less
self-serving publicity from a regime plagued by its own sense of weakness.
But such leadership, essential in any crisis, was necessary now to contain
the fear that had already played too large a part in the French Revolution.

Dread and suspicion had driven popular activism at critical moments,
whether by rousing the Great Fear of 1789 or fueling the awful Paris Massacres of September 1792, just as anxiety had encouraged legislators and journalists to endorse rumors of foreign and domestic plots. All of this coalesced
into a veritable conspiracy obsession during the Terror.[23]

Citizens had thought themselves done with conspiratorial fears after
Thermidor, but the anxiety of upheaval was not so easily conquered. It

came roaring back with this crisis to poison even the government. The directors' readiness to exploit anxiety in order to empower themselves would prove fatal because, rather than calming the waters as controversy grew, they threw oil on the fire.

The Editor, subsidized by the regime and widely regarded as its mouthpiece, led the charge. "Since the government revealed the conspiracy against the Republic and frustrated it by arresting many of its leaders, we have seen several newspapers whose editors are themselves suspect affect . . . disbelief about the case that would be wholly ridiculous if it were not so terribly guilty." Criminalizing any who resisted a rush to judgment, the paper added: "we would have thought the details contained in the Directory's two messages and the authentic texts it published [would be] enough to frustrate the skepticism that so clearly benefits the conspirators, but it appears that a few of these apostates are determined to cling to their self-interested doubts . . . until given tangible proof of these many crimes."[24]

As debate intensified, the directors spoke still more directly from the *Editor*'s pages. They gaslighted democrats by lying about arrest warrants and denying the panic sweeping France. "The Directory, in bringing the rigor of the law to bear on the guilty, will not criminalize the thoughtless man's opinions nor allow lists drawn up by a few conspirators to become rosters of condemnation." They brushed aside fears that a red scare would encourage royalism with the refrain they would sustain to the very end: democrats and royalists were equally hostile to the republic. "Such people pursue a common aim by a different path." Only the government, the directors insisted, could trace the narrow way forward and defeat all who "dare corrupt liberty's terrain."[25]

Unsurprisingly, given such assaults on critical talk, the regime was not long in reaching beyond the militants themselves to attack papers that questioned its pursuit of them. René Lebois, of *The People's Friend*, was tarred by association with Babeuf and "certain ex-members of the [Terror's] Committee of General Security" in the pages of *The Editor*, arrested, and interrogated. When he was released for lack of evidence, *The Editor* went after him again for "treacherous headlines" likely to excite "incendiary talk." A new arrest followed. *The Editor* attacked the *Free Men* as well, for "innuendo tending to justify the conspirators and legitimate their plans"; police arrested its printer and issued a warrant against editor René Vatar. Vatar successfully parried the charge that he was a co-conspirator, but his co-editor, P.-A. Antonelle, was not so lucky. Charged as an accomplice to the plot and forced into hiding, Antonelle began to knit himself into the case in ways that would affect everyone involved. Police went after smaller prey, too, arresting a woman in a Paris suburb, only to learn that the pamphlet she sold with Drouet's name on it had been published by the government's own printer.[26]

As these fraught circumstances intensified democrats' sense of persecution, more of them joined in opposition. The tightening of ranks was attested by an unlikely ally: Réal's co-editor at the *Patriots*, Méhée de la Touche. A mercurial figure best known for an obscene song against Robespierre that had been a colossal hit after Thermidor, Méhée took a stand. "The *Editor* tells us that those who raise doubts [about the conspiracy] are not themselves strangers to [it]. That claim, by making clear the danger of disagreeing with the *Editor*, proves there is no value in agreeing." Only a proper trial could determine whether there was a plot, Méhée concluded. Until then, he would stand by Drouet, "proud to denounce [the Directory's] errors . . . just as I was proud to denounce Robespierre . . . when he launched his terrible tyranny."[27]

Drouet's presence among the accused finally brought the case to the Council of 500, which alone was authorized to lift a deputy's immunity to indictment. It was a weighty decision, shadowed by memory of the purges that decimated the National Convention in 1793, 1794, and 1795. But rather than debate publicly to demonstrate their seriousness, the deputies secluded themselves in early June 1796. Three pamphlets stood in for their collective deliberations.

The first was Drouet's statement. A follow-up to the defense he had published immediately after his arrest, this one considered information made available since then. By what right was he arrested? Drouet asked. According to the constitution, a legislator could be detained only if engaged in activity "so obvious that the first person seeing the offender cannot doubt [that a crime is in progress]." But there were no weapons, no battle, no public outcry. The police found Drouet in quiet conversation with only a letter in his possession, as was proved by their arrest report. Drouet said no more on this point, probably because allies had already made clear that if he was not arrested while committing a crime, the Directory breached his inviolability.

What the police did have was material evidence of communication between Babeuf and Drouet: they found a copy of a speech Babeuf wrote for Drouet in the latter's home and identified drafts of two letters to the deputy among Babeuf's papers. Was this enough to prove conspiracy between them? As a representative of the people, Drouet reminded his colleagues, he was entitled—indeed, obliged—to "hear all ideas citizens may offer and adopt those I find suitable." That he did not deliver Babeuf's speech to the Council of 500 and left the draft torn in pieces was eloquent testimony to his opinion of it.

More striking still were the high-handed letters in Babeuf's archive that suggested a rocky relationship between the men at best. "Your speech is useless and unworthy of you," the tribune told the deputy in the first one, "if it does not outline the feelings I think you should express and which I tried to voice . . . [in] *The People's Tribune*. Review these pages and incorporate them . . . Anything you try to put in their place will have no effect whatsoever." The second letter had vented Babeuf's anger at Drouet for refusing to deliver the former's address. "Because you did nothing with my speech, citizen, substituting empty chatter for its truths; because you are *prudent*; because you are a senator like any other . . . I demand that you return the manuscript I confided to you . . . At least I know I did everything I could to save you from disgrace."

Finally, Drouet made short work of the statements of informant Georges Grisel. There was no material evidence to substantiate the captain's claim that Drouet and Babeuf met regularly or that Drouet hosted a conspiratorial gathering a few nights before the arrests. Yes, the deputy admitted, some friends dropped by, but he did not share in their conversation, which "did not seem to merit any more attention than [what] one hears daily in cafes, on the streets, and among groups of citizens discussing politics." As for "Grisel's vile . . . claims [that] . . . I meant to confiscate others' property," they were "too absurd to respond to with anything but ridicule."[28]

Deputy Antoine-Claire Thibaudeau, a regicide turned reactionary, made the public case for indicting Drouet in the second of the three pamphlets.

He claimed that the plot and his colleague's collaboration in it were readily proved. Grisel had informed the director Carnot, well before the arrests, that he "understood" Drouet to be at the head of the conspirators' insurrection, and later testified to hearing Drouet declare "anything . . . permissible to defend popular good," before advising the plotters to steal what money they required. Moreover, Babeuf himself had given Grisel the address where police arrested Drouet, and said conspirators were gathering there. Contradictory statements from several detainees about how each came to be at that house condemned them all.

That Thibaudeau thought Drouet's political history, acquaintances, and opinions more significant than his actions was made clear by the weight he gave them. Hinting at Drouet's status as a one-time Jacobin, Thibaudeau described the plot as that of a "faction" and adopted the reactionary chant that the Directory encouraged such men by accepting so many of them into its ranks. "What is most surprising is not the wickedness of the plot but the Directory's incredible blindness to the dangers that so long encircled it."

Turning to Drouet's associates, Thibaudeau argued that Babeuf's letters proved Drouet knew him and concluded that the deputy must have been familiar with the tribune's ideas. Drouet also knew Augustin Darthé, whom Grisel had named as another architect of conspiracy. "And yet," Thibaudeau added sarcastically, "Drouet remained innocent of the conspiracy while welcoming its leaders, feeding them, and declaring them his friends . . . !" Thibaudeau thought Drouet's own defense was incriminating because he mourned the loss of the democratic constitution. Falling back on the familiar equation of opposition and subversion, the deputy warned that "such opinions, permissible when their expression does not trouble public order, are wholly in keeping with the conspiracy's principal aim."

The revolution was over and anyone who denied that was a traitor, Thibaudeau concluded. If the Council of 500 failed to lift Drouet's immunity, it would risk all that France had accomplished. "Do not allow a handful of wretches, humanity's shameful dregs, to overturn in one day the astonishing glory realized by the generous devotion of the nation's intrepid defenders."[29]

Like so much else in this growing affair, the mood and rationale of the speech were painfully familiar. Despite his demand for positive evidence,

Thibaudeau revived revolutionary conspiratorial thinking by treating Drouet's personal history and political opinions as proof of his guilt. Like fellow legislators and the directors themselves, he recalled the darkest moments of Terror and Reaction, when men like Hébert, Danton, Goujon, and a whole coterie of Girondins were felled by charges that their opposition to official policy was the equivalent of taking arms against the nation.[30]

The only person to speak for Drouet before the Council of 500 was the author of the third pamphlet, the deputy's one-time fellow prisoner of war and a legislator himself, François Lamarque. Analyzing the evidence with more discrimination than Thibaudeau, Lamarque joined Drouet in emphatically denying that the latter had been arrested red-handed. Nor was this deputy persuaded by Grisel's testimony. What did the captain mean when he reported that "in the course of conversation" he was "able to figure out that Drouet should be at the head of the insurrection"? If Grisel were privy to the inner workings of the plot, why did he learn such an important detail so indirectly and so late in the game? What did it mean that no one said Drouet "was" to be at the head of the insurrection but that he "should" be? Grisel appeared to have shared conjecture for which there was no positive evidence.

Lamarque did not find Grisel's statement to the grand jury any more convincing. The captain described a meeting at which Drouet declared "anything . . . permissible to defend popular good" and urged his fellows to steal the money they needed. If that were true, the Council must indict. But, once more, there was no evidence to support these claims. "How unfortunate would be the fate of each citizen and every representative of the people if his safety, liberty, honor, and life depended on the simple statement of an informant, above all when that statement is contradicted by printed texts, writings, deeds, and every circumstance that preceded or followed?" Absent any positive evidence, and in light of Grisel's own dubious assertions, Lamarque concluded, "[T]here is nothing but naked slander to sustain . . . indictment."

Lamarque agreed with Thibaudeau on one point alone: that this case was a bellwether. He did not think that because be believed, like his colleague, that the plot revealed an eternal Jacobin threat. Rather, Lamarque saw evidence in this case of the polarization deepening around them. Yes, he admitted, Drouet was known for his political passion and a weakness for "exaggerated" ideas, but he was a "citizen who proved his devotion to the republic" and whose body was scarred by the chains he had borne for the nation as a prisoner of war. If the Council of 500 considered the facts coolly, Lamarque felt sure, it would dismiss the charges.[31]

Lamarque's faith was misplaced. The 500 voted by an overwhelming majority to lift Drouet's immunity. The Ancients followed suit by issuing an indictment. Because a sitting legislator could only be tried by a high court, they called one into being.[32]

Outraged democrats continued to discuss the case, intimating that Drouet was being mistreated in prison and debating strategies for his courtroom defense. It seemed that the conversation would go on like this until the trial began.

Then the deputy disappeared.

Guards found Drouet's cell empty just days before he was to be transferred to the provincial town of Vendôme, where the high court was to sit. The mystery of his whereabouts lingered until the *Free Men* published a letter from the man himself, explaining that he found the tools for escape when transferred to a new prison cell. But, Drouet continued, he refused to use them until stripped of his legislative immunity. Only then did he despair of receiving justice and take matters in hand by sawing through the bars of his cell, lowering himself to the street, and walking into exile.[33]

It was rumored at the time and has been since that Drouet was allowed to escape. If this is so, it is because his case had become a gross embarrassment for the directors. Disappointed in their hope of rallying public opinion by frustrating a dangerous plot, they found themselves mired in debate about a war hero famed for frustrating the flight of a treacherous king. Despite circumstantial evidence, despite Grisel's denunciation, despite condemnations delivered by the upper and lower houses of the assembly, Drouet's case remained a lightning rod. Perhaps the directors hoped that, by allowing him to escape, they could shift attention to the less popular Babeuf and still retrieve glory. If so, they were too late.[34]

The case had taken on a life of its own, revitalizing features of republican political life that the directors had vowed to banish. By equating skepticism about the plot with plotting itself, insisting that criticism was treason, the directors and their allies revitalized the polarized politics that all knew to be deadly. In so doing, they rendered impossible the reasoned debate necessary to resolve political crisis and find a way forward for a republic that included all citizens.

That the directors had failed miserably to rally citizens to the center was once again made clear by the unlikely figure of Méhée de la Touche, who volunteered to serve as Drouet's defender shortly before the deputy's escape. Mehée was an opportunist, known for taking a stand only when it benefited him. By inserting himself now, apparently on principle, he suggested how important the case had become. Even his colleague P.-F. Réal, Babeuf's bitterest democratic critic, changed his tune. Tarred by reactionaries for defending Drouet, Réal joined the radical editors of the *People's Friend* and the *Free Men* by abandoning vitriolic labels for Babeuf, such as "degenerate" and "con artist," to dismiss him like the others did as an impotent "hothead."[35]

The polarization that was tightening democratic ranks fed reactionary fears. Right-wing commentators saw not beleaguered critics rallying protectively but deadly opponents advertising opinions they had long shared quietly. Believing the plot was proof of a wider movement to renew the Terror, they must have found Réal's leftward shift especially galling. They could not know that his voyage was far from complete.

The case against Babeuf and his fellows, which the directors had expected would affirm their status as guardians of the law and reliable centrists, had pushed left and right into fearfully defensive positions. Indictments formulated, citizens turned their eyes to the provincial town of Vendôme where a high court was being organized to try the journalist Babeuf, the absent deputy Drouet, and a growing crowd of suspected accomplices.

SIX

The Case for Conspiracy

One hundred seventy kilometers southwest of Paris, Vendôme lies isolated on a flat, chalky plain, visible from afar thanks to a ruined chateau perched on a hill above it. The town itself is nestled on a tiny island in a branch of the Loire, shaped by the water that flows around and through it. The walled interior could be reached only by gated bridges that passed over the river's main branch, and the neighborhoods within were fractured by tributaries that urged foot traffic onto a few common roads, weaving some three thousand residents into a tightly knit community.[1]

The revolution touched Vendôme without fundamentally changing it. Despite periods of radicalism in the critical years between the king's flight of 1791 and Terror's end in 1794, the town was governed by the same wealthy elite who dominated in the last years of the Old Regime. They were cautious men: former nobles, merchants, and large landholders who praised the early Revolution for offering new freedoms and new wealth but disdained the radicalism that followed because they understood it to endanger those very same things. These citizens wanted stability above all, hoping it would preserve them from political extremes, whether restoration of the monarchy or resurrection of the Terror.[2]

The Directory chose Vendôme to host the high court, in part, because it satisfied the constitutional requirement that the special tribunal sit more than one hundred kilometers from the political hothouse of the capital. There were, too, the town's watery isolation and conservative elites, and the spacious buildings of its abandoned Trinity Abbey, which, according to the minister of the interior, were "ready to receive tribunal and prisoners." So the Directory appointed an architect to renovate the building, stationed twelve hundred soldiers nearby for security, and sent eyes and ears in the person of a police spy named Bourdon.[3]

Nothing proceeded smoothly. The abbey was in far worse condition than the minister had imagined, and the Directory as badly strapped for cash as ever, so work continued long after the inmates arrived. The troops sent to guard the court alienated locals by behaving like an occupying force, ruining gardens and stealing livestock. The Vendômois themselves seemed blinkered by provincial solipsism that rendered them impervious to national interests, or so said the police spy Bourdon as he kept watch. "Little used to great events . . . [they] think only of themselves, see only themselves, fear only for themselves, there is no other patriotism here." Worse still, at least from this man's perspective, the Vendômois were "wizards at calculation" who ensured that "everything is more expensive . . . than in Paris, especially the wine, whose price is out of sight."[4]

Despite such hardship, the high court managed to seat itself in early October with great fanfare. Magistrates and local dignitaries paraded through the town's narrow streets to the Trinity Abbey, renamed the National Palace, where prison and courtroom were located. Greeted by artillery, they were ushered into a freshly painted auditorium where the prosecutor, René Viellart, welcomed them with a speech that distinguished carefully between the court they inaugurated and the Terror's notorious revolutionary tribunal.

Although French law designated special courts to judge high crimes or treason after 1789, the revolutionary tribunal was unique among them. Created amid crisis and debate in the spring of 1793, the tribunal was meant to expedite prosecution of suspected counter-revolutionaries. It became still more politicized when the National Convention robbed it of independence by appointing members of the bench and requiring jurors to deliver verdicts individually and in public rather than allowing them to deliberate and vote privately. The tribunal's legitimacy was further impaired when the Convention limited rights to defense and denied all appeal of its judgments. The last innovation was especially troubling because those condemned by the revolutionary tribunal were often sentenced to death.

Although the tribunal worked carefully at the outset, its structure, quickening pace of work, and growing disregard for the rights of the accused doomed its credibility. At its nadir in the summer of 1794, the court ceased hearing testimony and defense arguments altogether, sending thousands of people to the guillotine with cruel efficiency. Even today, memories of the institution are indelibly linked to the Terror's violation of rule of law.[5]

Viellart did not mention the revolutionary tribunal by name, but that was clearly his point of reference when he promised that the high court would prove the Directory's integrity. High courts were authorized by the constitution, he reminded his audience, to ensure that legislators accused of wrongdoing be judged without prejudice or favor, and the procedures for appointing their personnel had been designed to preserve independence. Judges and prosecutors were chosen from the national court of appeals by a combination of chance and choice: nominated by a drawing of lots and elected by colleagues. Members of the jury pool were selected nationwide during legislative elections, and defendants would have ample opportunity to exclude any they thought subject to "prejudice, influence or error." Babeuf and the others would face a just and neutral court.[6]

What Viellart did not say was that, no matter how rigorous its organization and procedures for appointment, a court depends on real people to guarantee its proceedings. This one would prove as much a prisoner of politics and circumstance as the nation. The high court's liabilities were most visible in Yves-Marie Gandon, a former Breton advocate chosen to preside over the panel of five judges. As lead magistrate, he was expected to assess evidence, interview witnesses, and give defendants opportunities to challenge accusers, duties that demanded a delicate wedding of rigor and detachment even under the best of circumstances. Gandon was sorely lacking in both. Because his diffidence was nonsectarian, defendants and prosecutors alike ran riot in the courtroom. Because his opinions inclined sharply to the right, his judgments visibly favored the state. The combination proved disastrous. His failure to enforce order weakened the regime's standing among reactionary critics and his bias for the prosecution disqualified the proceedings among democrats.[7]

Gandon's colleagues on the bench were Bruno-Phillibert Audier-Massillon and Etienne-Vincent Moreau, who had both been liberal deputies to the National Assembly before joining the court of appeals, and Joseph Coffinhal and Charles Pajon de la Chambaudière, members of the appeals court since its founding. All were more politically moderate and professionally able than Gandon, but even seasoned magistrates like these were badly prepared by the rarified world of appeals for the chaos that was about to ensue. Hoping, like the directors, to end the revolution by restoring the social and political hierarchies they thought essential for order, they would surrender to their mounting antipathy for the defendants in ways that visibly undermined the dispassion necessary to legitimate such extraordinary proceedings.

Lead prosecutor René-Louis-Marie Viellart, another former legislator who had moved to the court of appeals, was an ambitious, conservative man with a poor second in colleague Nicolas Bailly. Although the police spy Bourdon praised Bailly's "impassive logic," the latter's scorn for the defendants and quick temper would produce shouting matches that horrified onlookers.[8]

The guidelines for seating a jury fostered greater equilibrium. Because the pool was generated nationwide during legislative elections, it encompassed a wider spectrum of opinion than the court of appeals from which the magistrates had been recruited. Because defendants were allowed to challenge as many as twenty-five candidates, whose names were drawn by lot, they could exclude those they thought most hostile. Even Babeuf admitted that high court juries had unusual autonomy.[9]

Better yet, when jury selection arrived, the defendants appeared fortunate in their choices. They approved two candidates as "republican[s], on the list of the good ones" and described another as simply "excellent." Some of their hopes were, inevitably, disappointed. Pierre Benoist, known to have protected patriots from violence after Thermidor, showed himself a reactionary upon winning a legislative seat in the spring, and the "excellent patriot" Jean Duffau disappointed early on by trying to avoid jury service until the court threatened him with arrest.[10]

The most illustrious juror of the sixteen was Jean-François Gaultier de Biauzat, yet another retired legislator. As a moderate determined to save the monarchy in the early years, he had been among the deputies who exonerated the king after his flight in 1791 with a false claim that the latter was "kid-napped." Opinions like those cost him his freedom during the Terror. And yet, if Gaultier was like many another in being changed by revolution, he was un-usual in moving left after Thermidor as he came to fear that reaction would undermine the republic, that "lovely structure raised in such a short time." He became an ardent defender, noisily singing the now unfashionable *Mar-seillaise* and advertising disappointment when his department failed to cele-brate the anniversary of the republican revolution.[11]

This does not mean, of course, that Gaultier embraced Babeuf. Like other democrats, he dismissed the *People's Tribune* as a paper "composed of slanderous, disgusting, and often violent articles" and condemned the plot as a "stupid, appalling project." But the accused admired his opinions, per-haps thinking that his relation by marriage to a former member of Robespi-erre's Committee of Public Safety hinted at a hidden wellspring of radicalism. He would prove an enduring ally.[12]

As the high court waited for jurors to arrive in Vendôme, the Directory pub-lished its material evidence in two thick volumes entitled *Papers Seized from Babeuf's Lodgings*. They reproduced more than four hundred docu-ments without comment, apart from notes that said which papers Babeuf or the others admitted writing. This was the most comprehensive evidence the regime possessed of the alleged plot.[13]

The hands of more than a dozen people appear among the letters, essays, and notes of the *Papers*, but the guiding intelligence was clearly that of Gracchus Babeuf, Charles Germain, Filippo Buonarroti, and Augustin Darthé. They were an odd quartet. Babeuf and Germain were the sources of inspiration, but Buonarroti and Darthé possessed administrative experi-ence, Jacobin convictions, and personal connections that the other two lacked. Indeed, Buonarroti probably encouraged the admiration of Robespi-erre that became visible in Babeuf's writing after the fall of 1795.

Filippo Buonarroti was a charmer. Puckish and warm, he had the easy confidence of someone who has been well loved and well fed, qualities that won friends and earned opponents' indulgence. A former noble descended from generations of Florentine jurists, he enjoyed a youth as privileged as

Babeuf's was hard. He served as a page at the court of Tuscany and then, while studying law in Pisa and reading the philosophy of natural right, fell under the spell of the revolution in France. Its "wild energy," he said later, "weakened thrones, astounded the multitude, and kindled hope in the bosom of unfortunate humanity's few friends."[14]

At the age of twenty-nine or thirty, Buonarroti abandoned family, fortune, and title to serve the revolutionary regime in Corsica, doing so well that France offered him citizenship. He traveled to the mainland in 1793 to be naturalized and then stayed, attending the Jacobin Club in Paris, reputedly socializing with Robespierre, and finally taking an administrative post in the recently annexed duchy of Savoy. He remained there well beyond Thermidor, until he crossed a powerful local in the spring of 1795. Then Buonarroti was purged, arrested, and imprisoned at Plessis in Paris, penniless but with his profound revolutionary faith intact.

Augustin Darthé was a taciturn northerner, like Robespierre in hailing from a modest but relatively comfortable family and studying law in Paris. As a young man possessed of ruthless ideological purity, he was temperamentally similar to Robespierre's colleague on the Committee of Public Safety, Louis Antoine Saint-Just. Appointed to administer his native Pas-de-Calais at the age of twenty-two, Darthé distinguished himself by hunting down draft dodgers' families hidden in the local woods. That won him an appointment to the local revolutionary tribunal and then a post as secretary to the notorious Joseph Lebon, who was ultimately executed for revolutionary excesses. When purged after Thermidor, Darthé appears to have landed in the Plessis prison alongside Buonarroti. It is fitting testimony to his ideological rigor that he was the man who read out Babeuf's column praising the September massacres to the Pantheon Club, and the one who dashed off the terrible injunction to "kill the five [directors]."[15]

The archive that these men brought into being was initiated by the *Act Creating a Directory of Insurrection*, drafted sometime in March 1796. "French democrats, sadly affected, deeply angered and justly revolted by the unprecedented state of misery and oppression into which their unhappy country has fallen . . . create . . . an insurrectional committee known as the Secret Directory of Public Safety . . . [to] guide the people in recovering its sovereignty." The authors say they are four in number, but do not name themselves. They were, almost certainly, Babeuf, Germain, Buonarroti, and Darthé.[16]

This Secret Directory, determined to abolish the Executive Directory its founders despised, appointed an agent to each of the twelve arrondissements of Paris and charged them with reporting on the popular mood, identifying friends and enemies among locals, and organizing conversations about the people's rights. They were to be seconded by military agents, who were ordered to corrupt troops by distributing seditious pamphlets and encouraging soldiers to talk about their rights and grievances. As if to confirm its status as a nascent government, the Secret Directory created forms to affirm agents' appointments with blank spaces for the man's name and date of assignment.[17]

Having identified its agents, the Secret Directory urged them on with letters that Babeuf copied for his files. "Never was a plot as holy as ours," one boasted. "Never did agents so merit the sacred confidence entrusted them. Never has anyone organized secretly against a treacherous government so long and successfully as we. The government's suspicions may encourage it to use torture and terrible Inquisitorial methods, but it will learn nothing." As the weeks passed, the Secret Directory gave its agents additional tasks, asking them to identify arms depots, locate writers to produce "rousing treatises," make banners for insurgents, and distribute newspapers and pamphlets.[18]

In reply, the agents sent neighborhood reports describing restless, unhappy people. Democrats in the fourth arrondissement were said to be consumed by "an unquenchable thirst for liberty and unending horror of tyranny" that good leaders could surely channel. Residents of the second were enraged by the Directory's having ordered the Paris police legion to the front, a state that "enlightened patriots among them exploit . . . to make [neighbors] appreciate the government's wickedness." Citizens near the city's central bridge were so favorable to radical opinion that they beat police when the latter tried to pull down the Secret Directory's posters.[19]

That the Secret Directory believed there were enough local men to galvanize popular energy was attested by the many pages naming "patriots . . . useful for administration and revolution," marksmen, and cannoneers, lists that included additional information on addresses, professions, and particular strengths—"good for many occupations, has character." The Secret Directory also believed these men could readily find arms and assistance, as attested by accompanying lists of weapons depots, arms manufacturers, and barracks housing friendly soldiers.[20]

As the agents took stock of Parisians' mood, the Secret Directory tried to shape it with the pamphlets and posters that had roused so much anxiety in the spring of 1796. *Must We Obey the Constitution of 1795?* challenged the government's legitimacy. A *Letter from Paris Citizens to Their Majesties, the Executive Directory* demanded death for the "constitutionalists of 1795!" *Soldier, Stop Again* claimed that the government deliberately sent enlisted men to slaughter. The *Statement of Babeuf's Doctrine* and the *Reply to a Letter signed M. V.* promised a new order in which the "few trades that suck up fortunes to entertain a couple of parasites will be replaced . . . by ones that increase the people's happiness."[21]

Finally, some pages spelled out how the Equals expected their day of insurrection to unfold. Activists were to bring people into the streets by ringing bells, organize some into regiments under the command of local militants, and appoint others to collect arms or invite soldiers to mutiny. Crowds would seize "the legislature and Directory . . . the national treasury, the mint, the post . . . every public and private storehouse," and "kill any deputy, director, administrator, judge, officer, or bureaucrat" who resisted. The Secret Directory hoped to win over new recruits by redistributing the possessions of "counter-revolutionaries."[22]

What would happen after the explosion was less clear. Although Babeuf had claimed in the *People's Tribune* that restoring the constitution of 1793 would be one step toward realizing "common good," his *Papers* say almost nothing about how the new order was to be organized. But the name of the insurrectional committee—the Secret Directory of Public Safety—and notes about resurrecting the National Convention and revolutionary committees like those of the Terror suggested that the Jacobins would be restored to power, as did Babeuf's proposal to rebuild their meeting hall. The latter was accompanied by a malicious suggestion that turncoats Fréron and Tallien, who had betrayed him after Thermidor, would be forced to help.[23]

Finally, some pages attested to an alliance between the Secret Directory and several former deputies to the National Convention, at least three of whom had been members of the Committee of General Security that oversaw policing during the Terror. Although Babeuf had once dismissed such men as enemies of democracy and "common good," he and the others appeared to have bowed to a need for allies. They agreed to resurrect the National Convention and restore ousted deputies in exchange for a right to name additional deputies. Lists were appended with the names of suitable friends, political allies, and renowned militants.[24]

The *Papers* give damning evidence of a conspiracy, confirming, at first read, the Directory's most frightening claims. Upon closer scrutiny, however, they appear equally likely to support the *Free Men's* mocking exclamation that the plot was "almost impossible to realize."[25]

The Secret Directory had chosen its agents carefully, appointing solid revolutionary veterans who included former employees of the Paris Commune, retired police, and a one-time member of the Committee of General Security. But no matter how much experience they possessed, twelve men could hardly rouse a city of more than half a million residents. In any case, there seem only to have been seven agents who worked consistently.[26]

None of them did more than impoverished stone setter and former police clerk Juste Moroy, who lived in the twelfth arrondissement. Although his part of the city included the famously radical working-class faubourg Marceau, Moroy worried that wealthy locals would corrupt their patriotic neighbors. So he organized small groups to read democratic newspapers together, distributed copies of the *Tribune* to local army barracks, and appointed men to paste up broadsides of the *Statement of Babeuf's Doctrine.*[27]

When Moroy's neighborhood witnessed an upturn in activism, he modestly refused to take credit, insisting that the Directory excited opposition itself by stationing more troops in Paris and threatening to reassign the police legion. "People shout out . . . *those who rule by crime are always afraid*, soldiers mingle with groups in the streets and are united with the people. *We can see*, they say, *that we have been misled about you . . . however much the government tries, its projects will fail.*" Satisfied that democratic circles were flourishing around him, he began making paper crowns with which activists could identify themselves during an insurrection. Shortly before the Secret Directory was arrested, he reported confidently: "garlands, crowns, courage, everything is ready."[28]

Jean-Baptiste Cazin was less successful in the eighth arrondissement, on the north side of the Seine and home to the equally radical faubourg Antoine. Purged from administration during the Terror and left in prison long after Thermidor, he was hobbled by poverty. "I must admit that I am in terrible need, half-naked, and without any means of support, having run through what little others could loan from their own meager resources and lacking work to feed myself, I cannot imagine being able to satisfy your wishes however much I would like to." Cazin was afraid, as well, of local authorities, especially after a justice of the peace warned him that anyone found distributing the *People's Tribune* would be imprisoned. The Secret Directory answered irritably: "Your excuses about justices of the peace . . . are not worthy of a revolutionary; we too are surrounded by inquisitors, but conspirators know how to allay their suspicions." Although Cazin pushed on, his timidity continued to grate. "You must . . . hand out papers openly," the Secret Directory told him. "Show a little daring to inspire others."[29]

Other agents drew up lists of "patriots" and "counter-revolutionaries," posted handbills, even organized an occasional discussion group, but none was more active than Moroy or Cazin. Most were far less so. Antoine Guilhem, who wrote just two letters from the fifth arrondissement, merely repeated local gossip. Jean-Jacques Pierron, in the tenth arrondissement, did nothing. Citizen Deray of the ninth did little more. The secret directors were silent regarding Guilhem, but they appealed to Pierron with the carrot of praise and prodded Deray with the stick of criticism. They flatly told Nicolas Morel in the first arrondissement that he was a disappointment. "When we invested our confidence in you, we believed you capable of understanding what that meant and having the qualities necessary to meet our expectations . . . [W]e have been frustrated by your conduct since you accepted the mission entrusted to you. It is careless, to say the least."[30]

Every agent who appeared before the high court would plead innocent and, indeed, no single act was illegal. They distributed pamphlets and newspapers, encouraged neighbors to talk about their rights, prepared banners with political slogans. Above all, they kept their eyes open and wrote reports that mimicked police bulletins, eavesdropping in cafés or wandering through city parks as police spies did and writing up what they overheard to speculate on the likelihood of a new revolution.

Babeuf's papers had been scrutinized by journalists and legislators in the spring of 1796, during the debate over Drouet's indictment. Those papers would again be a point of contest between prosecutors and defendants, who wove competing narratives from them before the high court. Prosecutors would argue that the crimes they pursued were not to be found in individual acts but in the coordination of those acts in order to topple the government and destroy the republic. The accused would counter that the *Papers* recorded the fantasies of patriots hoping to encourage the people to discuss and defend their rights. What both sides could agree on was that the French Revolution was not truly ended. In this common conviction lay the intensity of their conflict.

The Equals imagined they were preparing insurrection in a world like the one they had known in 1792 and 1793, in which well-organized militants raised crowds of citizens, whose energy sympathetic deputies translated into legislation. Just as Babeuf claimed in the *Tribune*, so he and the others truly believed that popular insurrection could redirect the course of the revolution as it had done so often since 1789. With one last push, they thought, they could rouse Paris and extend the republic's most radical achievements.

The Directory and its conservative allies feared that might be all too true. Having watched Parisians uneasily for years, irritated by their disruptive songs and public processions, dismayed by clubs and neighborhood sections that gave them political voice, horrified by their massed assaults on legislative assemblies, conservatives and reactionaries found a new source of fear in the depiction by the *Papers* of an agitated people eager to recover its influence. Memories of the long association between popular militants and Jacobins enhanced those fears, intensifying the conviction that the Secret Directory had been plotting a new Terror.[31]

What neither Directory nor Equals understood at the time is what appears so clearly in retrospect: the French Revolution was over and the people had been defeated. It was, ironically, the Jacobins themselves who initiated the popular demobilization, by hounding militants and attacking Paris sectional assemblies to consolidate their power during the Terror. Thermidorians, many of whom were themselves former Jacobins, built on the momentum of the Terror by closing weakened sectional assemblies, dispersing political clubs, purging radical deputies, imprisoning militants, and finally disarming working people. Hunger played its part by redirecting energy from activism to survival when not killing people outright. In the provinces, physical violence inflicted by right-wing vigilantes raised the stakes of radical activism far beyond what the ordinary person could bear.

In the wake of these steady assaults on popular militancy and in light of the changing complexion of the nation's legislative assemblies, it is hardly surprising that a neighborhood agent like Jean-Baptiste Cazin felt overwhelmed. No matter how carefully the Secret Directory had chosen, a few men like him were not enough to compensate for the dearth of popular energy that made anything more than grumbling or a brief strike unlikely. Nor could the Equals singlehandedly revitalize institutions and restore the friendly legislators who once buoyed popular activism. P.-A. Antonelle was right in his mocking retort to the Directory's announcement of a "terrible plot." What could a handful of men accomplish without troops, arms, or money? How could they pull off such an ambitious project in just a few weeks? No matter how determined the members of the Secret Directory, they were seconded by a pitifully small number of militants who had been reduced by circumstances to mere onlookers, men who could only count up friendly neighbors as they encouraged the airing of grievances.

What the *Papers* most clearly revealed was that the plotters had been put to the test in the weeks before the arrests. And they had failed.

In April 1796, Charles Germain was on the scene when the Paris police legion mutinied. He recounted the events in a series of breathless letters to the Secret Directory that described rebellious soldiers chatting with sympathetic onlookers and mingling with the troops sent to replace them. Local sans-culottes offered support, he said, and a carriage filled with arms was parked nearby.

Here was the opportunity the Equals had been waiting for. Knowing that the police legion was created to repel popular insurgency, the Equals had long hoped to persuade it to join the people in revolution. Now it was rising up.

"Quick, my friends," Germain exulted to his fellows, "give me my orders and the passage from life to death will be but a joyous leap if it is to serve the Equals."

Babeuf and the others scrambled to respond, promising a poster in support of the mutiny by the next evening. For the moment, Germain must labor on alone. He was instructed to encourage the rebels, confirm that retired generals Jean-Joseph Fyon and Jean Antoine Rossignol were at the ready, and prevent the hijacked arms from being removed.

It was a great deal for a single person to do.

It was, in fact, too much.

The window of opportunity closed as abruptly as it had opened, when the director Lazare Carnot ordered the arrest of the mutiny's leaders and promised to let the rest go home. The uprising melted away.

"What humiliation!" Germain wrote in frustration. "How we were played!"

But what exactly had he or any other Equal actually done? Germain, sounding much like the agents he employed, concluded: "how wise we were to watch before joining in!"[32]

SEVEN

The Equals in Vendôme

The first prisoners arrived in Vendôme in early September. Transported from Paris in barred cages like wild animals, they were stared at by "a large crowd of . . . every age and sex" as they passed through Rambouillet and mocked by "fancy boys" in Chartres. The streets of Vendôme were nearly deserted at journey's end. "What wearied the eyes, sickened the heart," Charles Germain remarked. "A few little royalist messieurs looked us over indifferently and shrugged off our singing. So we were delivered unto our prison."[1]

"We believed the government would make every effort on our behalf, or at least order that we be housed properly," Germain continued. "How often we expose ourselves to disappointment by expecting the best!" The renovations of the Trinity Abbey had only just begun, so the newcomers were placed in clammy, sunless cells. A couple of stoves produced gloom as well as heat because the shutters that secured the windows prevented smoke from escaping. There was an adjoining garden but it had not been properly cordoned off, so the only place of exercise was a narrow corridor between the cells. When autumn chill joined the damp and enforced idleness, inmates began to fall ill.[2]

Babeuf, Buonarroti, Germain, and Darthé were among the first to arrive, in the company of the Secret Directory's most conscientious agents, Juste Moroy and Jean-Baptiste Cazin. More prisoners followed, men and women whose personal histories suggest how much the hunt for accomplices had

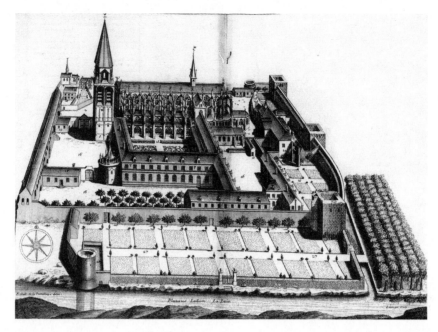

Michel Germain, *Monasticon gallicanum*, "View of the Trinity Abbey," 1694. Source: BnF.

become a settling of accounts with radical republicans. Six former deputies to the National Convention and almost two dozen officials active during the Terror had been indicted, as had five former jurors of the revolutionary tribunal, a couple of old Jacobin journalists, some radical printers, and owners of cafés known to be popular with democrats. Some were men whom Babeuf and Germain had met in the prisons of Arras. Others had encountered Buonarroti and Darthé at Plessis. It was quite a gathering.[3]

Thanks to the panicked search for suspects, many citizens were accused of conspiring on the thinnest evidence. Some were arrested for having subscribed to the *Tribune*, others because they were named "good patriots" in Babeuf's *Papers*. Maurice Roy and Pierre Fossard appear to have been guilty of enjoying the constitution's guarantee of free expression. Roy had received a pamphlet through the mail called *The People's Cry against Its Oppressors* and was overheard criticizing the government. Fossard shared his copies of the *People's Tribune* with friends. Grégoire Nayez, whom Germain had warned Babeuf against in Arras, probably condemned himself with the same nasty temper that grated on those two. Although Nayez was already in a provincial prison when the conspiracy was exposed, a justice of the peace told Paris police, "[I]f you find any letters from [him] among Babeuf's papers intimating that he was part of the plot, take whatever measures public security requires." No such papers turned up but the municipality sent Nayez to Vendôme anyway, happy to be rid of this "terror of our town." Needleworker Jacques Cordas was an outspoken radical. François Boudin was just poor. Like many democrats in these years, they were victims of purges that were decimating the last vestiges of popular activism. More than a generation would go by before their children, or their children's children, would rise up again.[4]

There were no women on the Secret Directory or among its agents, but their presence in the abbey attests to the vital part they had played in advancing revolution from the beginning. Jeanne-Ansiot Breton, the owner of a cabaret with a large democratic clientele, was arrested after a police spy heard her boast of her husband's militancy and declare that if he failed "to join in" (join in what exactly, she did not say), "she would go in his place." Marie-Louise Albin gave soldiers food and a place to sleep, which earned her the charge of encouraging desertion. Adelaide Lambert and her friend Sophie Lapierre were accused of encouraging desertion, too, and they may well have been guilty because they would behave as determined activists throughout the trial. Impoverished fruit seller Nicole Pognon allowed her daughter's companion, an ailing, demobilized soldier, to sleep in her home. For that, she was named an "enemy of military discipline."[5]

In all, sixty-five people had been indicted. Eighteen, including Drouet, managed to avoid arrest. The rest were crowded into the abbey, a cohort whose size and disturbing amalgam of genuine suspects with simple dissidents recalled the repression of the Terror.

The members of this motley group vented personal and political differences on one another. Some quarreled about the Terror, as when retired deputy André Amar criticized Jean-Baptiste Didier for sitting on the revolutionary tribunal. The latter shot back, "Which of us is guiltier? Why did you create a revolutionary tribunal? Why send so many people before it for no reason?" Thermidor was another sore spot. The Equals had long accused legislators of preferring personal interests to the democratic constitution after Robespierre was defeated, and the grievance returned under new guise on the night everyone refused their dinners as inedible. The wealthier ex-legislators compensated by purchasing food from town for themselves alone, which enraged Germain and his friends. "It's no surprise!" he shouted. "You've never been concerned for anyone but yourselves."[6]

The prisoners were equally divided over the looming trial. The innocents wanted quick proceedings and a speedy acquittal, so they chafed at the delaying tactics of the militants. The latter were determined to draw things out as long as possible, hoping to discredit the court and buy time should spring legislative elections bring a democratic resurgence. But the militants were divided, too. The ex-deputies blamed Babeuf's wild talk and damning archive for their arrest, worrying that he would continue to endanger them with courtroom scenes. Babeuf and Buonarroti mistrusted Nicolas Pillé, the scribe arrested with them in the rue de la Grande Truanderie.[7]

The business with Pillé dragged on for weeks, drawing in other prisoners and deepening tensions among them all. The scribe was a timid man who told police immediately that he had worked for the Equals because he needed money and became too afraid to quit once he understood what they were up to. To prove himself, he identified documents he had copied and pointed out prisoners he had met while at work. When Babeuf read all of that in the published indictment, he "leapt on [Pillé] like a madman." Then he, Buonarroti, and several others began to threaten the scribe and play cruel tricks that the prison warden connived at until another prisoner, Pierre Philip, took pity. Philip reported the whole thing to municipal officials, who moved Pillé to a different floor. By then, it may have been too late, because the poor man was "[exhibiting] signs of madness . . . insisting that an evil spirit in the form of a crow lived in the prison."[8]

This was a far cry from the camaraderie of Arras or Plessis.

And yet, alliances, even close friendships, did form. Inmates shared meals, walked and talked in the abbey's garden once it was secured, and joined in whispered conversation between cells when locked up. All of them sang patriotic songs on the anniversary of the king's execution. Pierre

Philip, who stood up for Pillé, was moved to another floor with him and remained the man's protector. Radicals Augustin Darthé and Adelaide Lambert may have become lovers.[9]

Most important, having been identified as a coherent group by directors, police, and prosecutors, the prisoners began to behave as such. They advocated for better conditions and began to craft a defense that would encompass them all: innocents and militants, ex-deputies and Equals.

First, they protested the haphazard organization of the abbey prison by demanding adequate food and less spartan housing, and objecting to isolation, nighttime searches, and the petty humiliations imposed by warden and guards. Then, they challenged the high court's reach with a collective petition arguing that Drouet alone fell within its jurisdiction because the constitution only demanded extraordinary tribunals for sitting legislators. Everyone else must be remanded to the cities and towns in which they had been arrested. It was a sound legal argument that simultaneously allowed the accused to maneuver for trials in ordinary courts, which were more likely to acquit political crimes.[10]

The high court's parry made clear that its magistrates were equally adept at negotiation. They gave the appearance of fairness by agreeing to consider the petition but barred the accused from making their case in person, so giving advantage to the prosecutor Viellart. The latter won his challenge handily by arguing that the constitution did not explicitly prohibit a high court from trying ordinary citizens, but the law did require persons charged with the same crime to be tried together. Anyone accused of conspiring with Drouet must appear before the court that heard his case.[11]

This affirmation of the high court's authority elicited new action from Augustin Darthé, Sophie Lapierre, and Adelaide Lambert. They accused the magistrates of violating the constitution and declared that they would not cooperate with an institution whose legitimacy they did not recognize, even if they had to forfeit their right to defense. This resistance prefigured the defense their fellows were in the process of elaborating: that the accused were not enemies of the republic but guardians of the law.[12]

As prisoners rallied inside the abbey, family, friends, and allies settled in Vendôme. Marie-Anne Babeuf, now five months pregnant, walked more than a hundred miles from Paris with nine-year-old Émile to stay in town and communicate with her imprisoned husband by holding up lettered signs on a nearby hill. Thérèse Poggi, an Italian noblewoman who left family and fortune to follow Buonarroti to France, hiked the same hill with a conviction that the mere sight of her would raise her lover's spirits. The wives of ex-deputies Vadier and Laignelot set up house together and became publicists for their husbands. Other defendants' family members declared themselves courtroom defenders. When a parlor was made available in the abbey for visits, these allies restored inmates' contact with the world by using physical proximity to smuggle letters in buttons, pockets, even tureens of soup.[13]

As such private efforts raised prisoners' spirits, three journalists kept their case in the public eye while laying groundwork for their courtroom defense. Babeuf's former sparring partner, Pierre-Antoine Antonelle, and newcomers Pierre-Nicolas Hésine and Marie-Agathe Hénault reported steadily through the months that stretched from Drouet's late-summer escape in 1796 to opening arguments in February 1797. All agreed that Babeuf and the others did not belong in the dock but parted company when explaining why, signaling differences over defense that would percolate through the trial. Antonelle sustained the argument he had advertised since May: the Equals were impotent dreamers. Hésine and Hénault hinted that the accused might have organized insurrection and, if so, were amply justified.

The former Jacobin Antonelle was already a prominent journalist and vocal critic of Babeuf when word of the conspiracy broke in the spring of 1796. Born a noble in 1747, he had followed the dictates of his caste until the age of thirty-five, when he resigned his military commission and retired to his estate in the south of France to take up the life of the mind. Antonelle immersed himself in philosophy and initially embraced the Enlightenment conviction that better education and improved mores would improve society. But, as the nation's fiscal crises deepened without resolute action, his critique sharpened. He came to believe that nobles were descended from the Franks, who had invaded Gaul centuries before, seized the land, and manipulated the language to make their domination appear organic. Antonelle's conviction grew that this decadent minority must be overturned.

Without an accompanying sense of how that transformation was to be effected, he suffered periods of debilitating depression.[14]

The revolution brought salvation by creating an arena in which ideas could become action. Antonelle joined eagerly, serving as mayor of his native Arles and organizing a local Jacobin Club before he moved to Paris in 1791 as a legislative deputy. During the republican crisis, he became a juror on the Paris revolutionary tribunal with such forceful convictions that, at one point, he delivered a speech against aristocracy to condemn a man whose lawyer seemed to have won the day. The depth of his convictions was so great that he refused to abandon them even when imprisoned at the height of the Terror. "Imagine our surprise," a fellow detainee recalled, "to hear him explain revolutionary justice, struggling to prove its purity to the very people being killed by it every day, and he did so with a good nature and sincerity hard to conceive of now."[15]

Liberated after 9 Thermidor, Antonelle tried to heal the polarization that threatened them all and to redeem vilified Jacobins. Himself a former Jacobin and opponent of Robespierre, Antonelle celebrated club members as "steadfast patriots" who led the republic through crisis and were among the first to criticize the regime's excesses. But he also warned his fellow Jacobins not to live in the past. They had to reformulate convictions, seek new allies, rediscover reasoned debate, and defend their achievements.[16]

Although Antonelle objected, in 1795, when the National Convention repudiated the democratic constitution of 1793, he pragmatically accepted defeat. The new constitution was "for the moment, our only means of order and strength," he told fellow democrats, but that should not prevent them from trying to liberalize it. He took an equally broad view of social equity. Rejecting Babeuf's radical egalitarianism, Antonelle called property a "necessary vice" that could not be abolished without great violence. At the same time, he warned that a yawning gap between rich and poor impaired democracy. There could be no "true and enduring liberty" without greater social equality, which the new constitution's authors ignored to the republic's peril. By making suffrage dependent on wealth and literacy, while withdrawing the guarantees of public assistance, work, and education necessary to make improvement possible, he argued, conservative deputies shamelessly enhanced the power of the rich and mercilessly consolidated the bondage of the poor.[17]

Antonelle's qualified acceptance of the Directory and commitment to free speech informed his complex dialogue with Babeuf when the latter resumed publishing in the fall of 1796. Believing Babeuf's stiff-necked refusal to compromise a threat to the united front republicans required at that delicate political moment, Antonelle censured the *People's Tribune* as "a spark of civil war" and declared its condemnation of property an invitation to violence. And yet, ever the advocate of free speech, he defended Babeuf's right to advertise the very ideas he found so troubling.[18]

When word of the plot exploded, the antagonism between the two intensified. Hoping to safeguard fellow democrats from reaction, Antonelle mocked the Directory's account of the plot by mocking the man it named as mastermind. "That Babeuf knows nothing, and has in fact never known anything, is obvious. Is it not widely acknowledged and indeed proven that he was never anything more than, in Réal's words, a revolutionary crank? An army does not confide . . . its campaign plans to a crank." That "defense," suffused with Antonelle's anger about Babeuf's reckless statements and archived notes, which exposed hundreds to police scrutiny, enraged the tribune. Babeuf remained bitter for months. It also enraged the authorities by calling into question their account of the plot. A warrant was issued, naming Antonelle a co-conspirator.[19]

The former marquis went into hiding and continued to defend Babeuf, Drouet, and the others in columns for the *Free Men* that he signed as "the Paris Hermit." At some point, Antonelle must have decided he would be more useful living among the accused, because he resumed his habit of strolling in central Paris dressed in a familiar hat and coat. He was arrested and whisked off to a smoky cell in Vendôme. Still, he continued to write for the *Free Men*. Signing his columns now as "the Inmate," he legitimated the Equals and expounded on the loyal opposition he had encouraged since Thermidor.

"Loyal opposition" seemed an oxymoron to many thinkers on both sides of the Atlantic in the eighteenth century. European philosophers warned against "faction," which, they thought, fostered fatal political division by giving priority to private interest over common good. The drafters of the American constitution wrestled with a similar problem when they asked how to prevent cliques from sowing "instability, injustice, and confusion" in the new republic.[20]

The long-standing conceptual difficulties of determining how to safeguard the common good of a sizeable, heterogeneous people were complicated in revolutionary France by the particularities of the nation's history. The legacy of the thousand-year monarchy sowed doubt about whether the will of the people could be as unified as the king's was supposed to have been, and memories of an Old Regime that accorded particular rights to specific groups rendered new coalitions suspect. Would not political alliances based on particular conditions or unique interests fracture a fragile general will and resurrect despised privilege?

The mounting crises of war and revolution after 1792 deepened the challenge of managing political difference by fostering the conviction, familiar to moderns, that defeating one's enemies demands rigid conformity. Fearfulness, suspicion, and troubled memories of the past mingled after 1792, joining Jacobins' ideological determination to identify a general will and their practical need to resist the centrifugal forces tearing the republic apart. The Jacobins came to define nonconformity as treason, a choice with the deadly consequence of transforming "loyal opposition" from oxymoron to delusion. There was, Robespierre insisted at the height of crisis in 1794, only one way to preserve the republic: absolute unity against enemies foreign and domestic. All else would lead to annihilation.[21]

This history informed Antonelle's reflection, after Robespierre's defeat, about whether Jacobins might engage the government from their novel position as political outsiders. His thinking sharpened as he developed a defense of the Equals that distinguished between subversion and principled opposition.

Antonelle's columns cast a searching light on the violations of liberty, equality, and justice he saw proliferating under the Directory. Babeuf and his friends were not the guilty ones, he told readers. It was the directors themselves who, with their privileged cronies and royalist suitors, sapped the

Alexis Chataignier, "The Directory's Public Audience," 1796–99? Source: BnF.

republic by corrupting its language. Claiming that France required "peace and order," those people dismissed "liberty" as an invitation to tyranny, charged that "equality" was a justification for expropriation, and condemned "patriotic enthusiasm" as unrest. Damning ordinary folk as too ignorant to appreciate their own best interests, the directors and their friends accused popular advocates of sowing chaos and claimed that they alone strengthened the nation. In sum, the Directory's "peace and order" was founded on "satisfaction of the rich . . . and blind submission of the people," or what the philosopher Montesquieu called "enduring servitude."[22]

True plotting, Antonelle continued, was to be found in the intrigue of supposedly "honest folk" against equal rights, the trickery of confidence men against upright citizens, and never-ending royalist schemes against the republic. Enthralled by the wealth and privilege behind those plots, the Directory allowed them to continue. When true patriots resisted them to defend popular sovereignty and equal rights, the regime called that "conspiracy." Then let it be so, Antonelle proudly declared. "[I conspired,] willfully and with forethought, in written and spoken words, for the consolidation and true glory of constitution and government, tirelessly demanding that all be directed to the greatest good of the people who . . . strengthen and perfect the former; improve, maintain, and preserve the latter." This distinction, between the malevolent plotting of republican enemies and the innocent conspiring of its defenders, would become a foundation of the Equals' high court defense.[23]

The embrace of patriotic conspiracy was not, Antonelle added carefully, violent. Since the Directory's inauguration, he had categorically dismissed popular insurrection as folly. In any case, what danger had Babeuf and the others posed? Recalling that the great crowds of 1789 and 1792 were no more, Antonelle asked what a few dissidents could accomplish without arms, money, or popular force. They were simple patriots who "thought only of the people . . . saw only the people's rights . . . wished only for the people's genuine well-being," and who defended the republic by exposing plots against that people. They had "no desire for upheaval," had engaged in nothing more than "wholesome," "generous" speculation.[24]

Taking head-on Babeuf's incriminating archive, littered with bold calls for insurrection and government slaughter, Antonelle argued that its very existence proved the defendants' naïveté. "Ask those who swore themselves to defeating liberty in the past eight years . . . Conspirators speak rarely, write still less, act often, and take care to burn what little they must commit to paper." The Directory's exploitation of such evidence proved not the prisoners' guilt but the regime's corruption, one so naked that even its reactionary friends wished the "slaughter of a few austere republicans" had been "more artfully imagined and more skillfully shrouded, conducted with less boorishness and haste."[25]

As he defended the Equals, Antonelle abandoned the label of wild-eyed crank to call Babeuf a "sober republican, incapable of indifference to the nation's ills, unwilling to excuse . . . the abasement and deepening misery of a people exploited by the corrupt, outraged by the impudent, and exposed to the efforts of the arrogant to subjugate them." But even in retreat from his ridicule of the preceding spring Antonelle's condescension lingered, to render the crank as a pitiable idealist. "Let others recall and exaggerate his faults and errors; I wish only to see [Babeuf's] intent and suffering."[26]

Antonelle began formulating his defense of the Equals while in hiding in the spring and summer of 1796. Once he was able to communicate more directly with them in Vendôme, his arguments are sure to have appealed to the indicted deputies eager to protect themselves. Buonarroti would prove his enthusiasm for Antonelle's defense on the floor of the high court. In sum, this clique of political insiders—men of roughly similar social origin, possessed of formal education, joined by association with the Paris Jacobin Club—were agreed.

Babeuf was, once more, the outsider. He loathed Antonelle's "theory of [the plot's] madness and extravagance," which had angered him in May as a squandering of opportunity. Believing that democratic resistance was close to the boiling point when he was arrested, Babeuf thought that allies should have encouraged the people to rise up, just as he tried to do with his bold letter to the directors. Instead, they offered ridicule at the very moment when the plot might have sprung forward. Babeuf's resistance to continuing down the path traced by Jacobin insiders would become one more complicating factor in what promised to be a tortuous trial.[27]

Pierre-Nicolas Hésine was a far more sympathetic ally than Antonelle, perhaps because he and Babeuf were equally unyielding in their militancy or possibly because they shared the common experience of scrabbling up from poverty. Hésine was educated in a village school, thanks to his father's work as a porter, and was destined for the church until, he claimed, a youthful awakening that was commonplace in revolutionary memoirs. "I read Rousseau . . . and idolized him. I found in his writings the germ of the republican character I nurtured during the Revolution. The priests accused me of philosophy. I escaped to Paris in 1782." After studying mathematics in the capital, Hésine became a teacher in the provincial town of Pontlevoy, about thirty miles south of Vendôme, where he met a gamekeeper's daughter named Marie-Agathe Hénault. They married in the year the Bastille fell.[28]

The math teacher radicalized quickly, like Antonelle and Babeuf and tens of thousands of others. He joined a local Jacobin Club and became a determined opponent of the church, his entry to and exit from government service moving in rhythm with the shifting currents of local politics. Dismissed from local administration when religious conservatives gained the upper hand in 1792, Hésine won a more important post when radicals stepped up the following year. Ebb and flow continued, bringing Hésine into the ranks of the Vendôme municipal government during the democratic resurgence after the Vendémiaire insurrection of autumn 1795 and sending him away amid the purge following Babeuf's arrest in spring 1796.

Hésine imitated many democrats in those years of declining activism by turning to journalism when excluded from formal politics. Answering the news that Vendôme would host the high court, he defiantly promised to publicize the proceedings. "Liberty will guide my pen. I will echo the truth." The cost of that gesture became clear within a couple of weeks, when the municipality insisted that because he had been purged from administration, Hésine must exile himself from the town during the trial. He retreated to nearby Pontlevoy, while Hénault stayed on to welcome allies, collect prisoners' statements smuggled from the abbey, and continue publishing their *High Court Journal*.[29]

If Hésine had a fearless partner in Hénault, he found in Babeuf a loyal comrade. "You have shown me many signs of affection my dear friend," the latter confided. "The admiration and trust you inspire . . . encourages me to share my most private thoughts with you." Babeuf appreciated that Hésine celebrated the Equals "with eloquence and feeling, as athletes generously laboring for the triumph of humanity's rights." It was, he continued, a striking contrast to the "broad and ridiculous strokes" with which Antonelle painted them. Driving the point home to cement the new alliance, Babeuf concluded: "you understand that [Antonelle's] latest account is meant to invalidate yours and deflect the attention it rightly deserves."[30]

Hésine and Hénault's plainspoken narrative complemented Antonelle's abstract reflection. Their columns took readers through the streets of Vendôme, down the corridors of the old abbey, and into prison cells where they met individual defendants. Charles Germain was the courageous soldier withstanding terrible hardship, and Filippo Buonarroti the genial romantic straining for a glimpse of his beloved through prison bars. Augustin Darthé was described as boldly defending his convictions before falling silent. So, too, was Sophie Lapierre. "My soul is impervious to fear," the paper reported her telling the judges. "Love of my homeland takes precedence . . . I challenge the [legitimacy of the] high court and will do so forever." On the *High Court Journal*'s pages, prisoners enjoyed an easy solidarity that too often eluded them in life.[31]

Hésine and Hénault conjured the Equals' opponents with equal skill. They depicted prosecutor René Viellart as a government stooge directing a play entitled *The Sacrifice of Liberty's Friends*, in which star witness Georges Grisel was the lead. The latter was "a miserable cheat" without "honor, morals, or homeland," and the whole production had such a terrible plot that many asked how it could possibly succeed.[32]

Hésine and Hénault denounced the "monstrous irregularities" of a high court they named as a new revolutionary tribunal. How could proceedings unfold fairly when magistrates refused to subpoena defense witnesses, interfered with jury selection, and denied defendants adequate time to consult with their advocates? Hésine's exile was but one more example of the corruption. "Every obstacle, no matter what its nature, will be overturned to insure the sacrifice of democracy's friends."[33]

Hésine and Hénault agreed with Antonelle that the Directory was rotten. But they denied his claim that the Equals answered the corruption with "extravagant" fantasy. They justified the revolt of fearless warriors by allowing Babeuf to make his own case for insurgency. In late fall 1796, they published a statement he had given to police the preceding spring and, presumably, smuggled out of prison. There, Babeuf retreated from his first avowals of guilt to spell out the fiction he would maintain throughout the trial: that his archive belonged to an anonymous group of democrats for whom he worked as secretary. Under cover of defending that collective, Babeuf defended the Equals. The call "to destroy the [Legislative] Councils and [Executive] Directory" that police found in his archive was not meant to excite violence, he explained, but to terrorize opponents. Challenges to the institution of private property were not incitements to pillage but promises to share counter-revolutionaries' goods.

And yet, even as he dismissed the manifest content of much of his archive, Babeuf conceded almost nothing on the charge that this "anonymous collective" had been organizing to "overthrow the aristocratic government of 1795 and replace it with the democratic government and constitution of 1793." On the contrary, he boldly justified it.

Should not the authors of such a plan be proud of trying to restore popular rights? he had asked police. Without the insurgencies of 1789 and 1792, the crown might have endured. If their republic was brought into being by insurrection, how could the government outlaw that activity? The right of revolt was so vital to the defense of liberty that the constitution of 1793 had guaranteed it. And if revolt was legitimate, then citizens might lawfully encourage it when they saw the republic under threat. Without it, "liberty cannot survive."[34]

Such justification of insurrection flatly denied Antonelle's claims about "wholesome speculation." But when published by Hésine and Hénault, in the fall of 1796, that was of minor concern. Hésine and Hénault were small-town amateurs producing a local paper. Antonelle was a former deputy whose columns appeared in the nation's most popular democratic paper. Although the *Free Men* reprinted some stories that appeared first in the *High Court Journal*, sharing them with other provincial papers, it did not breathe a word of Babeuf's interrogation. His springtime claims to police about a right to insurrection became visible to the select few who actually read the *High Court Journal*. What most democrats saw was the image that Antonelle publicized, one of peaceful patriots wrongfully suffering for their defense of the republic. The tension between that image and Babeuf's claims of a continuing right of insurrection would lie dormant until the high court trial began the following winter.[35]

EIGHT

Squaring Off

The trial opened in late February 1797, in a courtroom shaped from the abbey's former dormitory and decorated with all possible stateliness. The walls of the long, narrow room, newly covered in marbled paper and draped with fabric, recalled the elegance of royal law chambers. Great gilded chairs confiscated from the Versailles palace awaited judges swathed in white robes, and velvet benches were designated for the defendants. Local grandees in the audience brought decorative touches of their own: vividly colored vests, luxurious scarves, and extravagant hats that made manifest the wealth and social standing this ostentatious court protected.[1]

The prisoners who filed in from dank cells below must have seemed a species apart. Even the most polished of them would have been plainly dressed, in white shirts and simple coats, but the majority were working people ruined by inflation, unemployment, and long imprisonment, men dressed in rough shirts and straight trousers—shapeless things next to a gentleman's breeches—and women wearing simple skirts with thin, flat shoes. Such clothes, which once signaled the good republican, were now thought outmoded by people who had the money to keep up with changing fashion. The prisoners wore them proudly, parading the defiance of the sans-culottes.[2]

Courtroom protocol required each defendant to identify him- or herself before arguments began, but Babeuf scolded presiding judge Gandon when asked to do so. "You ask my name under pretense that this tribunal has been organized in accordance with conditions set forth by article 341 of the Penal Code . . . I will for now state simply that this case is not ready to be heard."

"Will you tell us your name?" Gandon replied, insisting that this was a formality.

"I am Babeuf. I tell you that only to begin arguments."

"What is your age?"

"After what I just said, I do not need to tell you anything more."

Gandon turned to the next defendant, who gave his name in order to lodge a protest: "We have not been given the materials guaranteed by law to the accused." Charles Germain asked to make a statement, but Gandon refused. Defendant Louis Blondeau bluntly snubbed the judge. "I am blind, deaf, and dumb. The court may not yet hear this case because it lacks [the requisite number of] jurors." Augustin Darthé repeated his by-now-familiar objection that "the founding laws of the republic deny you any right to judge me," and refused to say more.[3]

So it went, Gandon noting names and ages that were given and ignoring the rest.

The next order of business was to swear in the jury. The prisoners interrupted again, repeating Blondeau's charge that all of the jurors were not yet present. Two alternates had failed to show up, and a third, named Agier, asked to be recused because he had been named in Babeuf's *Papers* as a "treacherous enemy of public good."

The prosecutor Viellart dismissed the absences, saying that the court satisfied the spirit of the law by seating a full panel of ordinary jurors and they might lose some of those men by waiting for missing alternates. His associate, Bailly, brushed off Agier's request, saying that because the plot threatened all "public functionaries, honest men, and property-owners," it made no difference if one of them had been singled out by name.[4]

The judges' acquiescence to the latter argument wrung howls of protest from the prisoners. When the reluctant alternate was sworn in, he agreed to serve "because the court condemns me to," prompting Charles Germain to shout out to the audience: "People, you heard the citizen . . . say that the court *condemned him!*"[5]

Now Babeuf was on his feet again, demanding to address the jury. When Gandon allowed him to speak, he reviewed weeks' worth of protests against the court and urged jurors to resist hearing arguments until all had been addressed. The fate of the nation, he concluded, hung on this trial. "We must cease compromising our principles, to look long and hard at the negligence, abuse, and injustice that has brought the republic to the precipice."[6]

By the time Babeuf was done, it was late afternoon. The session closed.

The court managed no more on the first day than to identify defendants and swear in jurors. It was a turn the police spy Bourdon had anticipated, warning his superiors that the Equals would try to prolong the trial until spring legislative elections when, they hoped, a democratic sweep would weaken the court's authority. A reactionary newspaper charged that the accused were buying time until sympathizers could organize an uprising to save them.[7]

Some of this was accurate, some hyperbole. The Equals did hope that spring legislative elections would work to their advantage and raised objections with an eye on the calendar. More often, they simply tried to gain some foothold against judgments they could not appeal. And they used objections to censure the Directory, exploiting the extraordinary platform they had been offered to broadcast their opinions.

The Equals were not, however, the only ones to slow proceedings. Judge Gandon would prove devastatingly ineffectual, his seemingly quiet resolve decaying to disdain for the accused and disorientation in the face of their activism. His fellow magistrates were not especially adept either. Stunned by the Equals' combativeness, the judges seemed paralyzed by their own determination to let it continue, as if they would prove themselves evenhanded by indulging grandstanding. The tradeoff was disastrous. Regardless of how many speeches the magistrates permitted, their visible bias for prosecutors—colleagues from the court of appeals with whom they shared common values, political aims, and social standing—would convince democrats that the high court was railroading innocents. Meanwhile, the deepening chaos persuaded reactionaries that neither court nor Directory could contain the deadly radicalism that they believed threatened them all.[8]

Thanks to the trial's creeping pace, lead prosecutor René Viellart did not deliver his statement of the case until the fourth day. By then, he was simmering with impatience. A conservative man whose native convictions had been honed by revolutionary experience, he would pursue the Equals with nimble energy.

Viellart began the revolution as a cautious proponent of reform in the National Assembly and a moderate member of the Jacobin Club. He withdrew from the club as it gravitated toward republicanism after the king's flight in 1791 and, fearful of rising popular activism, joined the national court of appeals when his tenure as a deputy ended. The bench offered shelter from public life but no sanctuary from the Terror. Viellart watched helplessly as the National Convention attacked judicial independence and the guillotine bore away his colleagues.[9]

By Thermidor, the prosecutor's native reserve had been sharpened by bitter experience and his cautious optimism worn away, leaving him with the conviction that the revolution had reduced France to a state of nature resembling less Rousseau's unsociable utopia than Hobbes's war of all against all. As an ardent antipopulist by the time the Directory was inaugurated, Viellart was well suited to defend a constitution that promised to end the revolution by confiding government to propertied men.

The principal author of that constitution, deputy François Antoine Boissy d'Anglas, had argued in 1795 that the Terror was caused not by warfare and civil unrest, an ailing economy, or the clash of competing ideologies, but by an ill-conceived democracy. Radicals, he charged, made unrealistic promises of social equality that denied the natural asymmetries of strength, talent, and virtue on which hierarchy was founded. The best a society could hope for was equilibrium between rich and poor: "in their union lies strength, in their discord or harmony, the sickness or health of the state." The most a government could promise was equality before the law and the cooperation that came from "repress[ing] the pride and ambition of the wealthy and contain[ing] the jealousy, passion, and license of the poor." To attempt any more was to court disaster.[10]

Boissy thought that radicals had compounded the error of their convictions by adopting a democratic constitution in 1793 which permitted political clubs, popular societies, and crowds to compete with the National Convention. Although that constitution was never enacted, he insisted, with deafness to the oxymoron, that it had "organized anarchy." Legislators must put an end to such anarchy by strengthening the executive and limiting the challenges from below that were mobilized by rights of petition, assembly, free speech, and, most terrifying, insurrection. By confiding government to "the best . . . the brightest, and those with the greatest interest in preserving the law," Boissy promised, his constitution would empower the wealthy to safeguard stability, and sideline the poor and ignorant who would otherwise "rouse unrest . . . without care for its effect; impose . . . taxes deadly to commerce and agriculture without understanding, fearing, or anticipating their terrible consequences; and finally return us to those violent convulsions from which we have only just escaped."[11]

The prosecutor Viellart shared Boissy's conviction that government by elites was necessary to save the nation. Standing before the high court, he charged that the accused embodied the chaos that threatened them all and insisted that the only way to end the revolution was by taming them. To make his case, he reached back to 1789, rooting the nation's troubles in the very origins of the revolution. The attempt to guarantee liberty might have been worthy, he argued, but it created pandemonium. "Passions blasted unchained from all points on the compass . . . [A] corrupt brew fermented in the upheaval of social order, producing vicious beings and strange monsters" who called themselves patriots but who "divided, disfigured, consumed the nation." The worst of them were defeated at 9 Thermidor, but a "foul debris" remained. Much of that "debris" now stood in the dock.

Viellart had clearly read the defenses formulated by Antonelle, Hésine, and Hénault before preparing his attack. Insurrection was a sacred political act, he said, superficially agreeing with Babeuf, but only if realized by a "*universality* of citizens." When excited by a "fraction of the people"— whether Equals or Parisians—it was sedition. Attacking Antonelle's claim that the Equals were impotent dreamers, Viellart argued that their co-ordinated activity was visible in Babeuf's *Papers* and constituted far more than a "ridiculous fantasy." He refused, as well, the journalist's suggestion that "conspiracy" might be peaceful or patriotic. It was necessarily criminal, and particularly vicious if meant to "deliver the nation to the most terrible anarchy."

"Read *The Statement of Babeuf's Doctrine*, distributed, disseminated, posted in abundance by revolutionary agents at the behest of the insurrectional committee. We see the prohibition of the right of property, the tenet of community of goods," plans with terrible consequences. "Who can measure the ghastly effect of . . . [a] terrifying mass of proletarians, swelled by debauchery, laziness, and all the passions and vice that swarm in a corrupt nation, hurling themselves on property-holders, on wise, industrious, thrifty citizens? . . . No more property! What will become of the arts? What will become of industry? Who will cultivate the earth if it no longer belongs to anyone? Who will gather its fruits if no one can say, *they are mine?*" The abolition of property would destroy wealth, social hierarchy, and civilization itself, leaving survivors to roam like savages in the wild.

The defendants understood as well as anyone, Viellart continued, that there was no order without property. They only promised to abolish it in hope of empowering themselves. In the end, they would have "impos[ed] the yoke of tyranny on their credulous followers and quickly organiz[ed] some new order, leaving the cheated masses miserable, enslaved, and longing for property."[12]

It was in establishing this binary opposition between radical and conservative republics that Viellart found common ground with Babeuf, who inverted the order of value to repudiate the Directory as forcefully as the prosecutor condemned the Jacobin government of 1793–94. How, amid polarization that required citizens to defend republican ideologies purged of opponents' convictions as categorically as these two, could the nation find peace or stability? How was France to reconcile the radical aspirations of 1793 with the conservative tenets of 1795? How was it to find equilibrium between social justice and rights of property, transformation and stability?

Viellart's definition of legitimate revolutionary actors was as narrow as his conception of the republic. He dismissed all popular aspiration and popular achievement, to describe the revolution as a confrontation between demagogues and peacekeepers, claiming that the worst they had faced since 1789 was engineered by a sinister cabal and ended by a benign aristocracy of wealth. All of this accorded with the outsized fears of conspiracy the directors had trumpeted since the first arrests, for, if the revolution was the work of a few cunning men rather than a push-and-pull between vast social, political, and global forces, then a handful of agitators could well reignite the conflagration. Dismissing the pitiful numbers and meager resources that Antonelle alluded to, Viellart asked: "did the unpunished authors of the infamous 1792 September massacres plot so well? . . . Was 31 May [1793, when the Girondins were expelled from the Convention] . . . as carefully prepared as the [Equals'] proposed explosion . . . ?" And yet, in those moments, "a handful of crooks . . . managed to oppress, tyrannize, and defeat men who believed themselves able to withstand such terrible projects."[13]

The prosecutor exploited, as well, a conviction common across the political spectrum that revolutionary activism was not dead but dormant. Like Babeuf, Buonarroti, Germain, and Darthé, like the directors, like the Paris police and the fearful editors of reactionary newspapers, Viellart argued that popular militancy could spring back at any moment, despite overwhelming obstacles like those the Secret Directory had faced. He did not mention the indifferent service of bewildered agents, gave no word of Jean-Baptiste Cazin's reticence, Nicolas Morel's disappointing performance, Antoine Guilhem's disappearance. He did not highlight how arbitrary the search for suspects had been or admit that one-third of the Secret Directory's neighborhood agents were neither arrested nor indicted. Quoting generously from lengthy instructions, copious lists, and the minutes of meetings drafted by resolutely hopeful militants Babeuf, Germain, Buonarroti, and Darthé, he amplified their conviction that a vast plot had been on the eve of realization when they were arrested.

Viellart spoke relentlessly, despite defendants' outraged interruptions. When the word "conspiracy" passed his lips, Babeuf and Germain roared out that he was the real conspirator. When he compared the accused to the leaders of the September Massacres, a small crowd leaped up to shout objections that spilled over one another:
"But [those men] were judged . . ."
". . . and acquitted."
"Were we there in September?"
"We have always been on the people's side . . ."

"We are not the ones who starved and slaughtered them."

As the commotion mounted, driving out frightened audience members, a newcomer approached the bench and demanded to be sworn in. It was Babeuf's angriest democratic critic, Pierre-François Réal.

The judges interrupted Viellart to say that Viellart must not be interrupted, telling Réal to wait until the end of the afternoon to be sworn in. He took a seat near the accused and joined in the shouting. "My clients are innocent. Why surround them with armed guards like that?"[14]

It had been Réal's co-editor at the *Patriots of '89*, Méhée de la Touche, who first volunteered as Drouet's defender. When he dropped out, Réal stepped up, undoubtedly drawn in equal measure by the peril this case posed to democrats and its promise to serve his professional ambitions.[15]

A successful prosecutor when the revolution began, Réal had followed a path through the Terror much like that of his friend and ally, P.-A. Antonelle. He supervised the provisioning of Paris during the Terror, ran afoul of the Committee of Public Safety after opposing Robespierre in spring 1794, and spent months in prison. When released at Thermidor, he made a name for himself as a champion of free speech and rule of law.[16]

Although Réal opposed Robespierre and defended free speech, just as Babeuf and Antonelle had done, the political differences among the three suggest how fluid left-wing opinion became after Thermidor and how much this case once more rallied democrats. Antonelle stood firm on his conviction that the Terror had been a political necessity and that there could be no true liberty without greater social equality. Réal, more tepid in his embrace of popular democracy, had abandoned the sans-culottes after Thermidor and damned the Terror as pathological. But even when censuring the Committee of Public Safety for impugning rule of law, he had condemned reactionaries for continuing the Terror's deadly polarization and substituting new victims for old. He welcomed the Directory as an architect of compromise, for which Babeuf excoriated him.

Despite such tensions, Réal had come to see the Directory's pursuit of Babeuf and the others as an existential threat. He accused the government of persecuting citizens for their opinions and joined Antonelle in insisting that common aims and shared values united republicans across the political spectrum. Yes, he admitted, the Equals were dissidents, but only because they "longed for a time when the name of citizen was not an insult . . . when the people were happy, when soldiers were not reviled." They were not subversives but loyal opponents whom the Directory should accommodate. The republic could not survive, he had long insisted, without open debate and peaceful resolution of difference.[17]

As soon as he was sworn in as a defender, at the afternoon's end, Réal took charge by demanding that courtroom seating be reorganized. "First, [the defender] should be as close as possible to the accused; secondly, he should be able to see witnesses and jurors with equal ease; finally, he should be visible to the public as well." Gandon protested, weakly, that some of the places in question were reserved for soldiers, but Réal brushed him aside. "There are plenty of soldiers near the accused. The prisoners are not going anywhere."

This was only the beginning. Having come to Vendôme to represent Drouet and Antonelle, Réal joined seven defenders already present. The others were amateurs, prisoners' relatives or local militants. He was a successful Parisian lawyer and well-known journalist who would soon declare himself the "national defender" of all in the dock, squaring off alongside them against prosecutors, magistrates, and the Directory itself.[18]

By the end of the trial's fourth day, all of the actors were in place and bedlam mounting. Each step would be hard fought as weeks stretched into months, bringing France ever closer to the legislative elections from which each side hoped to win some advantage.

NINE

Witnesses for the Prosecution

B y default, high court trials unfolded like regular criminal trials, for no matter how exacting successive assemblies had been about how indictments were to be handed down or judges and jurors selected, none had bothered to detail the conduct of proceedings themselves. In keeping with its model, the high court's next phase was to hear testimony from prosecutorial witnesses. The list was long: in addition to plotters-turned-denouncers Georges Grisel and Nicolas Pillé, Viellart and Bailly expected to call handwriting experts, police agents, and militants incarcerated for other deeds.[1]

Normally, after a witness testified, defendants and defenders were allowed to challenge testimony and even question the speaker's integrity. Judges, prosecutors, and jurors could join in too, posing questions for clarification. Again, because of legislative silence, that order of business was not written in stone, so a free-for-all ensued before anyone came to the stand.[2]

Réal and the Equals objected to the order of business, arguing that challenges to a witness's character or reasons for testifying should precede testimony, to exclude unreliable men before they could poison jurors' minds. Réal even debated how the challenges were to be handled, attempting to expose the court's makeshift quality. Should witnesses hear challenges against them? he asked. Were defendants to be given the last word in these arguments, as in others before the court? What legal precedents would they defer to?

Babeuf, Buonarroti, and Germain focused on character, noting that many of the prosecutors' witnesses were police spies or criminals. What sort of trial, they asked, depended on testimony from "the vilest, filthiest, most corrupt members of society?" More troubling, they asked, with Réal, what kind of executive strengthened itself by denouncing plots—two more of which had been "revealed" since their arrest—and attacking its legislature in the person of a sitting deputy?[3]

As the debate churned on, prosecutors parrying at every turn, two things became clear. The accused were determined to block the testimony of Georges Grisel, who had participated in the plot before denouncing it, and they wanted at all costs to neutralize the phrase "kill the five," which topped a list of insurgents' tasks and was, in Babeuf's words, the "most striking," "awful" evidence the Directory had produced. To exclude Grisel, the defendants argued that he had a conflict of interest because he expected to be rewarded for his testimony. Indeed, he may have been a provocateur from the start. As for "kill the five," they pointed to a line drawn through the phrase, insisting that no one could be held liable for a thought that existed "only as long as it took to write it."[4]

They had no visible success. The magistrates heard every objection, retained every witness, and remained silent about "kill the five." The best the defendants could hope for was to have sown doubt in jurors' minds about what was to follow.

The first witnesses were handwriting experts Alexis Harger and Jean-François Guillaume. Harger, expected to verify authorship of some of the *Papers*, sat quietly as Babeuf, Germain, and Buonarroti acknowledged their contributions. His turn to speak came when the court reached notes and letters attributed to the uncooperative Darthé, who refused to acknowledge anything. Among those pages was the notorious list with "kill the five."

The court paused to scrutinize it, debating the origin of the line that cut across the damning phrase. Was it drawn by the author, who retracted the thought by scratching it out, or did it form part of the signature Babeuf had applied to all of his papers when they were inventoried by police? Réal insisted that phrase and line had been drawn by the same hand. Harger demurred: the line was part of Babeuf's signature.

In either case, Gandon asked, were the words beneath legible?

"Yes, citizen," Harger replied, bending over the paper to spell them out. "There is the top of the T, the bottom of the T, almost all of the O . . ."

"*What do you mean?*" someone called out.

"The lower part of the O in *tout,*" Harger replied. He had spelled out the word *tout* (all) rather than *tuer* (kill), reducing an injunction, "kill the five," to a simple description: "all five."

Realizing his mistake, Harger struggled to correct himself, only to buckle. He had expected to see the word *kill* before he first examined the note, he confessed, because the Directory had plastered it all over Paris.

Juror Gaultier de Biauzat asked Harger to repeat himself. "What you mean to say is that if it had not already been suggested to you that the word *kill* was present, you would [not] have found . . . that?"

"I would have said it was either *tout* (all) or *tuer* (kill)."

Buonarroti pressed harder. Had the director of the grand jury told Harger what to say? The latter denied that, but the question of tampering had been raised. It would return.

Whether or not Harger had been given explicit instructions, Babeuf added, he testified to the Directory's attempt to poison public opinion with its claim that a half-digested thought was a deadly order. "Such bad faith is incredible."[5]

Harger's colleague, Jean-François Guillaume, followed him to the stand and was asked to verify the handwriting on notes attributed to Darthé. Given one of the defendant's old account books, Guillaume compared it so quickly to the notes in question that Réal interrupted. Réal understood that the expert had done this kind of work for the grand jury, but knew, as well, that he was authenticating the notes with a new source so jurors could gauge his degree of certainty. Guillaume ought to be more careful, the defender warned.

The expert paused and stammered, then admitted that he had already seen this account book.

The prisoners erupted. This was a clear violation of courtroom procedure. How could the jury properly assess Guillaume's testimony if he had already made a comparison? When and where had he seen this account book?

Guillaume paused again. Gandon spoke up, to explain that he had asked the expert witness to inspect the account book to confirm that it would serve the court's purposes.

Outraged objections poured from the prisoners' benches as Réal's voice rose with cold fury. "But citizen president, how is it possible that the expert witness saw this account book in your home?" Had Harger inspected other documents? Were prosecutors present? What about other judges?

Guillaume tried to defend himself, but Réal cut him short. This was the sort of tampering Buonarroti had already hinted at. "It is clear to everyone . . . that this testimony is nothing but a performance rehearsed [in advance]."

The irate prisoners continued to shout until the judges ended the session in frustration.[6]

These were victories, of sorts, for the defense. Harger had called into question the damning "kill the five," and Guillaume did worse by alluding to a corruption of procedure by the lead magistrate himself.

Viellart scrambled to defend his case when the trial resumed the next day. Guillaume revealed no malfeasance, he argued, because the conduct of the trial was at Gandon's discretion. The only people corrupting the proceedings were the defendants themselves. "Have we not reached the fourteenth session and scarcely begun to hear the second witness? It is not hard to see how roles are being distributed to allow some [defendants] to prepare speeches that respond to others' seemingly impromptu questions."

Viellart asked the judges to take firmer control of the courtroom by forbidding defendants to question witnesses until the latter finished testifying. Otherwise, "you will see continuing disorder, confusion, scandal, and the slandering of a supreme court that defends the French social contract."[7]

That the judges were inclined to grant the request was visible in their refusal to allow Réal to respond. When they withdrew to consult, the defender vented his rage on the prosecutor.

"You slandered me, you slandered the jurors, you slandered the accused, and you don't expect anyone to reply? Never, not before the revolutionary tribunal, not under Robespierre . . ." Bailly tried to cut him short, but Réal would have none of it. "Roles are being handed out, but we are not the ones doing it." It was Viellart, he charged, who prompted witnesses, intimidated judges, tried to poison jurors' minds, and expected to proceed without challenge. Such behavior was worse than that of the revolutionary tribunal.

"I was not afraid of the king. I was not afraid of Robespierre," Réal concluded. He would not bow down now.[8]

If the judges did not hear his objections, Réal made sure that jurors did.

The magistrates returned and granted Viellart's request. Guillaume would continue testifying, and the defendants could not pose questions until he finished. Even then, they could not speak without express permission, which Gandon would refuse to anyone he believed to be needlessly prolonging debate.

Commotion like that of the preceding day mounted, prisoners shouting out questions and heckling magistrates as the voice of assistant prosecutor Bailly rose above them. "This is shocking. To think that the accused and their defenders call themselves republicans . . ."

"That's right, we are republicans," someone called back. "It's because we are republicans that you prosecute us, that you violate the law."

Overwhelmed, the bench called a halt to the proceedings. Prisoners shouted out, "Long live the republic!" and Charles Germain led them in singing the *Marseillaise*. When they reached the verse, "tremble tyrants! and you traitors," they raised their fists and shook them at the judges. Singing still, the defendants left the courtroom.[9]

Viellart had been right: the accused and their defenders did sow "disorder" and "confusion," putting the Directory itself on trial. By accusing the regime of assaulting popular democracy and social welfare, the Equals meant to prove themselves loyal republicans being railroaded by tyrants. They were not, however, alone in fostering confusion. The magistrates refused to discuss Harger's revelation and would not concede that Gandon's handling of the evidence was inappropriate, offering no response to the troubling testimony other than silencing defendants who raised objections. By so visibly abandoning the search for truth necessary to legitimate these proceedings and distinguish high court from revolutionary tribunal, the judges diminished their credibility. But they seemed to take for granted that the jurors for whose loyalty the Equals fought so fiercely would remain on their side.

Viellart and Bailly could reasonably hope to recover some ground with Georges Grisel, who not only had participated in the conspiracy but gave his all on the stand. For two days, the captain milked his testimony for the last dregs of celebrity that the case brought to his otherwise unremarkable life.

That Grisel rarely raised his eyes from personal interest to the far horizon of politics was clear from the brief account he gave of his life. Rather than telling the revolutionary's familiar tale of blinkered Old Regime youth and republican maturity, he catalogued disappointments among which 1789 passed unremarked. Born in 1765 to a modest provincial tailor and his wife, Grisel explained that he was a younger son with no hope of inheriting the family business. He joined the Royal Army, only to learn, when a truce was declared, that he was too short to serve in peacetime. Knowing his older brother remained in India, where he had gone for work, Grisel apprenticed to their father. Then the errant sibling returned.

"I was frustrated that the law gave everything to the eldest and nothing to the youngest," he admitted in court. "My brother returned much taller than I and with a very different build. There was also his long absence and my parents' special affection for him. Everything made me jealous. I had worked selflessly for my father for two years but was nothing when my brother came back." Calculating what he would have saved had he been receiving wages, Grisel stole the sum from his father and fled to Paris.

Life in the capital was no easier. Grisel shared a room with twelve men, continued to work as an apprentice tailor, and finally returned to an army that could no longer discriminate on the basis of height. He came back to Paris as a captain, in 1796.

This was the turning point of his testimony. Settling in, he began to tell the court about the plot he encountered that spring.[10]

Grisel said he found himself sharing drinks with an acquaintance named Monnier in early April. That fellow, surprised that Grisel had never heard of Babeuf, handed over an issue of the *People's Tribune* containing "a long, wordy speech meant to stir up troops." Grisel told the court that he was openly critical, saying that no one who understood soldiers would write like that. "Like me, the men in barracks will support our constitution as we promised."

Monnier's reply suggested that this was more than idle chat. "He started describing massacres in the South and exaggerating all kinds of things," adding that "true democrats" were distributing pamphlets, creating patriotic circles, and preparing to restore the constitution of 1793. Although Monnier did not know the names of any of these people, he was confident of their influence. "There are twenty-five thousand of us ready to go and waiting for the signal."

Grisel recalled saying to himself, "[H]ere is a man who may truly be part of a plot," and added knowingly to the court: "when someone confides [such a thing], you must pretend to be on his side or expect to be knifed." So, he said, he abruptly changed tone. "Great! I'm glad to hear it. There are a lot of patriots in the army right now waiting for the right time to prove their . . . allegiance to the constitution of 1793." Monnier shook the captain's hand and said, "Comrade, I want to show you more."

The two men set off, walking through the densely populated neighborhoods of the Right Bank to the café of the Chinese Baths. The regulars there stared suspiciously when they entered, but Monnier moved among them, murmuring, "[H]e's a good patriot; he's one of ours, he's a new recruit," until they returned to their conversations. A lone man talked privately to Monnier and then joined the pair to initiate a conversation about military morale. When he asked Grisel whether soldiers read the *Tribune*, the captain kept up his game by saying they were patriots of '93 but did not care for Babeuf, whose "words, turns of phrase, and figures of speech" made no sense to them. "I would use a completely different tone if I were to appeal to the army."

The stranger offered to print such an address if Grisel would produce it. Two days later, the captain handed over his composition and learned the man's name: Augustin Darthé.[11]

Grisel's *Letter from the Free Frenchman* is a plainspoken indictment of the Directory whose bitterness is far more deeply felt than what one might expect from an amateur spy working on the fly. "We are fucked, my poor friend," it begins. "Yup, fucked and left flat if we choke down the bitter pill that's been

forced on us. So much for . . . starving, fighting, sweating blood and piss, killing lice and [tyrants'] slaves for four years. It was all for nothing. Liberty, our
heart's desire . . . and sweet equality, its inseparable companion, are phantoms
. . . like wisps of smoke from my pipe." Ordinary soldiers were being betrayed
by the government and its aristocratic allies, public storehouses had become
morgues, and "the lovely Paris of '93, where liberty, equality, and abundance
bound the people into one happy family" was decaying to savage wilderness.
Their only hope was to resurrect the democratic constitution.[12]

Darthé was delighted. He had the appeal printed and, a few days later,
gave Grisel a stack of them with a certificate naming him an Equal.

The two men met several times after that, chatting at the Chinese Baths
or strolling in the Tuileries Gardens, where they ran into Charles Germain.
When Darthé introduced Grisel, Germain "congratulated me on my Free
Frenchman pamphlet, saying it was in the style that all such works should
be written." Grisel joined them and a third man, Jean-Baptiste Didier, to
read over a speech Babeuf had written for Drouet. As the captain listened,
the others worried that Babeuf was being too hard on the deputy, a "very
valuable man who must be managed carefully."

Then the visits stopped. For almost two weeks, Grisel said, work prevented
him from seeing anyone "or even going to the Chinese Baths." When he was
summoned again, it was not for more walking and talking, but to attend a
meeting at which Grisel found Darthé, Germain, and Didier, and was introduced to Babeuf and Buonarroti. "Here are the members of the insurrectional
committee," Darthé explained. "A few of our brothers will arrive shortly." As
they waited, Grisel spoke to Babeuf. "After all the boasting [the others had]
done [about him], I expected someone of a certain importance." But the captain was disappointed and, perhaps, haunted by his memory of sibling rivalry.
"I was shocked to find a man inferior in size as well as talent."

Grisel said he was loath to denounce anyone, believing he could set things
right himself. "Certain events in my life proved my influence over others," he
bragged to the court. "I even managed to quell sedition . . . I told myself I had
to do the same here." He urged Babeuf to petition the legislative assembly for
poor relief. "Right," the other answered dismissively, "we should act like beggars when we have arms!"

Former army officers Jean-Joseph Fyon, Jean-Antoine Rossignol, and Guillaume Massard arrived, and the group settled down to business. Babeuf read an *Act of Insurrection* and suggested that they print sixty thousand copies. Then the group turned to a decree urging insurgents to use force, and "there was talk . . . of changing a few phrases. Rossignol did not want the language to be too moderate, because he wanted people to understand what was necessary. Babeuf agreed, saying that they must commit acts from which there was no turning back." Before separating, the men organized a military committee that included Grisel, Germain, and the army officers.[13]

To this point, Grisel's testimony affirmed the tightly organized plot Viellart had described in his opening statement, his words corroborated by the *Act of Insurrection* and his own *Free Frenchman* pamphlet, both of which had been published in the *Papers*.[14]

But the captain lost momentum as he described a military committee that did little more than complain and gossip. Rossignol was running out of tobacco. Massard could not afford to get his boots from the cobbler. Someone said wealthy patron Félix Lepeletier would provide money, but another conspirator told Grisel privately that Lepeletier "promises a lot and delivers very little." Committee members sniped at those who did not show up, accusing Darthé of carelessness and Fyon of indifference. When Massard was alone with Grisel, he claimed that he was the mastermind of the plot. Grisel answered with backbiting of his own from the stand, dismissing Massard and even Babeuf as too stupid to have written the *Act Creating a Directory of Insurgency*. Alluding to a rumor that director Paul Barras was involved, Grisel hinted that a shadow leader had composed the incendiary statement.

Sometimes the military committee simply failed to gather. One meeting dissolved because Germain forgot to tell the others he was going to visit a military encampment. Then everyone was dismissed after days of idle talk to write up ideas for organizing insurrection. When Grisel showed up late for the discussion that was to follow, he found the others had scattered in less than an hour.[15]

These were not particularly menacing conspirators. Their disarray, like the drift visible in the *Papers*, blunted the prosecutor's account. Like the neighborhood agents, these men were idle, confused, frightened, rudderless.

"We talked," Grisel admitted, "chattering on because we didn't know where to begin."[16]

The military committee's lethargy may be explained by the revolution's decline. Its members, again like neighborhood agents, were experienced revolutionaries, former militants, bureaucrats, and soldiers, united in their hatred of the Directory. But the task before them was overwhelming. In 1793, militants like these had capitalized on crowds, popular institutions, and friendly legislators to win new policies. But Jacobins began to demobilize those networks to consolidate the Convention's power in 1793–94. Reactionaries finished off the work after Thermidor. Little remained by 1796 to buoy popular militancy against a hostile, exclusive political order.

If all of this is visible from the distance of centuries, it was not so readily apparent at the time. Anxious directors and fearful reactionaries saw in the first half of Grisel's statement evidence of the Equals' determination to reignite the French Revolution. Democrats found, in its second half, affirmation of Antonelle's claim that the Equals were mere dreamers. Jurors might yet bend either way.

It was during one more aimless meeting, Grisel continued, that he realized he could trust director Lazare Carnot with word of the plot. The others so clearly despised the man that he was unlikely to be involved. So Grisel wrote to the director, who welcomed him and waved away his offer of references. "A man who has not quit the defense of his homeland since freely embracing it in 1791 is no conspirator. Conspirators don't act like you do or speak as honestly and loyally." Carnot's colleagues were equally enthusiastic, "saying I had their complete confidence, and . . . encouraging me to use every means possible to realize my goal."[17]

Historians have argued that Grisel denounced the plot because the mattress in which he stashed the certificate naming him an Equal had been taken to a military warehouse so he spoke up before it could be discovered. His courtroom testimony suggests a more complex rationale. Grisel described his life as one of frustrated ambition and himself as a worthy man overlooked at every turn. His interest in politics was confined to what touched him personally: he praised the revolution for striking down inheritance laws that favored his brother and he joined the army only after exhausting all other options. Then along came Augustin Darthé. Generous with his time, his friends, and his praise, he offered Grisel a shot at something big.[18]

Perhaps Grisel had second thoughts and would have allowed the association to lapse had not Darthé recalled him. Or perhaps he really was too busy to return to the Chinese Baths. Regardless of what might have been, Grisel's experience of the conspiracy changed dramatically when he met the insurrectional committee. He felt his status diminished at every turn. Babeuf swept aside his proposal to petition the legislature, and the entire committee scolded him for asking whether an interim government would be installed after the insurrection. "Everyone looked at me angrily . . . Rossignol said: . . . remember, you were only brought in to advise us as a soldier, not to take care of anything else." No longer a valuable military insider or the publicist whose words were "in the style that all such works should be written," Grisel was once more a lowly apprentice outranked by elders, a neglected youth outshone by someone whose mediocrity he alone could see.[19]

It was not long afterward that he contacted Carnot, in whom he found a new patron with time, resources, and insight to cultivate his ego and direct him to new ends. As the Equals suspected, Grisel found money, too. Demobilized shortly before receiving Darthé's final summons, he did not return to active duty for more than six months. His work for the directors won a generous stipend that carried him through a dry spell.[20]

On the day he first met Carnot, Grisel continued, he learned that the Equals were negotiating an alliance with retired deputies from the National Convention. He told the director where the meeting was to take place, but a stakeout revealed nothing. When Grisel sent word of a second meeting, troops found only Darthé and Drouet sharing a bottle of wine. Blaming others for those failures, Grisel said he used the extra time to find Babeuf's hiding place and archives. He sent that address to Carnot with word of a third meeting between Equals and ex-deputies. As police moved in, he returned to barracks.[21]

"Overcome and exhausted, because I had slept barely two hours in the preceding fourteen days, I went home and fell . . . dead from fatigue. I didn't go to the Directory that day, but the next. The directors congratulated me.

Even . . . Larévellière-Lépeaux said it was impossible to reward me as richly as I deserved. I told him, and the rest of the Directory: *I did not serve you or even myself, citizens, but the nation.*"

On the stand in Vendôme, Grisel pointed to his heart as he repeated his last words to the directors. "*My reward is here . . . Anything more would be shameful.*" Then he fell silent.[22]

If Grisel hoped to make a good impression, the accused did their best to spoil it. "Powerful men used to amuse themselves by throwing liberty's friends to wild beasts," Antonelle interjected caustically. "Now they deliver patriots wholesale to the insults of wretched spies and the slander of paid liars."[23]

Other defendants linked Grisel's personal failings to those of the regime he served. Charles Germain mocked him as an anxious reactionary who became certain that a conspiracy was in progress once he saw "that shadowy lair" of the Chinese Baths, where "citizens of both sexes and all ages noisily shared hopes and dreams while relaxing companionably around a pot of beer, a pitcher of wine, a bottle of cider." What sort of person would think it criminal to be exasperated by the "shameless renewal of abuses like those feudal tyranny once imposed on France"? Who would think it wrong "to speak tirelessly to the people about its rights . . . to advise one's fellow citizens"? When "all that is declared conspiracy . . . we will see liberty flee and the defeat of the republic."[24]

Taking up the refrain that the Equals were gentle dreamers, Germain depicted their mistakes as inconsistencies that proved Grisel a liar. Would real conspirators welcome a complete stranger into their midst? Would true plotters do no more than complain? How were all the projects that Grisel described to be realized without money? Returning to Antonelle's insistence on the absence of means, Germain concluded: "three [coins] figure in this great affair: does that seem like enough for . . . the thousand . . . things necessary to effect such a terrible explosion?"[25]

Babeuf charged that Grisel had been employed by the directors from the very outset. They had been on the lookout for opponents since closing the Pantheon Club, he said, and found a flunky in Grisel, who extorted an introduction to the Chinese Baths and then used his proximity to democrats to invent a plot.[26]

Réal claimed to have found evidence of the government's collaboration. Although Grisel's first letter to Carnot identified neither Buonarroti nor Darthé, another hand had penciled those names into the margins. Then the government obscured the composite nature of the original by seamlessly incorporating the names into the printed version. Given the letter's importance, Réal concluded, jurors should examine the original and judges should attest to its having been altered.

Once more, the magistrates stonewalled. Thanking Réal for calling the court's attention to the discrepancy between Grisel's original letter and its reproduction, they insisted that nothing more was necessary.[27]

The singing at sessions' end continued, thanks to Sophie Lapierre. She had abandoned the rousing *Marseillaise* to take up a mournful *Goujon's Lament,* whose lyrics echoed the defendants' courtroom arguments. *With what corrupt lies,* she and the others sang, *did those evil-doers blacken our names.*[28]

Almost a dozen police agents followed Grisel to the stand. One said he heard Sophie Lapierre say "the most violent things" at a dinner with friends. Another was asked to move weapons he never saw. Several testified that defendant Philippe Blondeau gave them a generous meal and asked for help breaking Babeuf and Drouet out of prison.[29]

The Equals accused each witness of being a paid informant or provocateur. Réal returned to the charge of corruption, noting that one witness "never speaks in the first person" to intimate that his deposition had been composed by someone else and memorized. Of another witness, the defender asked: "who does not see that all of it was made up?"[30]

Despite such fierce criticism, no one backed down, admitted to being coached, or let slip damning disclosures like those of Harger and Guillaume.

Then Jean-Baptiste Meunier and Jean-Noel Barbier came to the stand.

Jean-Baptiste Meunier, arrested the preceding May for distributing subversive pamphlets, entered the courtroom singing Sophie Lapierre's preferred song: *Goujon's Lament.*

"You are forbidden to sing, that's not what you came here for," Gandon scolded.

"You should love that song as much as I do," the soldier countered. "The friends of liberty and saintly equality think it patriotic."

Struggling for control, Gandon demanded that Meunier testify.

"What do you want from me?" the man replied. "Praise for virtue shamed, innocence persecuted, the courage of the people's friends? I love them and I hate their oppressors. Let my tongue dry up in my mouth before I accuse the friends of their cause, of my cause, of the cause of all French republicans."

Gandon tried to cut the man short, but he would not be stopped. "It's true! . . . I did what I could to save myself from a panel of murderers and executioners . . ."[31]

Meunier said he had nothing to tell the high court because someone else had written his grand jury statement, a deception he accepted out of fear. When he informed Viellart, the prosecutor had done nothing more than produce a copy of the statement for Meunier to memorize again. Gandon had been no more helpful.

From the bench, Gandon repeated his demand for testimony.

"I said I don't know anyone," the soldier answered.

"How can you say you do not know anyone . . . ?" Gandon asked and proceeded to summarize the soldier's grand jury testimony with pointed questions. Had not the soldier claimed that Blondeau told him about a plot? Did he not accuse another defendant of giving him subversive newspapers? Did he not say defendant Félix Lepeletier told him to avoid wearing his uniform when visiting so as not to rouse suspicion?

Meunier denied everything. "[The director of the grand jury] dictated it all. I was weak. I was nineteen years old. I have suffered for eleven months. I am at your mercy. Do what you will."[32]

Viellart admitted giving Meunier a summary of his grand jury testimony, but only because the latter asked for help refreshing his memory. The court should know as well, he added, that the witness and his friend, Jean-Noel Barbier, asked to be indicted with the Equals because they believed that if tried for conspiracy and acquitted, all other charges against them would be dropped.

Bolstered by that information, the judges denied Réal's request to investigate Meunier's claims, charged the soldier with perjury, and told guards to take him away.[33]

Jean-Noel Barbier was next. An infantryman of twenty-three condemned for his part in the police legion revolt, he told a story that imitated Meunier's down to the word. He was suffering in prison, he said, "when the head of the grand jury asked me to sign a statement he had written. He promised to set me free very soon . . . I did what I could to save myself." Like Meunier, Barbier said he regretted the decision and appealed to Viellart, who offered him the grand jury statement to memorize. Claiming that he could not lie any more, Barbier threw himself on his sword. "If you need another victim, I am ready."

His wish was granted. He, too, was charged with perjury and led away.[34]

Given a promising opportunity to strengthen the court's credibility by investigating witnesses who had recanted in almost exactly the same way and who gave evidence—via Meunier's singing—of having communicated with the Equals, the magistrates forged ahead instead.

The last witness was the only one besides Grisel who had shared in the plot and cooperated with police: the scribe Nicolas Pillé. Prison bullying had worn hard on the timid man, who brought his grating deference to the stand. Trying to please everyone by affirming facts that prosecutors elicited but refusing to draw any conclusions from them, he freely admitted to working with some of the accused but demurred when Gandon said he was employed by "a group or insurrectionary committee." "I only knew . . . citizens Lepeletier and Babeuf." He acknowledged copying the *Act Creating a Directory of Insurrection* but could not say who wrote it. He confirmed transcribing letters to neighborhood agents but knew nothing about how they were distributed. He remembered visits between Buonarroti, Darthé, and Babeuf but said they took place "without any hint of secrecy." It was a clever strategy that someone had surely helped him formulate, each correction neatly sidestepping the collective activity upon which the prosecution founded its charge of conspiracy.

The critical moment came when Gandon asked why Pillé did not denounce the Equals after coming to understand what they were up to. The latter seemed to channel Antonelle in answering. "I would never have believed that a few men could excite all of Paris with nothing more than their voices. What seemed feasible on paper was impossible in practice . . . because the people had been through several revolutions by then and would not rise up at the first sound they heard." Babeuf's own behavior made the plan appear all the more fantastic. When they were alone together, Pillé explained, "I saw [him] wild-eyed, running around his room, jumping and shouting: 'We are risen up . . .'" He added, "[T]hat happened a lot."

Pillé continued, saying that the men he worked for were so demoralized by popular suffering that he could only pity them. "I thought a denunciation would hurt those who didn't need such trouble." In any case, he repeated, their success seemed impossible.

Despite such sympathetic assessments, the defendants blasted poor Pillé. Jean-Baptiste Didier, named as a courier, said he was crazy. Antonelle accused him of lying. Germain called him "an idiot who will say whatever he is told."

In the end, at Réal's insistence, Gandon asked Pillé about "evil spirits." The man said he had not wanted to go to Babeuf's home, but was compelled to do so by forces beyond his control. "I believe someone can make a deal with a devil to harm or protect someone else. I would like the court's permission to tell you more."

Gandon did not need to hear any more. He excused the witness.[35]

Prosecutors and defendants were at a draw. The case against the Equals had gained momentum as Georges Grisel described the conspiracy and police agents hinted at the political energy rippling through old activist networks to touch as many as two dozen people in the spring of 1796. But the Equals' charges of police and courtroom corruption gained force from the flustered admissions of Harger and Guillaume, the brazen testimony of Meunier and Barbier, and the magistrates' own clumsy supervision of interrogation and debate.

The most important stage of the trial was yet to come. More troubling than others' testimony about subversive comments overheard or menacing acts hinted at were the Equals' own words, contained in the hundreds of pages seized from Babeuf's hideaway and published for all of France to read in the *Papers*.

How would the accused account for that?

TEN

Reclaiming the Revolution

A fter hearing witnesses testify, criminal courts gave the accused an opportunity to challenge the evidence offered against them. Here was the heart of the matter, as the Equals explained their own words.

The statements in question were contained in Babeuf's *Papers*. Although the compilation included few newspaper columns, pamphlets, or posters—presumably because the Directory did not want to give them further publicity—it contained almost everything else police seized with Babeuf. There were notes on local troops, lists of men "suitable to command," drafts for decrees of insurgency, letters between Secret Directory and neighborhood agents, the damning "kill the five," and more, all treated as evidence of the coordinated activity on which Viellart and Bailly founded their case.

Faced with all this, the defendants pursued two lines of attack. First, they replicated their rhetorical assault on witnesses. Just as they had claimed that those men gave false testimony, so they argued that the *Papers* had been corrupted to give the appearance of criminal activity where none existed.

Buonarroti made his case by arguing that undated documents attributed to him were composed well before the "alleged" plot and had been tampered with since. He said that the *List of Democrats to Add to the Convention*, which prosecutors called part of a plan to resurrect the National Convention, was actually a roster of newspaper subscribers. It had no such title, he insisted, when he last saw it. He claimed that notes labeled *Men Suitable for the Movement* and *Men Suitable to Command* had been drawn up to answer the National Convention's call for allies at the time of the Vendémiaire insurrection. "I was very much surprised to find these sorts of papers among the evidence," he concluded gently.[1]

Charles Germain claimed that prosecutors purposely misrepresented his notes, which he fractured into discrete sentences and framed with shaggy dog stories to impart new meaning. He transformed a letter about negotiating with Drouet into talk about a debt owed a Belgian silk merchant, and reduced criticism of the military agent Fyon's proposed alliance with former legislators—"Perhaps . . . he will forget this ridiculous idea . . . of admitting three ex-conventionals among us"—to gossip about a dinner no one wanted to attend. He often laughed at his own invention.[2]

Réal, an agile critic of procedure, wove the claims into a charge of prosecutorial overreach. "I appreciate that one must make every effort to gather information . . . and formulate a theory based on recognized facts, but you show up with a ready-made theory into which you force every act, every bit of scribbling, every paper you find."[3]

Babeuf resurrected the fiction he had concocted months earlier and given to Hésine for the *High Court Journal*, insisting that much of the archive had been produced by an anonymous collective for which he served as secretary. As he justified the arguments within, he implicitly defended the Equals.[4]

There was, however, no doubt about the date and authorship of the notorious letter Babeuf had written to the directors within days of his arrest. Gandon began his interrogation of Babeuf with that. What was the court to believe, he asked, the defendant's declaration of conspiracy then or his plea of innocence now?

Babeuf tried to duck the question, complaining irritably about procedure. Gandon, finding the cool firmness he too often lacked, kept at it until Babeuf buckled. He had been trying to protect innocents by intimidating the police, he said, and so he inflated their fantasy of conspiracy. Seemingly blind to the ensuing panic, Babeuf congratulated himself on that supposed feint. "I think I spared a considerable number of men from persecution." But, he continued, he had since come to believe that the Directory had neither "the interest, will, or capacity to pursue the republic's few remaining friends," so "I see no point in sustaining claims contrary to my defense."[5]

Excuse given, Babeuf moved to the second line of attack on which the Equals were agreed, embracing a few critical documents to affirm that he and the others were servants of people and republic. As he did, a rift became visible. For Babeuf's increasingly radical statements veered repeatedly from the claims of peaceful, patriotic criticism that Antonelle had formulated and which Buonarroti defended in court, exposing simmering tensions among the accused.

The first pages on which Babeuf took a stand were notes that addressed "a small circle of virtuous men." Within those notes, he acknowledged the circle's wish to cure the nation's ills by rousing a revolution that would be "the last if it succeeds because it will satisfy all need," offered brief counsel, and surveyed the nation's achievements since 1789. After asking what kind of regime would "guarantee the social system we desire," he abruptly broke off.[6]

Viellart claimed these were notes for a speech, infused with a "prophetic voice that conquers the ambivalent, enslaves the weak, charms the anxious, beguiles the ignorant, and deceives the multitude." In short, they were notes for a speech "that creates fanatics."[7]

Not so, Babeuf countered. These were private reflections on virtue, justice, and social good. Was it a crime to voice his hatred of tyranny? Was he forbidden to ask whether political change was possible? "Can the citizen be forced to respect institutions he finds deficient and silence his reason when he believes the public is oppressed by a vicious government?" If so, he was guilty. But so, too, was Gabriel Bonnot de Mably.

Invoking Mably was a clever move. Although the philosopher had died in 1785, he found an enthusiastic revolutionary audience with the posthumous publication of his *Rights and Duties of the Citizen*. Composed midcentury but not made public until 1789, the essay challenged traditional defenses of the French monarchy that had dismissed even moderate reform as incitement to chaos, arguing instead that conflict strengthens a people and promotes liberty. Decades before the king's fateful revival of the Estates General, Mably imagined resurrecting that defunct institution to promote more stable, popular government.[8]

Such ideas seemed prophetic in 1789 and, phoenix-like, Mably's reputation soared. Pamphleteers sang his praises, publishers reissued his essays, legislators proposed statues in his honor. So well known did he become that a deputy who defended noble privilege to the National Assembly was told simply to "read Mably." So popular were his ideas that they flourished through Terror and Reaction alike.[9]

Babeuf, who had long admired Mably, recalled the philosopher's argument that laws are legitimate only so long as they serve society and keep pace with a people's growing enlightenment. "If citizens created ridiculous conventions and established a government incapable of protecting the law," Babeuf read from Mably to the court, "if they took a route contrary to the happiness they sought; if, lamentably, they permitted themselves to be guided by treacherous, ignorant leaders, would you cruelly condemn them to remain forever the victims of error or distraction? . . . Should laws created to enhance reason and sustain liberty debase and enslave us? Should society, meant to ease man's need, make us miserable?"

Mably answered those questions with a resounding no. "In every state, the citizen has a right to aspire to the government best suited to guarantee public happiness . . . He is neither a conspirator nor a provocateur if he proposes political forms wiser than those freely adopted or imposed by events, passions, or circumstance." Mably felt so sure that he insisted: "when a people does not see its menace . . . the most zealous citizens must act as sentinels, defending liberty if it is corrupted and raising barriers against despotism."[10]

Babeuf explained that these arguments informed his own thinking and encouraged him to ask whether the people would be better served by a new regime. Surely that was legal. Even Mably, who suffered the despotism of the Old Regime, was permitted to say such things publicly. If that was no longer permitted, Babeuf added, then the Directory need not have violated his privacy to find evidence against him. He had long advertised his discontent in the *People's Tribune*.

Continuing to align himself with Mably, Babeuf rejected the argument he imputed to Viellart: that asking how to improve the popular condition makes one an anarchist or demagogue. As an advocate for the people, Babeuf insisted, he was a philosopher and a patriot. His right to think, speak, and write about difficult issues was protected by natural law and their own constitution. How could the "cool calculation of the popular political condition" be conspiratorial?[11]

Assistant prosecutor Bailly interrupted. Mably might be a friend of liberty and equality, but his work was not "suited to all people." If a minority tried to change the government, it violated the constitution. In any case, how could Babeuf claim that the Equals hoped to improve the popular condition, when all knew they had been preparing to abolish the system of private property on which social order was founded?[12]

Réal interrupted. Bailly was pleading his case, the defender charged, not posing questions for clarification as the law authorized. Prisoners shouted their objections, too, but Bailly continued to speak. The judges let the uproar go on.

When the commotion settled, it was not Babeuf but Buonarroti who picked up the thread of argument. Echoing Antonelle's claim of loyal opposition, he declared: "if defending public sovereignty, liberty, and equality is conspiratorial," then "I am a conspirator." But, Buonarroti added, he thought the jury would ultimately vindicate them and make it impossible any longer "to call the defense of liberty a plot or to claim nonsensically that the nation's most ardent friends are . . . its enemies."

Returning to the contested notes, Buonarroti moved from Babeuf's claim of a right to challenge failing government to the more neutral terrain of civil liberties and popular sovereignty. Let them suppose that these pages outlined a speech. What did it contain? "The opinions of a man profoundly affected by public misfortune who finds the state in its present form deficient and at odds with the social contract." That man did not, however, try to promote change through trickery, force, or violence. "I see nothing but the supreme condition necessary for every project [the speech] details: popular consent."

And what was sovereignty? It was "the right to organize what is useful to society," which properly belonged to all of society's members. Accordingly, citizens were not just permitted, but obliged to discuss collective good. How else were they to share useful opinions? If they could not share opinions, how might they guarantee common good? "What do I see in these pages? I see a wish to change the present regime. I see discussion of how to enlighten others and persuade the public to adopt this or that system of government. Where is the crime? That right belongs to every citizen." Retreating from Babeuf's justification of censure and revolt, Buonarroti defended fundamental rights to free expression and popular sovereignty proclaimed in 1789.

As prisoners filed from court that day, Sophie Lapierre led them once more in *Goujon's Lament*. "Liberty, cloak us in honor / We will lay down ourselves for you."[13]

The court turned next to the *Act Creating a Directory of Insurrection*, which condemns "the unspeakable state of misery and oppression into which [the nation] has fallen" and calls into being a Secret Directory of Public Safety to "lead the people in recovering its sovereignty."

Despite its provocative title, the *Act* initially affirms Buonarroti's claim that the Equals were servants of popular will by arguing that "when a people is in full enjoyment of its rights and liberty is triumphant, no one may act for the general will without consulting [the people] and receiving its consent." But the text turns on a dime. "That is not so when the people is enchained ... Then it is just and necessary that the most courageous ... assume the dictatorship of insurrection, take the initiative, adopt the glorious title of conspirators for liberty, and install themselves as redemptive magistrates for their fellows."[14]

The only available copy of the *Act* was in Pillé's handwriting, and no one would admit composing it. The author was probably Babeuf, but he claimed it had been written by his mysterious collective. However, because it "belongs to some republicans somewhere and because all republicans are implicated in these proceedings," he would defend it.[15]

He began by reminding the jury of the circumstances under which this *Act* was written. Drafted before the Directory's inauguration, it testified to the abuses that followed in the wake of Robespierre's defeat, when "every one of liberty's guarantees" was attacked and the democratic constitution abolished, "despite the people's manifest wish."

Bailly interrupted again. This was no defense, he complained, but a justification of conspiracy. The speech itself was a form of plotting.[16]

Once more, Buonarroti redirected. Soothing the prosecutor like an anxious child, he observed: "the very word *insurrection* seems to haunt all those terrified of popular activism . . . But can one bring the world to its feet in a single day just by saying *I hope for insurrection?* Is it enough to declare an insurrection for one to occur? Before taking fright at the word . . . let us determine how the authors define it and how they mean to rouse such activity."

Continuing to distance himself from Mably's critique of despotism and Babeuf's creeping legitimation of revolt, Buonarroti turned to the dazzling gem of the Enlightenment: Denis Diderot's *Encyclopedia.* Composed by the finest minds of Europe, he explained, it was the work of a collective much like the Secret Directory. Like the Secret Directory, the *Encyclopedia*'s authors were united by a common wish to improve society and, like the Secret Directory, they appointed agents to lend a hand. But the Encyclopedists were far more successful than the authors of the *Act* because they mobilized "millions" to fight for liberty. "If we weigh the methods and accomplishments of one against the other," he concluded puckishly, "the prosecution's charges are better suited to the Encyclopedists than to our own over-confident democrats."

What both collectives had in common was a conviction that education improves society. "If we examine these works in all good faith, it is difficult to find anything other than a desire to nourish enthusiasm for a better political system." Natural law and their own constitution endorsed enlightenment and permitted regime change. How such change would be promoted might be up for debate, but the *Act* did not broach that. It merely encouraged citizens to read and talk about their rights.

Moving from the *Act* to the kind of loyal opposition Antonelle had advertised the preceding summer, Buonarroti continued. Any citizen might lawfully charge that the constitution failed to guarantee popular sovereignty, because the constitution itself "entitles [him] to hold such opinions and aspire to a system that better reflects his convictions." Indeed, the constitution went further still, by "impos[ing] on each citizen the duty to do everything he can to prove the wisdom of his convictions and persuade the people to act." Would the Directory violate its own founding principles to silence inconvenient critics? Would it do so when those critics wanted nothing more than to "secure . . . true law and perfect . . . government?"

Free speech was vital to the health of the republic, Buonarroti reminded the court. It was so vital that citizens might even encourage insurrection.

But, having appeared to endorse Babeuf's radicalism, he beat a hasty retreat by saying that he only raised that point for the sake of argument. The *Act* did not counsel insurrection. Its authors, like Diderot and the Encyclopedists, encouraged the people to read and to talk, hoping to counter that "old, bitter malady" of ignorance with "the eternal remedy of universal education."[17]

The judges must have heard enough, because Gandon suggested that they move on. Babeuf, however, insisted that he had more to say.[18]

Babeuf had thrown himself body and soul into this trial, spending long nights drafting petitions, preparing news items, and crafting courtroom speeches that he delivered during the exhausting days that followed. Throughout, he wrestled with his desire to speak openly. Having abandoned all reserve to defend increasingly radical convictions, he found himself silenced by his own allies and acquiescing to a defense he loathed. As he appeared day after day on the most expansive stage he had ever known, Babeuf joined his fellows in disavowing their project for revolution by claiming that the Equals had only dreamed.

The effort wore hard. Unable to voice his true convictions, he raged against courtroom procedure, challenged witnesses, damned the Directory, argued endlessly with judges and prosecutors. Downstairs, he quarreled bitterly with prison guards and fellow inmates. As the pressure of the trial mounted, Babeuf began to crack.[19]

He returned to Buonarroti's aside that citizens may use their right of free speech to encourage insurrection. Buonarroti, a former lawyer, shrewdly played it both ways by making the point with a wink to sympathizers and retracting it before opponents could object. The didactic Babeuf moved relentlessly forward, driving home his conviction that the controversial right of insurrection was still in force. "We will demonstrate . . . that . . . even if the authors of the *Act* could be proved to have organized something greater than *moral* insurrection . . . neither reason nor eternal justice would condemn them."[20]

The legitimacy of insurrection had been contested since deputies first argued about the defeat of the Bastille in 1789, recognizing that insurgents saved them from a likely royal coup but deeply troubled by a crowd that decapitated the prison's commander and paraded his head through the streets. When legislators finally endorsed insurgents' claims to express the will of the people, they joined an unstable alliance. Although insurrection protected the revolution, its authors challenged the Assembly's claim to be sole representative of the sovereign nation, and their violence threatened its promise of stability and justice. Every assembly from 1789 to 1794 wrestled with this paradox.[21]

The constitution of 1793 guaranteed a right of insurrection. However, once the Convention had defeated Robespierre without the crowd's help in 1794 and had survived the turbulent Prairial insurrection of 1795, its increasingly conservative deputies resolved to be done with such unpredictable, uncontrollable activity. They did not just purge a right to insurrection from the new constitution but pathologized the violence they had once celebrated as necessary to republican survival, infusing that pathology into their accounts of democracy. France required government by the "best," Boissy d'Anglas argued, to restore order by keeping an unruly people in its place.[22]

Babeuf recalled such disputes by challenging Viellart's claim that insurrection is legitimate only when undertaken by a whole people. The revolutions of 1789 and 1792, "exalted movements . . . described with such fine words as *great, generous* and *sublime*," were not initiated by all of France. They were realized by the very "Paris rabble" the prosecutor disdained. Why, then, did they not deserve "the fiercest, most exemplary punishment"? Because those revolutions served Viellart's interests. Like any "friend . . . of order and tranquility . . . who want[s] the weak and oppressed to cease troubling the strong and despotic," the prosecutor did not damn insurrection until his own ambition had been satisfied.

Returning to Mably, Babeuf praised the philosopher for recognizing the value of uncertain moments like their own. Mably argued that if a government renounces its contract with the people, and the latter do not resist, then any citizen may rouse his fellows to defend liberty and common good. Babeuf had made amply clear in his *Tribune* that he believed the Directory repudiated its contract by ignoring the people's crying need, excluding them from suffrage, closing political clubs, hounding the press, and choking public life. What were citizens to do if their welfare was abused, their rights denied, and all legitimate means of political expression abolished? What remained but insurrection?

Calling one's fellows to action need not create anarchy, Babeuf continued. Mably may have believed that citizens could easily be fooled by the powerful, but he also thought they were sound judges of their peers. The people would not rise up unless it were absolutely necessary, but even unnecessary activism was the lesser of two evils. "Better to sound a false alarm than to want an alarm when it is needed."[23]

Leapfrogging over moderate Enlightenment aspirations to educate, reform, and improve, rushing past Buonarroti's defense of revolutionary rights to free speech, open assembly, and popular sovereignty, Babeuf flew to the most controversial feature of the constitution of 1793. He defended its guarantee of a right to insurrection.

Buonarroti could not silence him.

The fits and starts, claims, counter-claims, and competing arguments that rippled through Babeuf's interrogation vanished when Gandon interrogated Buonarroti. A former lawyer at ease in the courtroom and a former noble used to exploiting the politesse of the privileged, this Equal smoothly denied the existence of a "Secret Directory," effortlessly brushed away the suspicious quality of lists in his handwriting, and, just as casually, acknowledged a damning note. "It is in my hand. I am the author. I gave it to a journalist [in the spring of 1796]."

The bailiff read out the note in question, a defense of the constitution of 1793 that endorses the right to insurrection and urges French soldiers to join in. "If you are not on the side of kings and nobles," it concludes, "you are with us." Here, in Buonarroti's handwriting, was much of what Babeuf had just defended. However, he reminded the court, he had not made these pages public. The Directory did so without his permission. Worse yet, it mingled them with unrelated writings to give the appearance of conspiracy.[24]

Buonarroti promised to explain everything but, first, he wanted to give the court some idea of who he was. With that, he launched into a personal history that defied Viellart's account of a catastrophic revolution by recalling youthful hopes brilliantly realized and cruelly defeated. Here was a very different portrait of what the nation had won and lost.

Born and raised in Florence, Buonarroti described himself as a disciple of liberty from a tender age and vividly recalled the opening of the French

Revolution. "Its impulsiveness rattled thrones, amazed the multitude, gave hope to unfortunate humanity's few friends. I devoured the news . . . I compared patriots' speeches in the Constituent Assembly with Rousseau's teachings and asked myself: *Is this how the reign of justice begins?*" He was so moved that he traveled to the French possession of Corsica, "renowned for [its] long, determined struggle against oppression," to serve the new order. France rewarded him with an offer of citizenship.

Buonarroti was naturalized on the mainland and stayed. "The constitution of 1793 became my religion. Even now, I fondly remember . . . the great popular assemblies it hallowed, how it encouraged the nation to abandon prejudice, avarice and pride for sweet equality, honest fraternity, friendship, sincerity, compassion, and natural virtue. I recall with delight the abolition of servitude, the promise of universal education, the guarantee of assistance to the poor and disabled, the creation of institutions to foster happiness and concord among the French people."

Admittedly, there were "harsh measures" and "a few deviations," but that was the cost of astonishing change. "What do storms matter if they produce truth? . . . Can we imagine that the many errors, biases, and barbaric institutions which overwhelm . . . most men could be attacked without agitation, clamor, resistance? If there must be victims to uphold the few principles necessary to stop spilling the popular blood that has, for centuries, flowed silently across scaffolds, through galleys and cells, and among despots' armies, I defy the evil genius who would put such a price on relief by sacrificing myself to public good."

Then came 9 Thermidor, Buonarroti remembered. The National Convention reversed itself, "disavowing principles once solemnly proclaimed, condemning laws decreed, imprisoning and executing men it had asked . . . to impart its doctrine and enforce its laws." At its nadir, the assembly replaced its own dazzling democratic constitution of 1793 with the code of 1795, abolishing liberty and universal male suffrage, once more dividing France between "rich overseers and poor slaves." Horrified democrats called for insurrection, but Buonarroti resisted, believing "a single drop of blood spilled . . . a terrible crime" and certain the Directory would set things right.

He was bitterly disappointed. The new regime continued the onslaught by closing public assemblies, violating press freedom, turning its back on impoverished workers, and catering to the privileged. Its offenses were too numerous to detail.²⁵

This glowing celebration of popular achievement and bitter defeat was the antithesis of Viellart's withering narrative of chaos and recovery. Viellart, who aspired to political reform and legal equality, thought the revolution should have ended when the king accepted the constitution of 1791. By then, however, popular activism and what the prosecutor considered unrealistic expectations of social equality were mounting steadily. The popular movement would have destroyed the nation, he thought, had not 9 Thermidor restored elites to power, renewed government, and reaffirmed property rights.

Buonarroti's revolution reached far beyond civil rights and legal equality to promise every man a voice in government and every citizen the essentials of life. The only way to preserve social good was by empowering the people, as the democratic and republican revolution of 1792 had done. The events of 9 Thermidor laid waste to all that, attacking liberty, democracy, and social welfare. Here was the real plot against the nation.

Buonarroti claimed that he saw widespread anger in spring 1796. Ordinary Parisians gathered "on streets and bridges" to demand the constitution of 1793. Thousands more such calls "arriv[ed] daily from the provinces." Believing the cacophony an expression of national will, he thought France was on the eve of a new revolution. If "what distinguishes a free from an enslaved people is the ability of the former to express its will in an orderly way," then his duty was to encourage peaceful demonstration. So he penned the essay before the court, begging soldiers not to turn their weapons on insurgents.

"I do not pretend to be infallible; I may have been mistaken," he added contritely. "But you must agree: convinced as I was that the nation was oppressed, liberty defeated, and the sovereign will opposed to the sitting government, I did my duty as a loyal citizen, exerting myself in every way to uphold the law and avoid bloodshed."²⁶

Having distanced himself from Babeuf's endorsement of a right to insurrection by defending the peaceful expression of sovereignty, Buonarroti did not deny his dissatisfaction. But he justified it by insisting he was in step with the people. He had used his right of free speech, he said, to address widespread discontent and to educate the people about its interests. He and the rest of the Equals acted peacefully and lawfully, advancing common good as any citizen might legitimately do.

A judge intervened to repeat Viellart's objection that Parisians did not represent the whole nation but "a tiny fraction" of the people. Implicit in that was the conviction that the only legitimate expressions of national will were those of enfranchised voters, at the polls, and deputies, in the legislative councils.

Buonarroti demurred, recalling that the committee charged with preparing to enact the constitution of 1793 had abolished it instead. "Those who violated the constitution of 1793 denied the will of the people. The right to demand the constitution belongs to each citizen. I did not say 'the people of Paris,' . . . because they did not act as representatives of all of the people but as simple citizens." If there was a plot against the nation, then any citizen might legitimately "conspire" to defend everyone's essential rights.

Bailly tried to silence the debate by defending the constitution of 1795. "Those who want to . . . overturn . . . the popularly-accepted constitution are guilty."

One of the accused answered from the floor, reiterating Buonarroti's claim that the sovereign people had been robbed of the constitution of '93. "Note down," he told the stenographers, "that the prisoners agree with that."[27]

Other prisoners spoke about their experience of revolution, echoing Buonarroti by describing worthy activism for popular rights and deadly plots against them.

Provincial democrat Pierre Fossard remembered that "there was bread in Robespierre's time," and suffering after Thermidor. "Patriots were murdered . . . liberty trees chopped down . . . the people were wretched and at one another's throats." Neighborhood agent Juste Moroy, who admitted hanging signs at dawn for people to read on their way to work, recalled similar desolation. "People didn't have any bread . . . [Bakers'] shelves were full, but with twenty-four-franc bread not three-penny bread." The wealthy few wallowed in abundance as inflation forced the hungry to strip their homes to buy food. "I bought a coverlet for forty francs in 1791. That's a fine thing for a worker. A coverlet doesn't lose half its value in five years. But you know what? I sold it [in 1796] . . . for [forty cents' worth] of bread."[28]

This was far from Viellart's salvation.

Printer Théodore Lamberté accused the Directory of disdaining rights he defended on behalf of all people. "These suspicious, anxious, dishonest men do not pursue me alone . . . My homeland's enemies want to destroy the palladium of liberty [through me], they want to topple the barrier that stands against approaching tyranny by attacking the free press I defend. [The press] has always obstructed the despotic schemes of those determined to usurp popular power, it has always been a weapon of the weak against their oppressors. If it is extinguished, the France of '95 will be more thoroughly subjugated than it was in '88."[29]

Others described gross miscarriages of justice that brought them to Vendôme. Grégoire Nayez, a small-town radical, explained that he was indicted despite having been imprisoned in the provinces when the supposed plot was unfolding in Paris. Pierre-Joseph Crépin, a respected administrator, was arrested after police stopped by to talk about something else and saw copies of the *People's Tribune* lying around. Joseph Cordebar, Pierre Fossard, and Jean-François Rayebois, friends from Cherbourg, appear to have been indicted for sharing newspapers and talking politics. "I am a good man. I must speak truthfully to explain the crimes of the monsters who sent me here," Fossard cried out. "As a republican who loved liberty and equality . . . I could not be still." Pierre Philip, Pillé's protector in the abbey prison, was a quiet man who had done his best to avoid all activism after having been wrongfully imprisoned during Terror and Reaction alike. He was arrested because police found his name among Babeuf's papers, and despite the Directory's promise not to use those papers to identify suspects.

Did anyone listening to Philip remember the prosecutor's argument against recusing the alternate juror Agier? Bailly had said, weeks before, that it did not matter whether the *Papers* actually named Agier an enemy because the Equals' plot threatened all "public functionaries, honest men, and property-owners." A similar kind of thinking seems to have applied to many of these defendants. Even when clear evidence against them was lacking, the simple fact of being a democrat was enough to justify detention, indictment, imprisonment, and trial in an isolated provincial town.[30]

The accused needed four jurors to acquit. Those inclined to accept the Equals' argument that everyone had been framed by a regime that consolidated its power by silencing critics could find ample confirmation among the prisoners who stood before them.

Having angrily described his long persecution by powerful men, Pierre Philip ended on a mournful note. "If the constitution cannot destroy [oppressors'] malignant influence over citizens, when will we see its end? When will we see the last of these vengeful men to whom France owes its ills and republicans their persecution? What government will guarantee peace . . . ?" He concluded, "I am firmly resolved to live far from all political activity . . . so that I might be forgotten by the enemies I made by loving the republic and daring to oppose tyranny."[31]

It had become commonplace by 1797, and remains commonplace today, to assail the Terror for devouring celebrated journalists, renowned deputies, orators, artists, composers, and scientists. Philip evoked the slow, ruinous consumption of ordinary people that endured well beyond Thermidor, a decimation of the popular forces who made revolution possible. Governing elites believed that such repression was necessary to restore order. And yet, the disenfranchisement and marginalization they enforced rendered that very order tenuous by making the peaceful defense of popular interests almost impossible. The irony is that the official repression to which men like Philip testified was given added force by the Equals' conspiracy. The panic roused by their plot had already been used to justify legal violations and would continue to serve as a weapon against equal application of the law long after the trial was done.[32]

If the conspiracy excited repression, however, the Equals' courtroom defense laid a foundation for new kinds of resistance. Buonarroti's insistence that they were loyal advocates of free expression, political liberty, and social justice was obscuring Babeuf's claims of a right to insurrection and his attack on the institution of private property. Buonarroti described the Equals as peaceful patriots who—faced with subversion of the nation's legitimate constitution; retreat from guarantees of work, education, and universal male suffrage; assaults on revolutionary rights of free speech and assembly— responded loyally, publicly, and peacefully. The Equals were not violent subversives, he said repeatedly. They were free citizens who encouraged the people to defend its rights and reminded the government of its responsibilities. In making that case, Buonarroti fostered a notion of loyal opposition that democrats would build on in years to come.

ELEVEN

Perfect Equality

In the early weeks of the trial, prosecutors and defendants kept their eyes on the approaching legislative elections, the former believing a quick courtroom victory would boost the Directory's candidates and the latter hoping for a democratic victory to discredit the proceedings. The elections arrived well before the trial was done, bringing results no one expected. After that, the prosecutors' sense of urgency faded.[1]

They should have kept the pressure on, because the proceedings were exhausting everyone.

Inside the abbey, inmates quarreled with guards who ransacked their cells and seized personal items. They quarreled with one another, too, venting the frustrations of an inconceivably long trial and continuing confinement in chilly, makeshift cells.[2]

Babeuf, in particular, was ailing. Always a man of extremes, he maintained an especially punishing regimen in Vendôme, working tirelessly on a defense he did not believe in and petitioning to have his son imprisoned with him so he could continue the boy's education. Perhaps to ease the memory of little Sophie's starvation after Thermidor, he deprived himself of food in order to share his prison rations with Marie-Anne and Émile. All of it took a toll. He was irritable, exhausted, and often ill. His legs and ankles sometimes swelled so badly that he had trouble walking and begged the court to suspend sessions. When those requests were denied, he required prison guards to carry him up several flights of stairs to the courtroom. It was not clear how much longer he could go on.[3]

Outside the abbey, locals were divided between suspicion of the prisoners in their midst and irritation at the unruly troops reputedly offering safety. Suspicion won out when prison guards seized a packet of smuggled letters that hinted at the possibility of a Paris insurrection and advised on corrupting jurors. Rumors of these letters suggested that the soldiers might be worth putting up with. More potently, the news fueled long-simmering impatience to be done with proceedings that were entering their third month and still far from over. The trial of the king himself had only taken six weeks.[4]

None of this prevented Viellart and Bailly from delaying further. They asked for a lengthy recess to prepare their closing statement and did not emerge until late April.

Bailly delivered the summation to a packed house. Beginning much as his colleague had at the trial's opening, he argued that revolutionary upheaval produced this plot. However, more wary than Viellart of seeming to condemn the entire revolution, he focused on the Terror. Good deputies were frustrated by the "weak, fearful men" who capitulated to Robespierre, he argued. "The helpless Convention [became] his slave . . . and we saw that disastrous state known as *revolutionary government* flourish . . . History will scarcely believe the horrors imposed by that abhorrent regime: the hundred thousand new Bastilles on French soil, the thousand scaffolds placed permanently in public squares, the appalling number of victims they consumed."

Like Viellart, Bailly claimed that Robespierre's heirs survived 9 Thermidor. He charged them with exciting the bloody Prairial uprising, attacking the constitution of 1795, and rallying others to their execrable "community of goods." Then, he continued, driven by greed, a mad desire for anarchy, and loathing of "republic and government," they organized the conspiracy before the court now. Had their project succeeded, he concluded, they would have plunged the nation into a crisis more terrible than the Terror.[5]

If this summation departed from Viellart's opening by more narrowly pinpointing revolutionary deviation, Bailly followed his colleague in holding a small clique responsible for everything. It was an approach that foreclosed all dialogue about the republic's form or future because, rather than parsing the complex amalgam of circumstance, ideology, and conflict that shaped the nation, the prosecutors depicted the revolution as a fight to the death between forces of light and darkness. In making that case, they revealed their own affinity with the Terror they condemned and insisted that elites alone should define the republic.

Equally telling, Bailly's summation echoed Viellart's opening in giving the lie to their claim that they only prosecuted acts. Just as the deputy Thibaudeau had done the preceding summer, when challenging Drouet's legislative immunity, high court prosecutors insisted that the Equals were guilty as much for what they believed as for what they had done. Government critics could not possibly be loyal opponents, only traitors.

The accused dared to call themselves patriots, Bailly declared. They insisted that the constitution's guarantee of free expression authorized conspiratorial notes, seditious pamphlets, posters, and newspapers. They claimed that citizens' right to instruction permitted them to condemn the regime's shortcomings. They argued that popular dissatisfaction sanctioned the promotion of a new order, because either "the people is in charge of changing its constitution and government" or "it ceases to be sovereign."

"But what is the sovereign?" Bailly asked. "Is it the whole people or a fraction thereof?" With that, he returned to arguments about democracy, political process, and activism that haunted not just this trial but the revolution itself.[6]

When the National Assembly declared, in 1789, that authority was delegated by the people, it did not mean that everyone would share in voting. Protestants and Jews were long excluded, as were black and brown men, women of any color, and the many white men whose incomes did not reach a determined threshold. In their exclusiveness, the otherwise iconoclastic deputies were in step with their century. For however much Enlightenment philosophers believed in broadening access to political power, they did not want to enfranchise everyone. Most feared that sharing political power among too many citizens would excite passions like those that had troubled ancient city-states, and they thought modern nations were too large for the direct participation that ancient democrats had enjoyed. So the National Assembly asked how to represent the people without giving them political voice and resolved the conundrum with the constitution of 1791, which declared legislators and a narrow electorate capable of articulating the will of all.[7]

By that time, radicals were exploring more expansive notions of participation. Babeuf complained privately, and deputy Maximilien Robespierre assailed publicly the Assembly's limits on male suffrage, calling them antithetical to the principle of equality before the law. "Is the nation sovereign when the majority of individuals who compose it are robbed of . . . political rights . . . ?" Ordinary Parisians experimented with more direct democracy by presenting petitions and organizing crowd action that urged representatives in one direction or another. In stark contrast to the moderates, who argued that "once [a free people] has entrusted power to its representatives, nothing remains but obedience," popular activists claimed with Rousseau that sovereignty could not be delegated. Workingmen insisted on their right to veto laws they disapproved and to recall deputies with whom they disagreed.[8]

Some democratic aspirations were ratified after the August Revolution of 1792 by the National Assembly's decree of universal male suffrage and new elections. Others appeared to receive validation from the democratic constitution of 1793, which affirmed "the [people's] right to express its will with complete freedom" and asserted that "when government violates popular rights, insurrection is for the people or any part of it, the most sacred of rights and the most essential of duties."[9]

Although the constitution was suspended as soon as it was adopted, because the Convention did not believe it could be implemented in wartime, conservatives accused it of undermining republican stability. Describing the code of 1793 as a threat to liberty, property, and public order, they abolished guarantees of universal male suffrage and a right to insurrection, restricted expressions of sovereignty to polling places, and reserved legislative power to deputies by adopting the constitution of 1795.

It was that repudiation of popular democracy that Bailly insisted on now. No one could act on behalf of the nation unless formally appointed to do so. "Only the legislator can prohibit activity he finds contrary to good social order or public peace. Once the law is decreed, there is no discussion, only obedience. To do what the law prohibits . . . is a crime." Bailly applied this narrow definition of political authority to the high court jurors as well. They could not interpret the law by ruling on the defendant's moral intent, he argued, but must restrict themselves to simple determinations of fact. "In cases of theft, intent is the will to take something from its owner; in cases of murder, it is the will to kill . . . In this case, it is the will to overturn the constitution and the government of 1795."[10]

This was a crude measure of political crime.

Having denied the Equals' claims of loyal opposition and the jury's right to consider intent, Bailly reviewed the evidence before the court. Eyewitness testimony and Babeuf's own papers affirmed that the accused had done far more than talk. After a group of men swore to overthrow the Directory, they appointed agents to assist them, and used "anarchic pamphlets, newspapers, and other writings . . . little clubs . . . rabble-rousers and poster-hangers" to "corrupt" and "exasperate the people," putting France on the verge of a new revolution. Babeuf's own words destroyed the defendants' claims that police and prosecutors fabricated the evidence against them. "*Never*," Bailly read from the *Papers*, "*was a plot as holy as ours.*"[11]

Turning to individual defendants, the prosecutor began with the plot's authors. Filippo Buonarroti "distinguished himself throughout the proceedings with decency and polish," so Bailly regretted to see him implicated. But the evidence was overwhelming. Once more taking political convictions as evidence of treason, he added that jurors should consider, too, "the care [Buonarroti] takes to elaborate on revolutionary ideals he remains proud of having professed."[12]

The prosecutor was less indulgent of the others. He denied Babeuf's claim to have been a secretary, describing him as "the very foundation of the committee of insurrection, . . . [who] conceived, developed, and organized the plot; weighed the balance of forces, planned, supervised, confirmed and corrected all that was to precede, accompany, and follow the insurrection." He called Charles Germain a devotee of "anarchy and bloodshed" who "acted in concert with Babeuf [and] . . . the secret committee, and with the same ends." But it was Augustin Darthé who bore the full weight of the prosecutor's scorn.[13]

Bailly recalled that Darthé was named by the informant Grisel as the man who recruited him and was identified by handwriting experts as author of the notorious "kill the five." But the jurors did not need to rely on that testimony alone. Darthé himself gave ample evidence of his wickedness. "Placing himself above the law . . . he repeatedly denied [its] authority" and celebrated his own supposed virtue by claiming that he "traversed the revolution without stain."[14]

Seizing on this fragment of Darthé's only speech during the trial, Bailly widened his attack. "We vowed not to say anything about what [Darthé] did under the tyranny of the Committee of Public Safety. But when a defendant looks beyond the accusation against him and asks jurors to consider his prior conduct, he demands that prosecutors do the same." Pulling out a letter Darthé had written during the Terror, Bailly read it to the court. "A powerful decree has jailed the wives of imprisoned aristocrats and the husbands of incarcerated women. The guillotine will not slacken, the heads of dukes, marquis, counts and barons, men and women will fall like hail . . . Now, more than ever, virtue and honesty are the order of the day."

Defendants shouted outraged objections, but the prosecutor raised his voice to continue. "The man who defined virtue and honor in this way was secretary to Joseph Lebon, one of Robespierrism's most despicable assassins. And yet he dares include himself among *humanity's defenders and martyrs to its cause. He dares claim that his revolutionary career was spotless, that his heart beat only for his fellow man!*"[15]

With this, Bailly closed the circle on a charge authorities had made since the first arrests in May 1796, offering proof in the person of Darthé that the Equals were Jacobins reborn. As such, they were savage demagogues with no other aims than to sow chaos and seize power.

In addition to the four members of the Secret Directory, Bailly named roughly twenty co-conspirators. Like Drouet's colleagues in the Council of 500, he found the deputy's political opinions as damning as anything Georges Grisel said. He declared that former noble Félix Lepeletier, described by Grisel as someone who "promises a lot and delivers very little," bankrolled the plot; found it proven that retired generals Rossignol and

Fyon conspired; and condemned the Secret Directory's most assiduous agents, Juste Moroy and Jean-Baptiste Cazin. He thought the testimony against Louis Blondeau, who tried to recruit men to spring Drouet and Babeuf from prison, was decisive and asked jurors, despite printer Théodore Lamberté's bold defense of free speech, to condemn him as a "willing accomplice to criminal activity."[16]

Then Bailly softened. "If the guilty deserve the full severity of the law . . . we have as well the sweet, sacred duty of celebrating innocence." Rejecting the very idea of women's activism, he urged acquittal of every woman among the defendants, even Adelaide Lambert and Sophie Lapierre, who had been as stubborn as Darthé in defying the court's authority. He brushed away Lapierre's amplification of her dissent with revolutionary hymns by calling her a "*revolutionary* singer" whose deeds "do not merit our attention." More accurately, he acknowledged the absence of evidence against "poor fruit vendor" Nicole Pognon, "whom we could not, unfortunately, acquit at the opening of arguments."

Returning to the men, the prosecutor dismissed charges against Antonelle, saying that despite his radical opinions and the Equals' respect for him, there was no evidence that he conspired. Bailly urged the jury to acquit poor bullied scribe Nicolas Pillé, a simple man wracked by delusion. Did Pillé's protector, Pierre Philip, feel relief or rage upon hearing himself declared blameless after a yearlong imprisonment?[17]

The prosecutor celebrated each dismissal as evidence of prosecutorial diligence and directorial mercy. Democratic onlookers could find affirmations of a national panic that had uprooted innocent lives, each of Bailly's dismissals giving further evidence that the regime did not frustrate a plot but purged critics. The Directory's eagerness to prove its strength, by inflating and seeming to resolve the threat the Equals had posed, sapped its own and its prosecutors' credibility.

Once the prosecutor had finished, defendants rose one by one to make closing statements.

Charles Germain, who had galvanized Babeuf's thought in Arras, failed to find similar focus in Vendôme. As rage overtook him, he became a secondary figure playing the angry clown. He offered nothing new in his final speech.

P.-A. Antonelle had no legal need to speak, having been absolved by prosecutors, and no practical need, because his defense had shaped so much of courtroom argument. But he seized this opportunity to vent his fury at an assault on democrats that he understood to reach far beyond the cramped courtroom in which he stood. "No matter how solemn the acquittal you pronounce," he presciently told the jury, "relentless slander more powerful than [you] and more pressing than the evidence will long prejudice public opinion against [the accused]." Jurors must do their best to restore peace and fraternity by acquitting everyone.[18]

Once more, Buonarroti and Babeuf carried the greatest weight of argument. Resisting prosecutors' representation of the Equals as incendiaries, they competed with one another to define opposition, conspiracy, legitimate government, and their own aims.

Buonarroti began by looking to the past. "What is this intractable impulse to demonize and condemn . . . those who dare to reflect on the long chain of human misery, who dare to exert themselves for the relief of their fellows? What is this devastating force that, throughout time, rouses itself against the most modest advance of reason and philosophy, calls truth, sacrilege; virtue, deception; compassion, hypocrisy; and [dismisses] appeals to sacred natural right [as] demands for sedition and revolt?" Righteous visionaries had always been demonized by governments envious of their power and ordinary people frightened by change. One such moment was unfolding before their eyes.

"We stand . . . charged with [the Revolution's] every ill." Why? "Do the prosecutors try us or [do they try] liberty itself? If they do not mean to put liberty on trial, making it loathsome in order to subjugate the people, why take such effort to depict patriots as *cannibals and thieves hungry for money and violence; enemies of all social order who, having nothing to lose, are ready for anything?* . . . If our prosecutors were inspired by justice alone, would they have looked beyond the trial to recall deeds that have nothing to do with us, blackening those deeds in every way to prejudice [you] by making us hateful . . . ?"

Viellart and Bailly condemned 1793, Buonarroti continued, but they did not acknowledge the crises that made its most terrible acts necessary or admit that extraordinary sacrifice saved the republic. They bemoaned the hardship of a privileged few but ignored the suffering of the patriotic many. And they laid every ill at the defendants' door, as if the Equals themselves were responsible for each injustice and every excess.

Picking up the thread of his defense of loyal opposition, Buonarroti argued that concerned citizens—like Diderot's Encyclopedists—could legitimately unite for benevolent purpose, "conspire" innocently. To prove that the Equals' "conspiracy" was not benevolent, prosecutors had to demonstrate that they could have succeeded in rousing insurrection and that they meant to harm the nation by such means.

Rejecting claims that the Equals were on the eve of a new revolution when arrested, Buonarroti repeated Antonelle's defense: they simply did not have the resources. Without guns, money, or men, they would have required vast crowds and a military mutiny to pull off the plot they stood accused of. "By what secret means might [the Equals] have mobilized so many people with whom they never communicated? . . . How to bring about that rebellion? How to win over eight to ten thousand soldiers?" These men had barely managed to publish their own newspapers, he reminded jurors, and prosecutors had produced only two pamphlets with which they supposedly appealed to the public. "Two pamphlets." He paused. "I will say no more."

Even had the Equals done everything prosecutors claimed, he said in direct challenge of Bailly, jurors might still consider intent. Were the accused anarchists bent on destruction? Or were they like men who rob a deserted house to feed the hungry?

The accused were "so affected by public misery, revolutionary events, and popular ideas that they would have needed superhuman strength" to remain silent. "Remember: [the Equals] were guided by patriotism alone. If they were inspired by a wish to improve the popular condition, if they reasonably believed a law was arbitrary, if they legitimately thought their plans were lawful, how can you . . . find them guilty of a free and conscious desire to harm society for their own advantage? When society demands that men fool themselves or find good where none exists, then it must show clemency . . . it must excuse the mistakes of those who only want to serve."

French jurisprudence offered few examples of taking sound motive into account, but the ancients had plenty. The Romans, "our masters in liberty, excused, even honored their fellow citizens' transgressions" because they understood that "this holy love of the homeland is sometimes violent, sometimes reckless, but never criminal. Beware of smothering [such love] by punishing dissent."

If they did not find that reason enough to acquit, Buonarroti continued, then jurors must consider the nature of their republic. Did the people have an inalienable right to sovereignty? If so, could a popular movement be subversive? Could despots legitimately condemn those who criticized their abuse of power? Or did critics' patriotism excuse them?

Having sweetly legitimated the Equals' challenge of the Directory, Buonarroti flatly denied their allegiance to community of goods. Prosecutors confused that "platonic idea" with pillage and slaughter, he said, but the *Act of Insurrection* quite clearly commanded strict respect of property. All food, clothing, and arms promised to insurgents were to have been paid for by the government or seized from émigrés. As for the anonymous *Manifesto of Equals* that prosecutors highlighted, it did not merit discussion. It was "the confusing product of an extravagant mind," penned by a stranger "in complete contradiction with the *Act of Insurrection.*" It was sent to Babeuf in the vain hope that he would publish it. In any case, why did prosecutors stress only the malicious parts of the *Papers* and remain silent about the many "plans for social good"?[19]

Jurors might well be forgiven if they believed that Buonarroti found the abolition of property almost as offensive as prosecutors did.

Babeuf was the last defendant to address the court, in a marathon speech that stretched across five days. Like Buonarroti, he acknowledged the weight of history, but did so by looking forward rather than back. The outcome of these proceedings, he predicted, would determine "the very existence of the republic . . . and whether [the people] will remain sovereign or bow beneath the yoke of a new slavery." And, again like Buonarroti, he insisted that a "conspiracy" might be benign and loyal.

Then Babeuf struck out on his own, heading in a more radical direction by arguing that jurors must take into consideration the legitimacy of the government against which a plot was organized. Carefully defining his terms, he pointed out that prosecutors had described the Equals' conspiracy as opposed to "established government," "legitimate authority," and a "freely established constitution." But these were not the same things, and such a confusion of terms had dangerous consequences.

To deny a people the right to overthrow "established government" condemned them to live with whatever they found in place. It reduced even 14 July 1789 to "criminal conspiracy." Nor was the challenge of a "freely accepted constitution" necessarily criminal, if a people had acquiesced to ill-advised laws out of ignorance. In that case, any citizen retained the right to enlighten his fellows because "the primary and essential condition of all human association is a tendency to perfect its civil organization," and no people could contract against itself or enchain future generations.

That left the challenge of "legitimate authority." "But what is legitimate authority?" Babeuf asked. "I understand it to be founded on and governing according to true principles of popular sovereignty and exerting itself for no end but the [sovereign's] good and glory and to preserve liberty." Someone who conspired to replace legitimate authority with tyranny should be punished. But the citizen who honestly believed "legitimate authority" could be improved was never guilty, even if mistaken.

Was the Directory a "legitimate authority" founded on a "freely accepted constitution"? Babeuf did not think so. The constitution of 1795 was imposed on France through deceit, he argued, and in violation of the popular will. It did not guarantee free press, free assembly, or the right to petition. It concentrated executive power and narrowed suffrage. It abandoned public assistance and public education. Accordingly, he might legitimately have conspired against constitution and Directory alike.[20]

But, he added, he had not.

The discord between what Buonarroti argued and what Babeuf claimed could make a world of difference to jurors hoping to acquit. By focusing on loyal opposition, Buonarroti redefined the Equals as peaceful critics who enjoyed their constitutional rights to speak freely. Babeuf, by stressing the

Directory's failings, explained why conspiring against it was not only legitimate but necessary. It did not matter that he concluded by denying conspiracy. After all he had just said, the claim was hardly plausible.

Babeuf did not stop there. He moved on, to address the most contentious issue of the trial, the one defendants had scrupulously avoided until then. He took up the subject of property.

All that revolutionaries had accomplished since 1789 hung in the balance by the fall of 1795, he told the court, because the people had come to long for the Old Regime. Believing the republic on a precipice, he called out. "Listen up," he read aloud to the court from an old issue of the *Tribune*, "those who have been convinced by this parade of public disasters that the republic is worthless and the monarchy better are, I admit, correct . . . WE WERE BETTER UNDER KINGS THAN WE ARE UNDER THE REPUBLIC. But what sort of republic? A republic like the one we have had until now is worthless. That, my friends, is not a true republic." A true republic would realize the revolution's promise of universal happiness.[21]

All but abandoning his plea of innocence, Babeuf set aside his appeal to popular sovereignty, his claim that the Directory violated the ideals of 1789, and his insistence on the right of insurrection guaranteed by the constitution of 1793. He broadcast the upheaval he had first imagined with Charles Germain in the prisons of Arras.

Since that moment in 1795, Babeuf had devoted two issues of the *Tribune* to making a case for "perfect equality." Some of the Equals' pamphlets advertised "community of goods" as well. But everyone retreated from the doctrine in Vendôme. Former Jacobins P.-A. Antonelle and Alexis Vadier kept the distance they had advertised well before Babeuf's arrest in May 1796. Others hewed to disagreements expressed privately. Even the doctrine's most ardent defenders, Babeuf among them, fell silent before the high court. No one challenged Viellart when he condemned community of goods as a "pernicious doctrine" founded on "murder, pillage, conflagration." No one answered Bailly when he charged that "perfect equality" would destroy civilization. Some actively disowned the idea by shouting, "[T]hat is one man's opinion!" when Bailly read from some anonymous pages entitled *Manifesto of Equals.* Buonarroti minimized the radicalism of the phrase "universal happiness" by alluding to its presence in the 1793 Declaration of Rights, which guaranteed property. Even Charles Germain retreated, arguing that his prison letters to Babeuf referred only to equal rights and equal taxation.[22]

Then Babeuf rose to make his final statement. He had struggled for months to respect the silence others demanded. Having spent his life in poverty, two of the previous three years in grim revolutionary prisons, and having seen his children starve, he believed his end was near. Even if acquitted, which he did not think likely, Babeuf knew his body was giving out. He did not think he would live much longer. Seeing his last chance to address the people, he threw caution to the winds and explained his most novel, most radical idea to justify a new sort of revolution.[23]

"The Revolution's purpose is to guarantee the happiness of the greatest number. Society's purpose is to guarantee universal happiness," he told the court. Nature promises every person an equal right to its bounty and imposes a common obligation to work, because "oppression exists when one person exhausts himself with labor and is deprived of everything, while another wallows in plenty without doing anything. No one may legitimately monopolize the goods of the earth or of industry." Society existed to defend natural equality. "In a true society, there is neither rich or poor . . . The Revolution's purpose is to destroy inequality and restore the good of all." But the revolution was not finished, "because the wealthy continue to monopolize wealth and power while the poor work in veritable slavery, languish in misery, and have no voice in affairs of state."

This was the doctrine that figured so prominently in the indictment and the one to which all other charges were subordinated, Babeuf continued. So let him pose the essential questions jurors would have to answer. Had he preached this doctrine? Was it pernicious? Was he its only advocate?[24]

Yes, he replied to the first question, he believed society's sole purpose was to resurrect the perfect equality found in nature and long since annihilated by inheritance, the buying and selling of labor, and the inflated value accorded to some skills over others. "Nothing is more evident than that *no one has too much without depriving others of enough,*" so a just society must sweep away private property and redistribute goods to guarantee "enough, but just enough" to every person. This restoration of natural equality would eliminate the need for fences, walls, and locks; abolish discord, theft, and murder; render courts, prisons, and scaffolds unnecessary; and expunge "envy, jealousy, greed, pride, fraud, duplicity." Most important, it would relieve citizens of the gnawing uncertainty suffered by rich and poor alike about their own and their children's futures.[25]

These were the convictions prosecutors called "terrifying," "abominable," and "subversive." They were not his ideas alone, Babeuf swore. Jean-Jacques Rousseau condemned luxury, making the case that everyone should live simply. Mably celebrated "the wisdom with which nature prepared us for community of goods," imagining public storehouses to collect everything and share it out equally. The abbé Morelly, whose anonymous treatises Babeuf believed were written by the philosopher Diderot, was "the most determined, the most intrepid, . . . the most ardent champion of this system," who defended "common labor" and insisted that "the sweetest, most humane nations, everywhere and always, are those without property." His own words, Babeuf volunteered modestly, "were but pale paraphrase of these three philosophers, these three legislators. So long as there is not yet an Inquisition under our republican government that prohibits their books, can it be forbidden to comment on and explicate them?"[26]

Having spoken so openly, Babeuf trimmed with uncharacteristic pessimism. He had only talked about all this and did not try to bring it into being, he said. In any case, the Directory need not fear such ideas. "Trust that the passions, prejudices, habits and vices that overwhelm us will maintain the system you adore . . . I will not insult the nation by calling it wholly corrupt, but I will dare to claim that it is not sufficiently virtuous to adopt an order of things that wise men say would endow it with pure, natural happiness and the simple, innocent pleasures it cannot now enjoy because so alienated from them."[27]

Babeuf was, undeniably, inspired by Rousseau, Mably, and Morelly. But he misread those thinkers as thoroughly as he misread the Jacobins, finding in their doctrines only what was useful to his own way of thinking. Rousseau criticized excess but did not propose abolishing property. Mably and Morelly spoke of abolishing property but did not believe it could or would be eliminated. They conjured perfect worlds of absolute equality to measure the imperfect state of their own, staking out imaginative spaces in which to promote reform. Whether criticizing luxury or advocating for representative government, none of these philosophers suggested that a world without property was on the horizon. Facing a powerful, long-lived monarchy, they hoped for moderate reform at best.

Babeuf lived in a world transformed by revolution. Given all that he had witnessed, all that he had experienced, it is hardly surprising that he believed perfect equality was possible. Like his audience, he knew how completely ideas could change the world. It did not take much to see that his claims to be like the philosophers of a defunct Old Regime were utterly disingenuous.

The prosecutors understood this. Understanding, too, the radicalism of Babeuf's advocacy of "perfect equality," they fell silent. They let Babeuf hang himself.

Having defended his convictions, Babeuf turned to the evidence. Now, prosecutors became impatient and demanded that he hurry up. The high court told him to shorten his speech.

At the very end of his days-long soliloquy, Babeuf implored jurors to consider the implications of condemning the Equals. "If my last hour is already fixed in the book of fate, I have waited for it a long time," he said. But he could not bear the thought of what his sentence would mean for those who remained. Addressing his children and, through them, generations to come, he spoke with tears in his eyes. "I have ... but one bitter regret. Having so very much wished to leave you liberty, the source of all good, I see only slavery before us and I leave you exposed to its ills. I have nothing to bequeath!!! I would not even leave you my civic virtues, my abiding hatred of tyranny, my deep devotion to Equality and Liberty, my keen love of the people. That would be too dreadful. What would you do with such a legacy under the royalist oppression that is coming? I leave you slaves and that thought alone rends my soul in its last moments. I would do better to advise you how to bear your chains, but I do not believe I am able."[28]

TWELVE

Speaking to the Nation

The Equals' trial took place inside a closely guarded prison situated within an isolated, heavily militarized town. Limited seating and lo-cal security restricted the physical audience to a privileged few. But the proceedings did not unfold before their eyes alone. The Directory and its democratic critics were as one in their conviction that the trial should be visible to all of France. Thanks to newspapers, pamphlets, and a novel form of court recording, it became so, knitting the trial into the identities of po-litical forces competing to define the nation's future.

The Directory was clearly determined to continue advertising the case as it had done since the first arrests, allowing the Equals to condemn them-selves with their own words. But what was relatively straightforward in the spring of 1796, when authorities had only to cull and reproduce the most damning pages from Babeuf's archive, became far more complex once pro-ceedings began. How to capture and reproduce the speeches that poured forth in the courtroom?

The inherently difficult task of "broadcasting" a trial was complicated by the prohibition of official transcripts. Transcripts violated the jury's author-ity, legislators had argued at the revolution's outset, because they intimated that readers could second-guess a verdict simply by taking in the content of the statements delivered in court. But jurors founded their judgments on "intimate conviction," an inner certainty that came from watching the "ju-dicial duel" between prosecutors, defendants, advocates, and witnesses.

That duel included testimony, to be sure, but it also encompassed tone of voice, gestures, facial expression, and perhaps an ineffable mood perceptible only to those present. How to capture all that in words? Better not to try, deputies had reasoned.

Until 1797, courts complied so assiduously with the prohibition of official transcripts that only the most celebrated trials were preserved with anything more than terse summaries of charges, statements, and judgments. Even then, more expansive records took the form of private observers' notes or newspaper reports. However, the directors deemed such cryptic summary inadequate to the momentous trial through which they hoped to prove their integrity and the defendants' treachery. So they violated the law by appointing stenographers to record courtroom talk and empowering a publisher to print and ship the record, in biweekly installments, across France and Europe.[1]

The stenographic transcript was loquacious but by no means transparent, which was why legislators had banned such things in the first place. A record of words stripped of the musicality of voice and variety of gesture, posture, and facial expression created a dense thicket of text that only sophisticated readers and the most devoted of trial watchers were likely to penetrate. Thus, having gone to such extraordinary lengths to preserve and publicize the proceedings, the Directory resorted to more traditional reporting as well. That took the form of coolly partisan summaries and pugnacious editorials in the government-subsidized *Editor*.

Democrats resisted the Directory's efforts with coverage of their own. Despite inferior means and limited courtroom access, they managed to communicate the trial as the Equals defined it and join the defendants in condemning government and high court.

Four journalists led the way, putting the case front and center from opening arguments in February 1797 until verdicts were delivered in May. Vendôme stalwarts P.-N. Hésine and Marie-Agathe Hénault regularized the once erratic publication schedule of their *High Court Journal* to produce issues on alternate days that detailed each turn in the case. Paris editor Paul Eon, piloting the *Free Men* as co-editors P.-A. Antonelle and René Vatar fought conspiracy charges against them, raised the trial to the status of legislative business by devoting a regular column to it. René Lebois did the same, reporting arguments on the front page of his *People's Friend* under a boldface title, **Vendôme: High Court**.

Collectively, these editors dramatized the battle they believed to be unfolding between liberty's valiant defenders and tyranny's partisans. Summarizing courtroom speeches—many of which must have been smuggled from the abbey prison or passed along by Réal with notes on the proceedings—they foregrounded defendants' complaints about procedural violations, reproduced their charges that the prosecutors' witnesses were provocateurs, spies, and shameless liars, and echoed their denunciations of magistrates' unprincipled bias. "The prosecutor [Viellart] showed himself not as judge but executioner and hired tough."[2]

When reporting testimony, democratic editors often compressed it and added details about performance that had no parallel in the official transcript. Recounting handwriting expert Alexis Harger's words about the phrase, "kill the five," Hésine and Hénault condensed a speech that was rich with hesitation in the transcript to a single bald statement. "In all truth, I was already familiar with this text because I had seen it plastered all over Paris . . . I can't really tell you what I would have seen had I not already been prejudiced." In the next issue of the *High Court Journal*, they lent guilty drama to Jean-François Guillaume's revelation that he had already seen confidential documents by describing Gandon as "flustered" when admitting his part in the business and claiming that the courtroom audience became "agitated" upon hearing it.[3]

None of the democratic papers was above withholding incriminating details. Neither the *High Court Journal*, nor the *Free Men*, nor the *People's Friend* gave any hint of the uncanny resemblance between the speeches of soldiers Jean-Baptiste Meunier and Jean-Noel Barbier when they recanted grand jury statements one after the other. All three papers alluded to the testimony of star witness Georges Grisel but gave far less space to his words than to defendants' charges that he was a provocateur. When they did report Grisel's statements, they minimized them by jeering at his "feigned confidence" or claiming that he appeared to be drunk. Working in these ways, democratic papers reinforced the Equals' claims that their trial was a travesty and the evidence against them doctored, fabricated, or willfully misrepresented.[4]

And yet, democratic editors did not so much invent as simplify and exaggerate. Every revelation they published appeared in the official transcript. Their descriptions of the Equals, by contrast, were more inventive. Some prisoners did not need much enhancement to achieve heroic status on the page. Sophie Lapierre's bravado in serenading the court with revolutionary hymns and refusing to address the judges was unmistakable, even in the official transcript. So, too, was Filippo Buonarroti's easy patrician grace. Other defendants were more visibly improved. Charles Germain, abrasive and impatient on the stenographic page, became "eloquent" and "courageous" in democrats' accounts. Darthé, whose silence effaced him from the official record, became democrats' physical embodiment of censure.[5]

Babeuf, as always, was a case unto himself as journalists he once called ambitious hacks protectively closed ranks around him. Like the prisoners of the abbey, these editors understood that to defend Babeuf was to defend the rest, so they abandoned old charges of ruinous militancy to burnish his reputation instead. Abridging rambling speeches for the limited space of their columns, they pared away Babeuf's digression and repetition to highlight the argument within. Condensing his cross-examination of Grisel, they described Babeuf as triumphantly "revealing" contradictions in the captain's testimony. Challenging the prison warden's account of rivalry among the inmates, they depicted the tribune as unfailingly patient and loyal. In so doing, they brought a headstrong, isolated, utterly idiosyncratic activist into the democratic fold.[6]

When the Equals moved onto the offensive in the courtroom, the publicists kept pace. Reporting Babeuf's interrogation, the *People's Friend* lingered over his memory of the famine that legislators had allowed to descend on Paris in the winter of 1794–95, which spared the wealthy but blighted his own children's frail bodies. "How many families suffered like this?" he continued in those pages. "How many resisted that annihilating plot as long as they could by selling their last shirt and last stick of furniture just as mine did?" The *Free Men*'s account of Buonarroti's interrogation included his description of the oppression he saw after the Directory's inauguration: the "persecution of writers; closing of citizens' assemblies; unbridled use of spies; protection of émigrés; encouragement of luxury, debauchery, and speculation; bankruptcy;

popular misery; disdain for the people; and unbearable dishonesty." That same paper took note when Charles Germain explained "what happy regeneration of public morale popular societies offer to government . . . [and] demonstrated how the Directory cost itself this fulcrum of republican opinion by crushing it."[7]

The Equals struggled for popular rights, the papers concluded, by demanding the constitution of 1793 when that was lawful and educating fellow citizens when nothing more was possible. They did so peacefully, patriotically, and legally. One after another, the democratic sheets reported the defendants' loyalty to the people and to constitutional rights of free assembly and free expression. Neighborhood agent Jean-Baptiste Cazin said he worked with "an association of democrats who gave their time to guiding and improving public opinion . . . to defeat liberty's enemies." His friend and fellow agent, Juste Moroy, spoke of a pressing need to "expose the outrageous schemes of treacherous men by distributing papers that revealed the dangers threatening the people . . . He invoked freedom of the press declared by law to prove there was nothing criminal in [this]." Printer Théodore Lamberté was described as insisting on "the duty of every French person to resist injustice, combat tyranny, and follow the letter of the law as prescribed by the constitution."[8]

Such claims to defend popular good hinted at the distinction between malevolent plot and salutary conspiracy that Antonelle had spelled out in print and Buonarroti celebrated in the courtroom. On the pages of the *People's Friend*, Charles Germain gestured to it shortly before the trial's opening by arguing that the only malicious plots were those against freedom and equity. Others imitated Antonelle by declaring themselves conspirators for liberty. "If loving the people passionately . . . is conspiratorial, then I declare myself a conspirator," François Cochet shouted from the floor of the high court. Louis Blondeau said he knew of no other plot but "the one forged at 9 Thermidor to slaughter equality's friends and destroy their homeland." The brother of Félix Lepeletier told jurors that "if there really was a conspiracy that intended, usefully and legitimately, to amplify popular rights, consolidate the reign of liberty and equality, and honor those who devoted themselves to this glorious cause, then of course, citizens, my brother was part of [it]."[9]

If the readers of democratic papers had trouble putting the pieces together from one issue to the next across the trial's many months, Jean-Nicolas Pache summed up. A former Jacobin mayor of Paris, Pache published a pamphlet dated one year to the day from Babeuf's arrest and gave it a title that mingled present controversy with long-standing revolutionary antipathy: *On Factions and Parties, Conspiracies and Plots.*

Promising to define words whose meanings he believed were dangerously confused, Pache began with "faction" and "party." Both were political sore spots. Revolutionaries feared that coalitions corrupted the expression of a uniform national will and encouraged citizens to prioritize personal alliance over virtue and talent. For that reason, France had eschewed electoral campaigning since 1789, and charges of "factionalism" became deadly during the Terror. Pache tempered these ideas.[10]

A faction, he argued, was united by a shared ideology. Party focused on acts and persons. Factions alone were dangerous, because they preferred tyranny to good government and were almost always organized by those who already held political power. Members of factions, he warned, "tend to profit from their position to alter the government, thanks to the unhappy weakness that inclines the unenlightened to hope for conservation and enhancement of their influence." Parties could play a more beneficial role, Pache continued, because even the most popular government was not likely to please everyone. Some citizens inevitably "see certain circumstances differently than others," so parties could channel their opposition and even improve the polity by calling attention to a government's shortcomings.

Moving on to "conspiracy" and "plot," Pache echoed Buonarroti before the high court, voiding the words of revolutionary horror. Conspiracy, he argued, might be a mere sharing of common hopes, a simple "inclination of mind." Indeed, "people [may] conspire without knowing one another, without communicating, without being related in any way." Plotting was more active, rooted in a collective vow to pursue a common political aim. Neither conspiracy nor plot, Pache repeated with Antonelle, was necessarily malicious. Historically, they had been judged by their aims. A plot in defense of popular government was laudable and would be remembered as such. One that promoted tyranny was noxious and worthy of punishment.

Finally, like Babeuf in Vendôme and Mably decades before, Pache insisted that a plot organized by private citizens against good government was essentially harmless. The majority understood that their government served them and would come to its defense if necessary. In this way, the former mayor of Paris joined his voice to a growing democratic chorus that sang the praises of loyal opposition and envisioned a republic capable of accommodating political difference.[11]

If democratic journalists, and pamphleteers like Pache, rallied readers to the Equals by casting them as patriotic critics of authoritarianism, the refashioning came at staggering cost to Babeuf. It robbed him of his most novel idea: that property could be abolished through concerted political action.

Babeuf spent hours defending "universal happiness" in his final speech to the high court, celebrating shared labor and equal enjoyment. Democrats reported almost none of it. The *Free Men* published a few generic allusions. "[Babeuf] faithfully sketches the principles he advertised in his writing and the notes seized with him. He proves . . . that his writings contain ideas proclaimed by Jean-Jacques [Rousseau], Mably, and Diderot." Hésine and Hénault were equally elusive: "[Babeuf] explained . . . why and to what end he published his doctrine of universal happiness. He found it in the books of the greatest philosophers, which he simply followed and echoed; he meant it as nothing but pure speculation." Even René Lebois, imprisoned at least once for advertising Babeuf's ideas, breathed not a word about property in the *People's Friend*. Only those who had already read the *Tribune*'s defense of "common good," and properly understood it, could grasp the meaning behind these elliptical statements.[12]

By obscuring Babeuf's defense of "perfect equality" or dismissing it as utopian speculation, democrats conjured away his utterly original argument that citizens might abolish poverty using concrete action and familiar political institutions. They recast him as one of their own, an activist who wanted only to enhance popular sovereignty and ameliorate social inequality.

Readers frustrated in their wish to learn something more of "perfect equality" from democratic papers had no hope whatsoever of finding enlightenment in the Directory's supposedly complete transcript. That official record contained only a fragment of Babeuf's final defense, tailored to the prosecutors' narrow definition of conspiracy. Characterizing the tribune's speech about "perfect equality" as "more political treatise than true defense," the Directory cynically pretended that its silence was a favor to Marie-Anne who might yet "derive some benefit" by publishing a speech that celebrated ideas the Councils had outlawed on pain of death. Almost a hundred years would pass before Babeuf's full speech appeared in print.[13]

Perhaps Hésine and Hénault, Paul Eon, and René Lebois kept quiet for pragmatic reasons, knowing that the law threatened them with death if they spoke up. J.-N. Pache did more than hold his tongue. Like Filippo Buonarroti before the high court, he denied that the Equals had advocated for community of goods. That charge was slander, he swore, like the Old Regime claim that Jews profaned Catholic sacraments. "I know each of these men too well not to believe in their honesty, their patriotism, and the soundness of their convictions."[14]

Babeuf's legitimation of insurrection suffered a similar fate. He spoke of it defiantly to the high court, justifying himself with Mably and the constitution of 1793. A pale vestige of his claims survived in democratic papers. Lebois offered only a few words. Hésine and Hénault referred readers to long-gone issues of their *High Court Journal*. The *Free Men* simply denied it. "Babeuf . . . elaborates on the same truths about the nature and aims of democratic society as Buonarroti." If such brief allusions to insurgency recalled Babeuf's convictions to those who remembered his columns in the *Tribune* or his comments to police that Hésine and Hénault had published the preceding fall, readers not already well informed, like those unfamiliar with "community of goods," had no hope of learning more.[15]

This muting gave the last word to Babeuf's old adversary, Antonelle. The latter had publicly softened his opinion of the tribune without fully endorsing him. Or perhaps the former marquis thought he took the sting out of casting Babeuf as a holy fool by labeling himself a hopeless pessimist. "I am always struck by two things when considering that old dream [of perfect equality]: the impossibility of the thing itself and the awfulness of the means necessary to achieve it . . . Babeuf . . . was . . . not as ready to despair of his fellow men. I saw him delight in his illusions; I saw him trying hopefully to realize his dream, looking toward an uncertain future. He did not make plans, he did not sketch a project, he did not think about how to execute it . . . Nothing was more innocent or more frivolous than [his] dream of the imminent return of a golden age."

Here was Babeuf as Don Quixote, spinning utopian fantasies for family, friends, and knowing readers, not Babeuf the revolutionary making practical arrangements to transfigure the world. In this way, the reputation Babeuf had so painfully forged for himself, as a pioneer determined to banish need forever, was subsumed by the image that cultural elites and old revolutionary insiders cultivated to save themselves and their democratic allies. Thirty years would pass before the public saw Babeuf once more as the unique militant he was.[16]

Redefining Babeuf was part and parcel of redefining the Equals. Rather than accepting the Directory's charge that the accused plotted secretly to restore the democratic constitution, revive the National Convention, and abolish property, sympathetic newspapers advertised the image that Antonelle, Buonarroti, and Pache proposed: the Equals as loyal opponents who only talked and encouraged the people to do the same. By silencing the true nature of the conspiracy, high court defendants and their allies dissipated the last traces of revolutionary radicalism and laid a foundation for the loyal, peaceful activism democrats would pursue in coming years.[17]

Hésine and Hénault, Eon and Lebois served the Directory's wish to publicize the trial and imitated the government-subsidized *Editor* by shaping accounts of the proceedings to reflect their editorial opinions. And still, authorities pursued them. If that pursuit failed to silence democrats, it gave further credence to the Equals' charge that the regime would stop at nothing, not even the violation of its own constitution, to impose itself.

René Lebois may have suffered most, hounded by the minister of justice himself, Merlin de Douai. Merlin, a former Jacobin whose commitment to order far exceeded his ideological affinities, ordered Lebois arrested in spring 1796 as a suspected accomplice to Babeuf. The journalist was released for lack of evidence, but the minister, whether driven by inner certainty or simply infuriated by Lebois's unflagging radicalism, appointed new investigators to continue digging. When those men came up empty-handed, Merlin used a police spy's claim that the *People's Friend* dampened military morale to justify another imprisonment.[18]

René Vatar fared slightly better. An arrest warrant was sworn out when his name was found on a list of subscribers to the *People's Tribune*. That list identified several sitting deputies and all five directors as well, none of whom suffered for their association with the *Tribune*, and ten days elapsed before the warrant against Vatar was executed. These facts suggest that the journalist may have been targeted more for his public skepticism about the case than from any genuine evidence of conspiratorial activity. Although spared a prison stay, Vatar was denied access to his home, office, and business papers for a month. And so, he concluded, "in a country with courts and procedure, laws and a constitution . . . individual liberty and freedom of the press are deprived of . . . public safeguard." Vatar was arrested again the following spring and forced to leave the *Free Men* in the hands of co-editor Paul Eon.[19]

Pierre-Nicolas Hésine initially seemed more fortunate. Despite his sympathy for the accused and open ridicule of the high court—after being exiled from Vendôme, he publicly claimed to have attended the trial disguised as a dandy—Hésine remained free to hector magistrates, prosecutors, and directors for months. Local authorities finally brought him in on a technicality, having found that the farm on which he was living was beyond the Vendôme perimeter when traveling by local roads but within it as the crow flies. Marie-Agathe Hénault, like Paul Eon at the head of the *Free Men*, continued publishing the couple's newspaper. Three months after trial's end, Hésine was still in prison.[20]

Advertising a devotion to liberty and rule of law, the Directory imprisoned journalists who dared to criticize. It is not entirely clear why. After all, democratic newspapers were outsold two, three, even five issues to one by conservative and reactionary sheets. Left to themselves, most democratic editors could expect to be done in by financial ruin or reactionary violence.[21]

The Directory may have attacked Parisian papers like the *People's Friend* and *Free Men* because they were almost alone in celebrating the Equals to provincial readers. Democratic editors of small-town newspapers said almost nothing about the trial. Perhaps they found it difficult to justify rousing right-wing ire without moving the people for whom the Equals claimed to speak, because that people—all too often poor, disenfranchised, and exhausted by scarcity, inflation, and police repression—ignored much of what was going on in Vendôme. Their indifference gave the lie to reactionary claims that France was rotten with Babeuf's disciples. In these years of melancholy reversal, Hésine and Hénault, Lebois and Eon spoke, above all, to fellow journalists and to a shrinking cohort of seasoned militants left by the ebb of revolutionary enthusiasm.

Democrats who did follow the case continued the tightening of ranks initiated during the first bitter debates in spring 1796, resisting a hostile regime and alienated by news from Vendôme of judicial prejudice, prosecutorial malfeasance, and legal harassment. François Poultier was the most visible such figure. As editor of the government-subsidized *Friend of the Laws*, he loyally accepted the Directory's first accounts of the conspiracy and reported the trial in its early weeks with evenhanded caution. But the bias and corruption visible in official transcript and democratic papers finally broke his spirit. Declaring "the character of the Vendôme affair . . . wholly changed since arguments opened," Poultier insisted that "witnesses' testimony and material evidence prove the minister of police and his subordinates to have been leading provocateurs of the conspiracy and authors of several parts of this case." According Babeuf grudging respect, he more vigorously highlighted the court's errors and breaches.[22]

Journalist Jean-Baptiste Louvet, a moderate democrat who never wavered in his conviction that Babeuf posed a terrible threat to the republic, was as troubled by the court's conduct as Poultier. "Friends of the constitution and public order . . . want the conspirators to be punished," he opined, but "they also want the accused to enjoy the right to defense accorded them by nature, law, and the constitution."[23]

Journalists were unusually visible figures, but they were not the only citizens whose political opinions were shaped by this case. Militant democrats discussed it privately and would allude to it publicly for years. In the spring of 1797, the most dangerous impressions were probably those of Jean-François Gaultier de Biauzat, a high court juror experiencing a change of

heart. Gaultier had denounced the conspiracy when it was exposed as "stupid" and "appalling," but the Equals thought themselves fortunate to have
this resolute friend of republican principle on the jury. They must have
been pleased, too, when he joined the questioning of handwriting expert
Alexis Harger about whether the Directory's account of the plot influenced
his work. As the trial progressed, hostile locals began to claim that he spent
more time with prisoners than with colleagues, but that may have been angry gossip. Charles Germain lent credibility to such talk when he attested to
his warm feelings for this "good man" in one of the letters seized near the
trial's end, adding ominously that "it would be a great loss for us and the
homeland" if Gaultier were ambushed. Authorities who read these letters
worried what this meant for the verdicts Gaultier was preparing to deliver.[24]

Reactionary editors understood as well as their democratic counterparts that
the defendants' renown depended on them, so they said very little about a
trial they had already judged. Those who did speak up vented outrage at
"fifty shameless wretches reveling in their disgrace," or damned Babeuf for
"advertising his hatred of the current government and his plans against it."
Such antipathy did not, however, generate warmth for the Directory. Having doubted early on that police could identify all of Babeuf's accomplices,
reactionaries intimated that the court's failure to contain the prisoners
proved the government's vulnerability. One journalist complained that "the
judges show a moderation and circumspection that too often looks like
weakness. The accused are assured and possessed of a confidence that looks
like cold-blooded insult or deliberate contempt." Another dismissed the
whole trial as "a joke."[25]

The directors had tried to have it both ways, claiming that police had defeated the Equals' conspiracy but depicting its radical impulse as an undying threat. Caught in a bind of its own making, the regime saw it tighten
with the approach of spring legislative elections.

The elections of 1797 marked the nation's first unrestricted balloting in almost five years. Although voters had gone to the polls in summer 1795, they
were hobbled by the requirement that two-thirds of the outgoing Convention

be appointed to the Directory's incoming legislative councils. If many saw the Two-Thirds Decree as a breach of sovereignty, that was far from being their only source of discontent. The economy was in shambles, inflation and urban unemployment continuing to spiral upward as agricultural production stagnated. Economic woes were coupled with a general breakdown of order, visible in crowds that demanded food with arms in hand, and bandits called "firemen," who attacked isolated farmhouses and burned victims' feet to gain whatever money was available. Endless warfare sapped the treasury and, more poignantly, stole away a generation of young men. Corruption flourished.[26]

Reactionary newspapers cheered that elections would bring an end to this "reign of fools and crooks" and return "the old Convention . . . to the obscurity it fears." Even exhausted conservatives ready to accept the republic as a *fait accompli*—and they were myriad—refused to endorse the Directory's candidates, flirting with danger by urging voters to "help" the directors start afresh by electing "new men" to the legislative councils. The nation required deputies unspoiled by politics, the argument ran, who could save France from a government that was incompetent at best and, at worst, corrupted by the very radicals it claimed to police.[27]

Hope for what the elections might bring was matched by fear that it would be frustrated. Reactionaries worried that "anarchists"—by which they meant Jacobins, Equals, and other advocates of the popular democracy they demonized—would do their best to interfere. Jacobins, *Perlet's Journal* wailed, were "organizing to prevent or dominate the elections by means of a new Terror." The conservative Dupont de Nemours warned vaguely of "plots . . . being hatched under cover."[28]

Such allusions to "Jacobins" were objectively confusing. Who, exactly, were these people? Robespierre, most of his allies from the Committee of Public Safety, and almost every member of the radical Paris city council active during the Terror had been put to death by the guillotine in the days after 9 Thermidor. More friends and allies followed or, like Babeuf's malicious patrons Fréron and Tallien, turned coat to save themselves. The Paris Jacobin Club was shuttered in fall 1794, and the last of its provincial affiliates closed by spring 1795. The handful of democratic newspapers that survived barely got by. It is difficult to see "Jacobin" as anything more than an epithet by 1797, a shorthand smear of advocates for universal male suffrage, public education, and social welfare.

As with so much else in these years, the retrospective view is deceptive. Reactionaries saw radicals everywhere, inflated their power, and exploited the fear they roused, often rendering Babeuf and the Equals as icons of the enduring Jacobin threat. Campaign talk was rich with allusions to the defendants. The *Evening Messenger* asked whether Drouet would run for re-election despite "the law that considers ex-deputies absent without leave . . . to have resigned," and Dupont raised the specter of Babeuf in his *Historian* by publishing the speech of a prominent conservative deputy who insisted that "the people want senators, not tribunes." This kind of talk was accompanied by unprecedented activism. Disdaining revolutionary suspicion of political campaigning, reactionaries created local associations to mobilize voters, published opinions about candidates in broadsheets and newspapers, and asked friendly clerics to offer guidance from the pulpit.[29]

Meanwhile, demonized democrats held their tongues. With attention consumed by the Equals' seemingly endless trial and nerves shattered by renewed violence against old provincial militants, Parisians René Lebois and Paul Eon published the names of a few outgoing deputies and worried that returned émigrés were preparing to vote. But they did not advise readers on electoral choices or even encourage them to go to the polls. Their small-town counterparts were equally reticent.[30]

These men had good reason to be discouraged. Political malaise and cynicism had reached even that last outpost of radicalism, Paris. "Here are the elections," working people were overheard to say, "the parties are at odds, commerce is paralyzed, workers are unemployed, and public calm may well suffer from the combination of such unhappy circumstances." The government fared no better. "The members of the Council of 500 . . . are believed to be more interested in serving a party than producing wise laws to meet the people's needs . . . The Directory is also criticized . . . [for] favoring one extreme or another when it should give precedence to sound morals over factionalism."[31]

If people believed all politicians were deaf to the nation's best interests, how were they to make good choices? Weary of revolution and war, chaos, inflation, and uncertainty, many seemed to weigh their options as the prosecutor

Bailly had done when he warned against democracy's perils. Imagining themselves forced to choose between Jacobin "anarchy" and royalist "despotism," voters seemed to share the prosecutor's conviction that the latter would at least bring stability. As one reactionary put it: "Ninety-nine percent of royalists are . . . more concerned with their tranquility than with counterrevolution." Seen in this light, right-wing candidates appeared not as proponents of tyranny but as guardians of peace and prosperity, capable of overcoming revolutionary social change, revitalizing a stagnant economy, and quelling the banditry that was wreaking havoc in the countryside.[32]

Electoral polling lasted from late March to mid-April. As voters chose electors in the first round, and electors chose legislators in the second, high court jurors listened to the interrogation of Babeuf and Buonarroti. By the time Vieillart and Bailly asked for a recess to prepare their summation, the final tallies had been published.[33]

They were devastating.

Of the 216 newly elected deputies, only 11 were incumbents. The rest were "new men" devoid of legislative experience, almost all avowed reactionaries or outright royalists. It was an extraordinary repudiation of the Directory, the republic, and the revolution. There were enough royalists in the legislature to organize a voting bloc. And they did.[34]

Conservatives reeled at what they had wrought. "Now they seem to be what we have always been," the republican *Friend of the Laws* commented bitterly. "Their latest writings are infused with republicanism and the sincerest attachment to the constitution. They successfully backed a party they knew to be dangerous but which was useful to them; that party shows its teeth and threatens its most devoted supporters."[35]

Democrats and even centrist republicans were furious. "Royalists are being given public offices; patriots are disdained and reviled, liberty is threatened, the constitution is about to be overturned."[36]

As republicans demanded that the Directory take action, the high court asked its jury to deliver verdicts.

THIRTEEN

Trial's End

G iving the jury its charge continued the court's chaos.
French jury trials were founded in 1791 by legislators determined to bring popular sovereignty into the criminal courtroom. If the law expressed the will of the people, they had reasoned, the people must play an active part in administering it. To that end, the assembly replaced learned magistrates, who relied on sophisticated categories of proof to judge cases, with citizens who used common sense to assess evidence and judged according to the intimate conviction that came from watching the trial. To facilitate judgment, deputies required presiding judges to pose multiple questions of fact. Had a particular act taken place? If so, was the defendant in question proved to be its author? Finally, did the defendant mean for that act to do harm? Affirmative answers to all three questions constituted a guilty verdict that was subject to penalties fixed in advance.[1]

Presiding judge Gandon hewed to the usual formula for the first two sets of questions. Was there a conspiracy in the spring of 1796 to trouble the republic by arming citizens against one another? he asked the jury. Was there a conspiracy to trouble the republic by inciting citizens against the constitution of 1795? Was there a conspiracy to abolish the legislature?

If thirteen of the high court's sixteen jurors answered yes to any of those questions, which defendants did they find guilty of the deed?

Having asked about the "what" and the "who," Gandon moved on. It was here that trouble began.

Revolutionary magistrates typically asked whether the accused had acted with malice, giving jurors the possibility of negotiating harsh mandated sentences by affirming that a crime had been committed but delivering an acquittal by denying the intent to harm. As everyone in the high court knew, revolutionary jurors had increasingly used this question to exonerate citizens accused of political crimes. Reputed leaders of the radical September Massacres and the reactionary Vendémiaire insurrection had escaped condemnation the year before, because jurors accepted defendants' claims that they believed themselves to be acting for the nation's good. More than a dozen royalists accused of conspiracy had been acquitted on the same grounds just weeks earlier. This was, in part, why Babeuf, Buonarroti, and Antonelle had insisted so vigorously on the Equals' patriotism and why Viellart and Bailly did their best to cut short those kinds of speeches.[2]

It was against this background that Gandon conspicuously took the prosecutors' side. Setting aside all question of malice, he asked jurors not to gauge "moral intent" but simply to determine whether anyone proved guilty of a deed had acted with forethought.

Then he opened the floor to comment. A free-for-all ensued.[3]

Jury president Jean-Ambroise Rey-Pailhade was the first to speak. As a former justice of the peace, Rey had discussed formal points of law with magistrates and defenders during the trial. He now seemed intent on preserving some latitude for the jury. But he did not ask Gandon to reformulate the question of intent. Rather, Rey suggested that the judge add further charges and pose the question of malice about them. The law of 27 Germinal year IV, he noted, outlawed advocacy for the democratic constitution of 1793 or any form of government other than the Directory. Why had Gandon not referred to a decree that "seems intended for the case before us" when formulating the charges?

Intimating that he knew the jury's mood, Rey continued. "Suppose a conspiracy to excite civil war or overturn the government is not proved. Suppose, too, that testimony and evidence prove there were speeches and writing calling for restoration of the constitution of 1793," the very crimes targeted by the law of 27 Germinal. The public would be deeply troubled to learn that the court gave jurors such a narrow charge that they could not condemn a crime that was proven.[4]

This was a risky solution. Adding charges might permit conviction by giving the jury greater latitude to negotiate the penalty, but it would violate the letter of the law by denying the accused any chance to answer the new accusations. As well, the charges Rey proposed were at odds with the spirit of the law because they were based on a decree adopted at the height of the Equals' pamphleteering. In other words, the law appeared to have been designed to target specific acts rather than to formulate a general principle. Resorting to such an expedient would risk turning the high court into a new revolutionary tribunal.

Surprisingly, P.-F. Réal—who had built his name on preferring legal consistency to particular political aims—seconded Rey's unorthodox recommendation. The law of 27 Germinal was barbaric, he admitted, because it proposed capital punishment for an expression of opinion. But it had the merit of restoring jurors' right to weigh defendants' intent, latitude that was essential in times like these. "Is this the moment to restrict the question of intent? On the contrary . . . its healing generosity has never been more necessary than in this time when revolution continues to brew." This was all the more true of a court that was judging not common crimes like theft or murder but contested ideas. France could not end the revolution until partisans of all stripes acknowledged their opponents' good faith and the state showed lenience to those who challenged it on behalf of society at large. If royalist conspirators could be acquitted on such grounds, were good republicans to be denied the same consideration?[5]

Viellart and Réal seemed to have switched places, because it was the prosecutor who stepped up to defend legal principle by recalling that the penal code forbade last-minute charges. That he was less concerned with a point of law than winning his case became clear when he addressed the question of intent. Just as Bailly had done, Viellart insisted that ideological opposition was no different from any other crime. "[I]t would be absurd to ask a juror who convicted someone of [premeditated] murder . . . whether the defendant acted *consciously and with malice* . . . Yes, criminal intent is necessary to convict . . . but what is *criminal intent?* It is the formal and undeniable will to carry out a deed the law defines as a crime."

Réal was right to say that France must end the revolution, Viellart admitted. But these were not the means by which to do so. What the defender called "clemency" was a travesty of justice that would encourage others. If courts permitted such "ghastly crimes" to go unpunished, the nation would stagger from one insurrection to another as their leaders claimed to be patriots. France needed stability, even if that came at the cost of liberty.[6]

Having listened to it all, the judges ruled in a way that highlighted their priorities. They upheld Gandon's narrow formulation of intent. However, perhaps fearing that jurors would refuse to convict if denied all room to maneuver, the judges added new charges. Invoking the law of 27 Germinal, they asked the jury to rule on advocating for the constitution of 1793. Had there been spoken incitement to its restoration? Written incitement? If so, who was guilty? Finally, did the jury admit extenuating circumstances?

The jurors were sequestered in a small apartment. Over the course of the afternoon and evening, they deliberated, paused for meals, and took catnaps as the heat of an early summer pressed in.

In the basement of the Trinity Abbey, the accused waited anxiously.

At four o'clock the following morning, jurors sent word that they had finished deliberating. As the law required, Viellart and a high court judge met with them to verify the verdicts. This was a formality usually fulfilled quickly. Now, however, delays set in and stretched on. Morning came and went, the court announcing that it would not reconvene until late afternoon. Then it postponed to early evening. Then it postponed again. Rumors circulated in Vendôme that no one had been condemned to death, then there was talk of jurors revisiting verdicts on the new charges.[7]

It was not until five o'clock the following morning that the jury returned, twenty-five hours after it had declared deliberations complete and more than thirty-six since it had withdrawn from the abbey courtroom.

Judges, prosecutors, and defenders expected jury foreman Rey-Pailhade to deliver the verdicts, but he was too visibly distraught to speak. Instead the magistrates tapped juror Pierre-Marie Pajot, "undoubtedly because he appeared the least affected." Pajot began by fumbling the dates of the revolutionary calendar in a way that suggested his general disdain for the radical invention. Then he announced that the first three charges were dismissed.

"The conspiracy of 21 floréal . . . Babeuf's conspiracy . . . all of it was a fantasy, no one can imagine how blood might have been spilled."

Turning to the last-minute charges, Pajot declared that Babeuf, Darthé, Buonarroti, Germain, and four others were guilty of promoting the constitution of 1793 with spoken words. Because the jury admitted extenuating circumstances, the sentence was exile.

Pajot prepared to deliver the final verdict but an exhausted colleague collapsed, forcing the court to delay for another hour.

When the man returned, Pajot took up the thread. Babeuf and Darthé were guilty of advocating for the constitution of 1793 in writing. The jury admitted no extenuating circumstances.

The sentence was death.[8]

When the prisoners were brought in to hear the verdicts, Babeuf quickly took in the scene. "Do not keep anything from me," he appealed to Réal. "Be blunt, I beg you."

"You are condemned to death," the lawyer replied.

Believing he had been convicted of conspiring, Babeuf was stunned to learn that it was for promoting the constitution of 1793. "Death for written words! . . . What can I say?"

He stood by, uncharacteristically silent, as Buonarroti and Réal improvised.

Buonarroti suddenly remembered that the law of 27 Germinal was void because the constitution required any law restricting free press to be renewed annually. The legislative councils had not revisited this one since adopting it fourteen months earlier.

Réal abandoned the position he had defended the preceding day to make Viellart's case that a jury could not rule on last-minute charges. "Neither Babeuf, Germain, nor any of the others was accused of any crime related to the law [of 27 Germinal] . . . The last two sets of questions target speech and writing, but [speech] when and before whom . . . ? Of what writing do we speak? . . . It is vague law that criminalizes spoken and written words. Must we compound its murderous impulse with a still more murderous question that does not scrupulously define the crime?"

Knowing that high court judgments could not be appealed, Réal begged the magistrates to consult with the legislative councils about whether a verdict based on a defunct law could be executed. "Will you endanger the republic by postponing a judicial murder for twenty-four hours? The brutes who want this death will criticize you . . . but just men will applaud."

As the magistrates conferred once more, the exiles comforted those condemned to death. The judges returned and refused all recourse to the legislative councils. Babeuf and Darthé would be executed as soon as possible.

Darthé broke his long silence by shouting, "Long live the republic!" and plunging a knife into his chest. As courtroom guards wrestled him to the ground, Babeuf silently drove a blade into his own body. Guards immobilized him, too.[9]

The men had staged their final act of defiance with pitiful weapons fashioned from stolen silverware and scraps of metal, emulating ancients who wrested control of their lives from a state whose legitimacy they denied. Frustrated, they were returned to their cells to await a traveling executioner who was trundling his mobile guillotine from the nearby city of Blois.

The executioner arrived in darkness, and the prisoners were taken from their cells before dawn on a spring morning. Darthé remained defiant to the last. Fighting the guards who cut his hair to expose his neck for the guillotine's blade, he reopened the wound in his chest. Bleeding heavily, he was tied to a chair and carried to the square in front of the abbey where the guillotine stood. As soldiers looked on in the growing light, he shouted, "Long live the republic, liberty, and equality!" before the blade fell.

Babeuf walked silently to the instrument of his execution, his dagger still lodged in his chest. He lay down and "received the blow with an innocent calm that might even be called indifference."[10]

The corpses were spirited away and secretly buried to prevent the graves from becoming sites of pilgrimage. The remains of the two men have never been found.

The trial that ended in Vendôme with the thud of a guillotine echoed through the press in the weeks that followed.

Reactionaries suddenly had a great deal to say as they denounced the verdicts. The editors of the *Evening Messenger* told readers that only four jurors rejected the conspiracy charges, insisting that the rest affirmed what all right-thinking citizens knew to be true: the Equals had plotted. The next day, they added that one juror changed his mind to condemn Babeuf and Darthé at the last minute, and damned him. "Either you meant to embarrass the government with your first [verdicts] or you allowed yourself to be influenced in the latter. In either case, you sacrificed conscience to passion, principle to personal consideration, things to people."[11]

More surprising, the reactionary *Republican Courier* condemned the high court for "judicially murdering" Babeuf and Darthé with "a law that no longer existed." Admittedly, "both men deserved death because they plainly conspired against the government," but "once acquitted of conspiracy, they ought to have been freed." The *Evening Messenger* chimed in with a caustic remark that "to convict reputed arsonists at the very moment one declares there was no fire is . . . the height of barbarism and madness." Such partisan verdicts that targeted acts and people rather than defending legal principle, editors argued, laid bare the regime's contempt for its own constitution.[12]

Rather than uniting reactionaries and democrats, however, the verdict became new cause for blame. "The example of Babeuf and Darthé," the *Evening Messenger* continued, "should excite unhappy reflection among [the Jacobins] who last year decreed, eagerly and by acclaim, the death penalty for authors promoting anarchy or royalism. That law is barbaric and revolutionary, the [*Free Men*] said today. But was it not the Jacobins who demanded and legislated it? Did they not oppose its recall? Jacobins are responsible for the exile and death of your friends."[13]

The long, noisy, costly trial had accomplished nothing, reactionaries concluded. Drouet was free, Babeuf had become a martyr, and dozens of subversives were turned loose, "enlightened by their mistakes" and so better prepared for future efforts.[14]

Democrats condemned the verdicts too. But first, they mourned.

The *People's Friend* and the *Free Men* praised the bold attempts at suicide and celebrated Babeuf and Darthé for their courage before the guillotine.

François-Jean-Baptiste Topino-Lebrun, *The Death of Caius Gracchus*, 1792–98. The democrat Topino-Lebrun probably began this painting in 1792 but did not resume work on it until 1797. It depicts the suicide of Caius Gracchus, a Roman tribune who lived in the second century BCE and, with his brother, advocated for agrarian law. Theirs was the name Babeuf adopted in 1794. The painting depicts the moment when, according to Plutarch, Caius and his servant killed themselves rather than suffer defeat by aristocratic senators. There is evidence that some democrats understood the contemporary allusion when this ostensibly historical painting was shown at the Salon of 1798. Photo: Jean Bernard. © RMN-Grand Palais / Art Resource, NY.

Colleagues published spare, bereaved accounts. "Darthé . . . cried out: long live the republic. A rush of blood announced that he had struck himself . . . Babeuf silently pierced himself with a sharpened wire and fell, dying . . . [H]e breathed still at eight o'clock . . . and throughout [his] long agony, called in vain to see his wife and son." On the streets of Paris, "Babeuf's partisans . . . are disgusted by the sentence and make angry predictions about the republic's future."[15]

Democrats damned the high court jurors as vengeful, the magistrates as despots, and the prosecutors as royalists, arguing that the verdicts confirmed the Equals' charge that the proceedings had been corrupt from the start. Just as reactionaries claimed that jurors who acquitted defendants on the original charges did so for partisan reasons, democrats insisted that jurors who condemned men on the last charges were pressured into doing so. The *Toulouse Journal* described Viellart as having become "enraged" when he learned that the conspiracy charge was dismissed. "Seeing the collapse of the scaffolding he created to . . . guarantee the deaths of as many as possible," he was said to have hounded a juror until the man buckled. The *Free Men* upended reactionary claims that the holdouts were slaves to faction by celebrating those men as guardians of conscience.[16]

To democrats, the trial's outcome stood in shocking contrast to the recent acquittal of more than a dozen royalist conspirators and so proved the Directory's reactionary character. They resented the continued suffering of men like Drouet and fellow defendant Félix Lepeletier who, although exonerated, were charged as émigrés after fleeing imprisonment and suffered confiscation of their property. Worse yet, "the murder of republicans in Vendôme must have been the signal for new massacres [elsewhere]. Four citizens were slaughtered in Mamelart, near Avignon, and the most horrible atrocities committed on their corpses. In Lille . . . three more citizens were murdered . . . In Lyon, the butchery continues with equal fury."[17]

Réal weighed in from the pages of the *Free Men*, hustling to save his reputation by insisting that he had not been alone in believing the new charges necessary. He devised that strategy with fellow defenders and the accused themselves, he said, because it permitted jurors to disavow the empty claims of conspiracy with which the Directory empowered itself "without freeing men [they] believed dangerous." No one, he insisted, could have imagined that the jury would return a death penalty "for written words" or that the high court would enforce a law that was lapsed.[18]

Reactionaries and democrats were equally bitter about the trial's outcome, but, as always, they could not find common ground. Instead, they blamed one another. Reactionaries accused Jacobins of corrupting the judiciary and reaping what they had sown. Democrats charged that their opponents shed crocodile tears over Babeuf and the rest. If all of the accused "had been condemned as conspirators and guillotined according to the penal code," Réal wrote to the *Free Men*, reactionaries "would have applauded that butchery." René Lebois agreed: "these gentlemen only attack the high court judgment because it didn't kill enough people."[19]

Réal burned the last of the bridges he had tried to build at the Directory's inauguration by arguing, in company with the *Free Men*, that the real source of reactionaries' outrage was their knowledge that the law that condemned Babeuf and Darthé could be turned against them. Reactionaries were "moralists of the moment," he charged, who only joined the fight for "sound principle" once the regime had freed them of men they despised. The law of 27 Germinal could, indeed, target right as well as left, because it criminalized advocating for any form of government other than the Directory. It is likely that the editors Réal accused of shedding crocodile tears were doing just that. But it is equally true that Réal himself had succumbed in Vendôme to the partisanship he condemned in others. He had subordinated legal principle to short-term gain while maneuvering for advantage in the high court.

Seen from every side, the Equals' trial was a debacle. It did not simply fail to rally citizens but quite plainly alienated them, renewing polarization and an almost universal sense of victimization. Conservatives and reactionaries, unable to believe the regime capable of steering France to calmer waters, remained convinced that Jacobinism posed an eternal threat. Democrats, despairing of the Directory's ability to tame the past, feared that its hostility to them would poison the republic's future.

What was to become of this revolutionary nation?

Babeuf was haunted by that question to the very end. As he lay awake the night before his execution, blood spilling around the knife lodged in his chest, he pleaded to see Marie-Anne and Émile one last time. His jailers refused. His last words to them were in the letter he wrote while awaiting the verdict.

"Farewell my friends, I am ready to enter the eternal night . . . Dying for my homeland, leaving family, children and beloved wife, would be easier if I did not see the destruction of liberty and the prohibition of everything true republicans hold dear at the end of all this. Ah, my sweet children! what will become of you?"[20]

Speaking to his own family, Babeuf addressed all democrats. He had long fused painful knowledge of his own children's suffering with empathy for his fellow citizens' hardship, believing he could save everyone by instituting "perfect equality." Having failed, he thought he had won nothing.

What he could not know was that his status as a martyr to democracy and the Equals' passionate defense of loyal opposition from the floor of the high court would mobilize new activism. Although his commitment to radical egalitarianism would be obscured for decades, the trial's notoriety would preserve Babeuf's memory until a truer account of his thinking was put in service to the seemingly endless struggle to extend political rights and material security.

FOURTEEN

The Republic Imperiled

Once the corpses of Babeuf and Darthé had been spirited away, the acquitted were released into the arms of local supporters who paraded them through Vendôme and hosted a festive meal. Then, abandoned by the government that had transported them to this isolated town, the former prisoners had to find their own way home. Wealthy men like Antonelle could afford carriages, but few others had resources for such luxury. Most returned on foot.[1]

The exodus continued, judges and jurors, prosecutors and defenders moving on. As Vendôme grew quiet around the men condemned to exile, Charles Germain fell into deep depression. "He doesn't see anyone, doesn't say much, doesn't talk about anything without the greatest sadness," the prison warden informed his superiors. "We found very clear plans for suicide in his letters. Even the most careful supervision cannot foresee all means of self-destruction."[2]

Germain, like Buonarroti and fellow exiles Jean-Baptiste Cazin, Juste Moroy, Louis Blondeau, and Marc Vadier, feared he would be sent to another continent. The English blockade kept them closer to home. They were returned to the mobile cages that had brought them to Vendôme and sent north to the dilapidated Fort National, perched on a tiny island in the Cherbourg harbor.

The makeshift prison was accessible only by boat, and still the exiles' movements were narrowly restricted. Their hardship was aggravated by official indifference because administrators, assuming that the prisoners could somehow purchase food for themselves, provided such meager rations that they were several times in danger of starving. The minister of the interior finally authorized additional funds, but local merchants were unreliable and the fort's hostile cook served what did arrive in revolting condition. "Can you believe I have found tufts of hair, slugs, feathers three or four inches long in [my] soup?" Vadier cried out. "Even a fat spider in my [water] bottle."[3]

More profoundly isolated than ever, the men did not enjoy the camaraderie of Arras and Plessis, nor did they recover the common purpose that had finally united them in Vendôme. They were at each other's throats. Former agent Jean-Baptiste Cazin, who had managed to overcome his fear of the police to distribute Equals' pamphlets in 1796, fell prey to deeper dread as dementia convinced him that Charles Germain was a police spy and fellow agent Juste Moroy an assassin. Germain became a bitter rival of former activist Louis Blondeau, who responded in kind by calling Germain "a wretch he would just as soon kill if the other did not get him first." Juste Moroy got along with Blondeau, but disliked Cazin. Everyone resented Buonarroti after authorities allowed his companion, Thérèse, to move into the prison and gave the two a private room. If these men had thought themselves at the ends of the earth in Vendôme, they found fresh hell on that windswept pile of rocks in Cherbourg.[4]

Babeuf and Darthé were dead, the "exiles" cast away, the rest legally acquitted. But the accusation of having been an Equal would haunt many for the rest of their lives. The case would haunt the Directory, too.

The regime had been brought into being in 1795 by usurpation of the democratic constitution and the Two-Thirds Decree that guaranteed legislative seats to unelected men. These acts, which violated political process and excluded citizens from exercise of their sovereignty, were the foundation on which the Directory continued to build after the Equals' trial. Refusing to negotiate with critics to the left and right, who demanded inclusion and reform, the regime would erode what remained of the republic's legitimacy by staging a series of coups. Memories of the Equals abounded in these sad years, democrats embracing the peaceful image the defendants

Entre deux Chaises le Cul par Terre.

I. S. Lemonnier, "Between Two Stools," n.d. Banners that identify claims to the figure's right include "glorifying émigrés" and "civil war." Those on its left name "the people's happiness," "defense of rights," and "reward to the homeland's defenders." Beneath the tumbling figure we see "public confidence banished," "murder of republicans," and "closing of patriotic societies." Above it all is a quotation from the philosopher Montesquieu: "Decline is imperceptible, the restoration of good demands effort." Source: BnF.

had forged in Vendôme as directors assaulted the republic by exploiting the anarchic figures perfected by prosecutors.

The first act of this tragedy began when 205 novices, most of them reactionary and all elected in the shadow of the Equals' trial, took their legislative seats in May 1797. Republicans demanded a response to the right-wing surge, but the directors seemed paralyzed as deputies elected rigid conservative François Barthélemy to their ranks, appointed a royalist to preside over the Council of 500, and repealed revolutionary legislation. In the provinces, newly elected judges turned a blind eye to vigilante violence that was intensified by reactionaries' laments about "escapees from Vendôme."[5]

Left to their own devices, private citizens crafted a republican front. At the pinnacle of Parisian society, diplomats, philosophers, journalists, and — unofficially because of her sex — the intellectual Germaine de Staël resisted the legislature's rightward tilt by organizing a club in support of the Directory at the Hôtel de Salm. Although the Salmists advertised their political moderation by vilifying the Terror, several gave speeches that recalled Equals' talk in Vendôme. One imitated Buonarroti with a complaint that "we see the republic advancing everywhere beyond our borders" but "engulfed in shame [within]." The founders of the republic were "reviled," he mourned, and "the sacred title of citizen disdained." Another Salmist recalled Babeuf and Mably by urging fellow club members to act as a vanguard for citizens distracted from politics by "the thousand problems of a hard life." The defender P.-F. Réal was said to belong to the club.[6]

More modest circles formed elsewhere. Some simply offered places to read or reprinted Salmist speeches, but others, especially in Paris and a few radical strongholds in the south of France, rallied citizens with political talk. Seizing on the latter, reactionaries complained that this "mass of associations" would provoke "civil war" and argued that Antonelle's presence in one of them proved the Equals to be organizing anew. Right-wing deputies took up the cry. Warning in midsummer that "plots are formed in groups . . . plots are executed in groups," they ordered the circles closed.[7]

Perhaps legislators thought they could attack free association without exciting visible resistance, as the directors had done in closing the Pantheon Club in 1796. This time, republicans objected loudly. Although the deputies justified themselves with the constitutional article that forbade associations disruptive of public order, many citizens saw their decree as an assault and voiced rising anxiety in noisy café talk, letters to democratic newspapers, and petitions to the directors. Activists demonstrated peacefully in the provinces and brawled with royalists in the capital. The general Napoleon Bonaparte offered to bring troops from Italy "to maintain the Constitution, defend liberty, [and] protect the government."[8]

Antonelle joined the cacophony from the pages of his new *Constitutional Democrat*, celebrating civil liberties and censuring the "royalist hypocrites" who would violate them. Like the Equals in 1796, he published his opinions on posters for passersby to read. But rather than condemning the constitution, as the Equals had done, he urged citizens to defend it. "Will you stand by as vicious cliques barter away your liberty?" he called out. "Republicans, men of 14 July and 10 August, stand guard, keep your arms handy!"[9]

Many people worried that the endangered republic would be overwhelmed if the annual elections scheduled for spring 1798 returned enough reactionaries to give them a legislative majority. But circumstances were not yet dire. The new deputies had managed to repeal laws against priests and émigrés, but failed to do much more because they were divided among themselves and hamstrung by lack of political experience. Even if more reactionary candidates won legislative seats in 1798, constitutional safeguards against hasty revision would remain.[10]

For the moment, republicans had the legislative majority. Given the circumstances, they might have encouraged allies to stand for Council seats in the next elections and worked to improve voter turnout. But too many deputies, like the directors, saw the terrifying possibility of renewed revolution in the political effervescence rising around them and so accepted a desperate violation of the constitution.

In September 1797, directors Paul Barras, Louis Larévellière-Lépeaux, and Jean-François Reubell claimed that a royalist plot was afoot and used that excuse to stage a military coup. Troops occupied Paris, permitting the directors to expel conservative colleagues Carnot and Barthélemy, oust reactionary legislators, and dismiss right-wing judges. Once purged, the legislative councils completed the executive's work by ordering sixty-five men into exile. Many old enemies of the Equals were among the disgraced. In addition to Lazare Carnot, who initiated and guided the case against them, there was former police minister Cochon de l'Apparent, who gathered evidence of the plot; police inspector Jean-Baptiste Dossonville, who arrested Babeuf and Buonarroti; even Boissy d'Anglas, author of the constitution of 1795 that the Equals had so despised. The councils outlawed forty-two right-wing newspapers as well, many of which had condemned the Equals as anarchists throughout the preceding year.[11]

The coup, remembered by the revolutionary date of 18 Fructidor year V (4 September 1797), appeared to nourish the new republican front as democrats and centrists joined their voices in praise. "18 Fructidor! Day of deliverance that avenges crime!" Antonelle crowed. "I salute you!" The Marseilles *Anti-Royalist* damned any who would "call the revolution anarchy," and a newspaper editor in Nancy counseled the government to "never lose from sight . . . that *republicans are your friends and your only friends.*" Avowed anti-Jacobin Benjamin Constant resurrected the language of the Terror to justify the directors' assault on the constitution: "those who do not believe in the rights of the people, must be deprived of them."[12]

The Directory appeared to move left. Laws against émigrés and hostile clergy were resurrected, director Larévellière-Lépeaux recalled radical aspirations by praising republican festivals' capacity to win hearts and minds, and the minister of justice promised to review recent legal judgments to ensure that innocents had not been wrongly convicted. Drouet's old friend in the 500, François Lamarque, even won the promise of an indemnity for prisoners acquitted in Vendôme after their persecution by "bloodthirsty royalists."[13]

The new climate encouraged the Cherbourg exiles. Charles Germain sent a letter to the directors that cheered their victory but warned of continued danger. "And here am I, forced to watch my blood curdle in the horrible shadows of this Bastille when it should be spilled for the beloved cause of liberty! Here am I, forced to watch these vigorous arms wither when they should be raining terrible new blows on liberty's enemies!" He begged to be sent to the front, "to throw myself at the enemies arrayed against us and prove how worthy I was of [their] hatred." When the directors failed to reply, Germain joined Buonarroti, Moroy, and Blondeau in petitioning the legislative councils for review of their case. Using language like Lamarque's, they described themselves as victims of royalism.[14]

The constitutional circles that had been shuttered in midsummer were revived and expanded. Their commitment to a more democratic republic, like the one the Equals defended in Vendôme, was visible in defenses of free speech and free assembly, and efforts to renew political engagement by sharing out newspapers and encouraging talk of public good. Many circles went further still by petitioning officials about abuses, registering new voters or reinscribing old ones purged from the rolls, and encouraging electoral turnout. Their determination to foster a more equitable society was visible in advocacy for public works, progressive taxation, and universal education.[15]

That some circles felt self-conscious allegiance to the democratic Equals they had come to know through the trial was visible in their continuing censure of the high court proceedings and welcome of those who had suffered. Antonelle was once more said to be attending a constitutional circle in the faubourg Antoine. *Free Men* editors René Vatar and Paul Eon joined former juror Gaultier de Biauzat at a circle on the other side of Paris, and Félix Lepeletier, whom Grisel once named as the Equals' banker, belonged to a circle in Versailles. Democratic papers cultivated an Equals martyrology by reporting on the trials for perjury of soldiers Meunier and Barbier, who had disavowed their grand jury statements before the high court, and lamenting the original defendants' suffering. Two editors even appropriated the title *People's Tribune* for their pages, which encouraged democratic enthusiasm and mourned the high court's "illustrious" victims.[16]

In keeping with their embrace of democratic rather than radical Equals, citizens repudiated "perfect equality" as firmly as had Buonarroti, Pache, and every high court defendant but Babeuf. Indeed, some democratic writers deemed the doctrine so pernicious that they sounded like high court prosecutors in denouncing it. "The most certain outcome of community of goods or any system other than that of property," one of them argued, "would be to discourage work, leaving the populace without labor, diplomacy or defense; diminish all productivity[;] and degrade all talent to make nature itself sterile."[17]

Such convictions were genuine. Like Rousseau, like Antonelle, like the Jacobins of 1793, the democrats of '97, '98, and '99 believed that luxury perverted citizens and gross inequality corrupted society. But they were not levelers. At the same time, however, the ferocity of their disavowals suggests how the memory of the Equals was being turned against them. For the tragedy's hopeful first act of republican unity was giving way to an unhappy second act, in which the union crumbled as directors and reactionaries turned against the left.

The first cracks in the façade of republican bonhomie appeared in fall 1797, just days after the Fructidor coup. When the Council of 500 debated exiling defeated "royalists," one of their number suggested that Antonelle and two more high court defendants be included to frustrate the "intrigue" they were surely "taking up at this very moment." Cracks widened in winter, when the indemnity for exonerated prisoners that had sailed through the Council of 500 died in the upper house of the Ancients. At no moment would either council consider the petition from Germain, Buonarroti, and the other Cherbourg exiles, which Réal explained to them by saying, "[T]he legislative assembly hears your names and those of royalism's apostles with equal horror."[18]

Hostility reached more moderate democrats early in 1798, when conservatives accused constitutional circles of stirring up the people, and police closed some down. The Council of 500 shackled the survivors by prohibiting collective petitions. The democratic press, weakened by a stamp tax that had driven small sheets out of business in late summer 1797, took another hit in the winter of '98, when authorities silenced five papers with claims that they encouraged unrest.[19]

The harassment of democrats reached dangerous new heights as legislative elections approached in the spring and the directors began to tamper. Shortly before primary assemblies opened, the directors warned voters against choosing "terrorist" or "royalist" electors, demonizing all challengers to the left or right of a center they unilaterally defined. The next executive circular targeted democrats, in particular, as "disordered spirits, instruments of destruction, fanatical liars whose exaggerated notions and past crimes sow terror among citizens." Recalling reactionary legislative candidates who raised the specter of Babeuf while campaigning in 1797, the directors in 1798 hinted darkly at electoral opponents who looked favorably on "universal leveling."[20]

Centrist Salmists might have stepped up at this point to preserve republican union. They had, after all, joined democrats in celebrating the Fructidor coup and were known as loyal government allies. They might have discouraged the directors' brazen slander of legislative candidates by pointing out that, no matter how lively democrats' criticism, they were fellow republicans.

Instead, the Salmists took the directors' side and bared their teeth.

On the very day the Directory charged that democrats were anarchists and levelers, Salmist Benjamin Constant issued condemnation of his own. Excusing the Jacobins of the Terror as "ardent souls who . . . ceded to an indignation too long contained," he damned the more moderate and far less powerful democrats of 1798 as "minstrels of sedition" and "speculators of massacre." Equating them with the Equals, he dismissed the lot. "[Those] who exaggerate everything, have no opinions; [those] who proscribe property, do not want the republic; [those] who threaten the constitution, do not want liberty; [those] who detest enlightenment, do not want equality." Like the prosecutor Viellart, Constant denied that his opponents possessed genuine convictions. He charged that, devoid of principle, they were driven by greed and ambition. With that dramatic expulsion from the national community, Constant approved in advance whatever the Directory might do against its challengers to the left.[21]

And still, dozens of primary assemblies designated democratic electors for the second round of voting. At best, those men might have seated a vocal legislative minority. Humbling for the Directory, to be sure, but by no means fatal. And yet, having already purged right-wing men who might have provided ballast in the Councils and panicked by early word of primary assembly choices in the capital, the directors meddled further. They warned electors against "partisans eager to overthrow the state" and instructed supporters to secede from legitimate assemblies to choose their own men if they deemed it necessary.[22]

There were stormy debates and noisy secessions across France, but no place saw more trouble than the electoral assembly gathered in the Parisian Oratoire church. In keeping with the capital's status as a radical haven, the Oratoire included many democratic electors, several of whom were former Equals or Equals' associates. Antonelle was there, as was Réal, former juror Gauthier de Biauzat, former defendant Claude Fiquet, old subscribers to the *People's Tribune*, and a handful of men identified in Babeuf's *Papers*, without their knowledge or consent, as "patriots."[23]

The directors used the presence of such men to discredit the entire assembly. A poster entitled *Attempts to Realize Babeuf's System by Means of Elections* named twenty-six electors and the page in the *Papers* that identified them. A "remarks" column labeled Réal, incorrectly, as Babeuf's defender; branded the general Fion, despite his acquittal, as a member of the insurrectional committee; and raised rumors about former high court juror Gaultier de Biauzat to the status of fact by claiming that he had been "Babeuf's protector." The directors promised more information shortly, "because these messieurs, determined to win the elections . . . have allies in every department."[24]

The campaign sowed chaos. Oratoire electors, fearful that democratic deputies would be purged, preferred more moderate candidates with the rationalization that "we must not spoil our chances." Even Antonelle was cowed. Seeing his fellows prepared to put him up for a legislative seat, he begged, "[D]on't do any such thing, you will ruin me."[25]

The Directory's men forced a schism anyway and elected their own candidates.

When the directors learned that democrats had prevailed in other electoral assemblies, they staged a second coup. Moving more quickly than in the preceding year, they pressured the Council of 500 to invalidate elections before deputies could be seated. François Lamarque was among the few who resisted. Demanding respect for voters' choices, he exhorted colleagues to resist a name-calling "dictated by hatred and vengeance." His words fell on deaf ears as deputies turned the name-calling against him, accusing Lamarque of wanting to "admit . . . Babeuf's and Robespierre's men" into their ranks. He resigned before he could be expelled.

The deputies who annulled almost one-third of electors' choices in 1798 continued the assault on rule of law and popular sovereignty that was begun before the Directory's inauguration and continued with the Fructidor coup of 1797. In the wake of the legislative nullifications, police closed more constitutional circles and democratic newspapers.[26]

This coup was known, too, by its revolutionary date: 22 Floréal in the year VI of a dying revolution.

The charge of "Babouvism" was a common excuse for the violations, as is suggested by the slander of Lamarque and the directors' vindication of purge with lurid allusions to men "bathed in blood and carnage, preaching *common good* to enrich themselves on the ruin of all, speaking of equality only to become despots . . . in short, men who were Robespierre's agents before 9 thermidor and . . . Babeuf's acolytes [afterward]."[27]

Why these epithets? Accusing democrats of being Jacobins was incendiary but perhaps understandable. Many 1798 democrats had, after all, once been Jacobins. More to the point, Jacobin deputies had presided over the revolution's most traumatic year, organizing wartime government, subordinating property rights to subsistence, and violating rule of law for reasons both practical and ideological. They had been extravagantly demonized for all that since 9 Thermidor. By 1798, "Jacobinism" was the directors' preferred excuse for the republic's ills.

But what of the charge that democrats were "Babouvists"? Babeuf made a splash after the Directory's inauguration by condemning private property, there were notes among his papers that endorsed violence, and Grisel had repeated compromising conversations to the high court. But the Equals' plot was frustrated without a shot fired, a drop of blood spilled, or a shout raised. And still, the frustrated conspirators were equated with legislators who led France through its greatest crisis in centuries.

Fear explains some comparisons, but not all. Cynical opportunism was the more likely motive. Centrists and reactionaries used the word "Babouvist" to sow panic, disable opponents, and justify their own excesses, exploiting a smear to foreclose talk of political and social equality. Drawing patently false parallels between Robespierre and Babeuf, they insisted that Babeuf's repudiation of private property was the logical outcome of Jacobin social welfare, and claimed that violations during the Terror proved the Equals' aspiration to tyranny. By linking democratic electoral candidates to conspiratorial Equals, the directors cast lawful critics as subversives and slandered their relatively moderate convictions as aspirations to "pillage and violence," "universal happiness," and despotism. It was part and parcel of a process aimed at ending the French Revolution by making politics narrowly exclusive. In 1796, high court prosecutors had attacked the Equals' claims to serve the people by arguing that the only legitimate sites of popular political activism were polling places. With the coups of 1797 and '98, the directors and their legislative allies attacked even that.[28]

The French republic entered the third and final act of its unhappy decline in the spring of 1799. Electors sickened by government corruption and a stagnating economy dismissed the directors' continued warnings against "royalists" and "anarchists" to turn their backs instead on the regime's preferred candidates. This time, the Council of 500 refused to annul their choices. The executives were further disgraced by a cascading series of military defeats for which they were held responsible. A sizeable democratic minority took their seats in the legislative councils, joined with the conservative majority, and forced out two directors.[29]

These events were named the coup of 30 Prairial year VII (18 June 1799). Although equally dangerous, Prairial was distinct from the coups that preceded because, this time, legislators asserted themselves to rein in an abusive executive. Their coalition held in the wake of that act, promising renewal as deputies appointed new ministers, negotiated reform, and addressed France's faltering war effort.

The Councils' energy was matched by a dazzling popular revival in the summer of 1799. It seemed, for a brief moment, that the republic might not only survive but flourish. Democratic newspapers were resurrected, and constitutional circles renewed. Once again, former Equals and their allies played a part. Réal and Antonelle, the editors of the *Free Men*, and René Lebois, formerly of the *People's Friend*, joined three thousand men at the outspoken democratic club of the Manège to endorse free speech and free assembly, and to applaud proposals for progressive taxation, universal education, and public works. Antonelle promoted moderate reform on the pages of the *Free Men*. René Lebois advertised more radical opinions in his *Defender of the Fatherland*.[30]

In this hopeful moment, Antonelle resumed his reflection on republican political life, which had been interrupted by the Equals' arrest in 1796. Popular democracy, he argued, was the best antidote to rising authoritarianism and deepening political apathy. The drafters of the 1795 constitution had been mistaken when they claimed that restricting suffrage was necessary to prevent anarchy. On the contrary, permitting all citizens to vote stabilized a republic by making its governors accountable and encouraging its people to support a nation they saw as their own. Former defendant Félix Lepeletier had suggested that the popular ignorance conservatives feared could be vanquished by education. Antonelle added that suffrage itself was a form of education, giving citizens practical experience of politics, fostering fraternity, encouraging conversation, and enhancing civic commitment.[31]

Antonelle did not, however, consider the restoration of popular democracy sufficient. Troubled by polarization, he returned to the discussion of "faction" and "party" that Jean-Nicolas Pache had initiated in 1797. Like Pache, Antonelle shared the republican conviction that factions endanger a popular regime by promoting oppositional ideologies, fostering "grasping, rebellious, troubled minds that jointly attack an established government's founding principles." Accordingly, "in a civil society like our own . . . whose constitution is founded on equality of rights, a faction can only be vicious because it sustains itself by . . . sowing division within the collective."

"Party" was altogether different. As "an association of dissatisfied citizens" who challenge particular personalities or government action, rather than founding principles, a party could play a "useful, even necessary" role. It might do so by disciplining officials who breached liberty, bringing them back into line before they could do serious harm. If a censured leader answered loyal critics by slandering them, the people must stand firm alongside its true defenders. "Governors are not the government . . . [T]o attack the deceit of the one is not to insult the principles of the other."[32]

Most imaginatively, Antonelle envisioned parties that grew beyond moments of crisis and were integrated into public life. "In every well ordered republic . . . patriots united by the same love of [their] government or . . . its founding principles, may be divided between parties by disagreement about individuals or their governors' acts." However, political disagreement need not be a fight to the death as directors, and radical revolutionaries before them, imagined.. Accepted as the natural outcome of fluid, changing opinion rather than a fatal confrontation between patriotism and deceit, political disagreement could be channeled through parties and peacefully resolved by elections.[33]

It was a powerful defense of representative democracy and a hopeful legitimation of opposition, a forward-looking vision of a stronger, more inclusive polity like the one some republicans were promoting in North America. In France, the promise died on the vine. In late summer 1799, the heady excitement that had inaugurated the republic's third act vanished. Democratic deputies, determined to root out corruption, demanded that the ousted directors be tried. Wishing to overcome military crisis, they campaigned for emergency measures that reminded conservatives of the Terror. In the Manège, a speaker proposed taxing the rich and arming the people, calling on the "illustrious shades of Vendôme" to guarantee justice.[34]

Finding all the excuse they needed in such rhetoric, conservatives turned on their democratic allies with the accusation that they had not changed since the Terror. *Get rid of the Jacobins, no more guillotines . . . no more revolutionary tribunals!* one pamphlet screamed. Another warned of a *conspiracy to overturn the Directory . . . [and] restore the constitution of 1793*, and a third accused resurrected "Babouvists" of plotting with Jacobins and royalists alike. The familiar shuttering of democratic clubs and newspapers resumed.[35]

This was the republic's death rattle. Just as Antonelle had predicted, the most dangerous plot came not from ordinary people defending their sovereignty and material well-being but from elites determined to preserve their own wealth and power. Conservative director Emmanuel Joseph Sieyès, who had joined the executive the preceding spring, led the charge. Convinced that more authoritarian government was necessary to restore peace and prosperity, he conspired for it with about two dozen others. Sieyès's group was roughly similar in size to the Secret Directory and its agents, but it possessed far greater resources. These conspirators had money, influence, powerful allies, and the armed forces that the Equals had always lacked.

Over the course of two days in early November 1799, Sieyès's coterie struck their final blows. He and two other directors stepped down as allies advertised the familiar tale of an imminent Jacobin coup. The Ancients acquiesced to the accompanying demand for exceptional measures with hardly a murmur. When democrats in the 500 objected, Sieyès's fellows charged that this was the very violence they had warned of. With troops at the ready, the conspirators dissolved the Councils and installed three consuls, who included the popular general Napoleon Bonaparte. These events, too, were remembered by their revolutionary date: 18 Brumaire year VIII (9 November 1799).[36]

The republic was not formally abolished until 1804, but the Brumaire coup marked a defeat for which the Directory had long prepared the ground. Napoleon would elevate himself over the other consuls, posing as the revolution's defender. The Consulate, and the Empire that followed, would postpone restoration of the French monarchy for almost a generation, but at what cost? That achievement pales in comparison to all they swept away: free press, free assembly, habeas corpus, popular sovereignty. If the Directory's legacy was indifference to rule of law, that inheritance was visible in the Consulate's response to an attempt on Napoleon's life in 1800.

Following the explosion of an "infernal machine" that missed Napoleon but killed eight others, police opened their archives on "irreconcilable enemies of the government" to hunt down suspects. They arrested almost six hundred democrats in Paris alone, many of them old Equals or Equals' allies. One hundred thirty people were deported without trial and before the investigation was complete. When police proved shortly afterward that royalists had been responsible for the attack, no effort was made to recall the innocents being borne across the Atlantic and Indian oceans. Most of them died in far-flung colonies, thousands of miles from family, friends, and home, destroyed like the republic for which they had sacrificed so much. It was a bitter end to a decade inaugurated with such high hopes of liberty and equality.[37]

FIFTEEN

Buonarroti's Gospel

Thirty-eight men and women were released from Vendôme's Trinity Abbey in May 1797 to resume lives ruptured by arrest, imprisonment, and trial. Many had long since lost their jobs. Some found their homes stripped, contents sold to support families and ease the costs of detention. Clothes were moth-eaten, properties fallen into disrepair, spouses dead.

Pierre Fossard, whose offense had been to share copies of the *Tribune* with friends, could not return to Cherbourg after he broke his leg because he was too poor to hire a carriage. Sophie Lapierre and Adelaide Lambert were destitute. Perhaps poor, bullied Nicolas Pillé made a long-hoped-for move to Saint-Malo to care for his mother. Maybe his protector, Pierre Philip, realized a despairing wish to "live far from every sort of politics" because his name vanishes from police archives.[1]

In Paris, Antoine Guilhem, tried in absentia by the high court and defended there by Charles Germain, attempted to repay his exiled friend's loyalty with a steady stream of letters he wrote with his wife Julienne and their friend Janette Ponser. But the good intentions were complicated by Germain's feelings for Janette, which she did not share because she and the "handsome Guilhem" had become lovers. "He had my virginity . . . and while you know that no one sleeps together just once, it's only the first time that counts . . . His wife is not jealous and we get along as best we can. I am convinced that you look like him," she told the isolated man, adding with blind naïveté, "and that you are not jealous either."[2]

Few defendants ever fully put the affair behind them. Even those who had nothing to do with the plot—and they were in the majority—suffered for having been labeled extremists. In a nation whose mighty crowds had already been dispersed and whose newspapers and political associations would be silenced by century's end, such people became the "usual suspects," their commitments to liberty and equality repaid with harassment, purge, and prison stays that stole more of their precious days. If the growing isolation of some exposed them to persecution, the growing sophistication of others anticipated secret societies and public activism that descendants would build in the next century.[3]

The precarious condition of men and women once identified as Equals became painfully clear during the last great assault on revolutionary democrats: the hunt for suspects that followed the assassination attempt on Napoleon in December 1800. Police assumed democrats were responsible for the "infernal machine" that exploded in a Paris street because they "never stop complaining about despotism [and] the loss of liberty." Hundreds of suspects were arrested, and, within weeks, legislators ordered transport without trial for 130 of them. Among the exiles were at least sixteen high court defendants and several old allies. They included former general Jean-Antoine Rossignol and retired deputy Jean-François Ricord, both of whom had probably conspired but were legally acquitted. Mathurin Bouin, condemned by the high court in absentia, was part of the cohort, as was Jacques Cordas, apparently sent before the high court because the Equals jotted his name onto a page in Babeuf's *Papers*. There was poor, hapless François Dufour, whose crime had been to welcome Drouet and his associates for a simple lunch of fresh radishes on the day police descended in 1796. All but Ricord died thousands of miles from their homes and families.[4]

The defiant printer Théodore Lamberté, who so passionately defended free press before the high court, escaped a penal colony in Cayenne and made it to New Orleans, where he became a printer once more. *Free Men* editors René Vatar and Paul Eon were not so fortunate, nor was R.-F. Lebois, whose name had long appeared on the masthead of the *People's Friend*. Those three died in exile.[5]

Charles Germain was sent to Guiana in 1802 and escaped by signing on with French pirates. When taken prisoner by the British, he was said to have preached republicanism among them until freed and returned to France in

1814. After that, he vanishes from history as abruptly as he had entered with his letter to Babeuf in 1795.[6]

Pierre-Nicolas Hésine flourished until the empire's end in 1815. After that, the restored monarchy's police pursued republicans whom Napoleonic officials had missed. They accused the aging journalist of "revolutionary excesses," "ill humor," and exercising a "dangerous influence . . . over a certain class," and gave him two weeks to leave home and business in Vendôme. Hésine died isolated and penniless in Rouen. Of his intrepid partner, Marie-Agathe Hénault, no word remains.[7]

P.-A. Antonelle retreated to his native Arles after the brilliant summer of 1799 to "cultivate his garden" by easing local poverty. When he died in 1817, clerics refused to ring bells for the old anti-Catholic, which raised a "general cry" from mourners in the street: *Is this how one treats a father to the poor?*" An onlooker later recalled that "many unfortunates lamented the passing of their benefactor with tears in their eyes and loudly prayed for divine mercy on him, in striking contrast to the chilly reserve of the priest who, against all usual practice, read a prayer so quietly that no one could hear it. An even more scandalous scene awaited at the church: not one lighted candle." There, "the crowd's agitation reached its peak. I feared an explosion any minute from the assembled people offended by such proceedings."[8]

So the impress of revolution lingered, exposing many of those who had been associated with the Equals' trial to further suspicion, exclusion, imprisonment. Two managed to rise above the distrust. The very different trajectories of Pierre-François Réal, who amputated himself from the conspirators, and Filippo Buonarroti, who glorified his status as one of them, suggest how revolutionary hopes were betrayed and reconfigured in the next century.

Pierre-François Réal, who had declared himself the Equals' "national defender" in Vendôme, renewed his fortune with the kind of speculative practices Babeuf once deplored: he became a military contractor. But his political dissatisfaction deepened. Although the directors spoiled democrats' electoral chances in 1798, Réal blamed his old allies in a way that suggests how persecution pits activists against one another. Claiming that former Equals in the Oratoire assembly had "prefer[red] their accomplices to their defenders," he mined a rich vein of self-pity. "Equally stung by reactionary bigots who consider me a terrorist and patriotic bigots who shun me as a counter-revolutionary," he vowed to live "without seeing one or the other."[9]

Réal turned to Napoleon, pushed by his own frustration and pulled by the latter's military success. "The floundering republic has lived on your victories for two long years," he complained to the general in 1798, "and, I swear, even today, men of principle drowning in this noisy unconstitutional chaos, borrow against your future successes." Réal so admired Napoleon that he joined the plot to install him as consul in 1799. In following years, he was rewarded with administrative appointments, a seat on the Council of State, and, ultimately, a title.[10]

Perhaps the man who became the Count Réal did not see his alliance with Napoleon as a compromise of principle. He might have defended himself by pointing out that he objected when democrats were accused of responsibility for the "infernal machine," and even led the investigation that exonerated them. Years later, he challenged Napoleon's proposal for a Legion of Honor, which many feared would restore the nobility, and protested a motion to enhance censorship. But, having voiced his reservations, Réal stood aside. He not only acquiesced to the Legion of Honor but accepted a place on it, and he abandoned his commitment to free speech with the specious argument that censorship might be considered acceptable if submitted to "voluntarily."[11]

Those who knew Réal claimed that "the Jacobin in him disappeared by leaps and bounds" after he joined Napoleon's Council of State. Perhaps this is how he became the sort of man who not only endorsed censorship but complained that "the common people have never been properly put in their place!" Was that a complaint long harbored? Had Réal's defense of the Equals expressed genuine conviction, or was it just one more ambitious gesture by an ambitious man?[12]

The former lawyer was not alone, of course, in presiding over liberty's corruption. Other democrats served Napoleon, believing they could ameliorate his government's tyranny, or searching for wealth and power, or seeking outlet for frustrated political energies. Unable or unwilling to effect a new revolution, they served the regime that defeated the republic and enhanced the lie that it had done so for the nation's good.[13]

Philippe-Auguste Jeanron, *Portrait of Filippo Buonarroti,*
n.d. The Picture Art Collection / Alamy Stock Photo.

Réal may have turned to Napoleon in despair at the Directory's flagrant
violation of its own constitution. He might have stayed out of loyalty or ambition or greed. It is possible he even believed he did some good. But he cannot
have been innocent of the cost. This once principled man, who challenged
Robespierre, directors, prosecutors, and high court judges, who defended free
expression and rule of law, finally gave his loyalty to a government that exiled
innocents, resurrected arbitrary imprisonment, repudiated popular sovereignty, and assaulted civil liberties. Whom or what did Réal serve other than
himself?

Filippo Buonarroti knew quite well what he served. Having abandoned
family, fortune, and birthplace for the French Revolution, he spent the rest
of his life defending it.

After years of internal exile, Buonarroti settled under supervised residence in Geneva in 1806. He renewed his activism by creating secret societies that only revealed their communist aims to the most trusted members, leaving the rest to believe they were organizing for democracy. He reached beyond Geneva through an elaborate network of correspondents that he sustained for years until his own carelessness exposed them. As happened in 1796, it was an archive that proved his undoing. Buonarroti sent sensitive documents across the Swiss border with a youthful protégé who fell into police hands, costing the courier ten years in prison and earning the aging activist expulsion from Geneva.[14]

Buonarroti arrived in Brussels in 1824, at the age of sixty-three, to find a homecoming among revolutionaries exiled by restoration of the monarchy in France. He renewed his friendship with Marc Vadier, a fellow inmate from Vendôme and Cherbourg, and socialized with retired legislators willing to overlook his undying radicalism. The exiles gathered in local cafés and strolled through the city's central park, talking of the world they had tried to create and the one that came into being. Retreating to the silence of homes and libraries, they wrote memoirs to explain their revolutionary choices before it was too late. Buonarroti joined them in putting pen to paper.[15]

> Shortly before we were condemned, I made a promise to Babeuf and Darthé from the benches of the high court in Vendôme, in the shadow of the aristocratic blade that was to strike them down. I promised to avenge their memory by publishing an exact account of our collective project, which factions have so strangely misrepresented. As I near the end of my life, I must acquit myself of that debt.[16]

Almost all of the Equals were dead. Old age was pressing in. Buonarroti looked back across three decades to place the conspiracy of Equals at the heart of the French Revolution. Offering up his greatest secret, this perennial intriguer disavowed the claims of innocence he had so doggedly defended in Vendôme. The Equals had conspired against the Directory, he told the world. They had been on the eve of realizing the French Revolution's true aim, "perfect equality," when they were betrayed and arrested.

Promising to preserve that frustrated project for future generations, Buonarroti crafted the gospel that would shape how Babeuf and the Equals were remembered for almost two centuries.

Babeuf's Conspiracy for Equality consists of three parts. The first narrates a history of revolution and conspiracy that identifies the Equals as the Jacobins' political heirs. The second takes Babeuf's notion of "perfect equality" as the foundation for an elaborate communist utopia. The third offers evidence for the first two by reprinting pamphlets, posters, and private papers originally published in 1796.

According to Buonarroti's history, a "party of equality" emerged in 1789 to realize the French Revolution's greatest deeds. Inspired by philosophical principles, that party was composed of Jacobins, who Buonarroti identified as the Equals' predecessors. Those Jacobins fought a vast "order of egoism," unmasking plots and rallying patriots to reach the victory of 31 May 1793, when the Girondins were expelled from the National Convention. Then, Buonarroti explained, Robespierre, Saint-Just, and their allies could prepare for a "new order in the distribution of goods and duties."

Admitting that the constitution of 1793, adopted under this leadership, contained "old, desperate ideas about the right of property," Buonarroti speculated that the Jacobins had been trying to mislead enemies about their true purpose. But the constitution was, he added, forthright in giving democracy to the people. Metamorphosis ensued. "Men who were once pleasure-seeking, greedy, superficial, and arrogant readily renounced a thousand foolish pleasures to offer their comforts at the homeland's altar, mass against royal armies and demand nothing more than bread, iron, and equality." The new order was within reach when "false friends of equality" destroyed its champions on 9 Thermidor.[17]

All might have been lost had not Robespierre's heirs rallied, ultimately to become Equals. They organized all opposition to the Directory, Buonarroti claimed fantastically, rousing democrats, organizing the Pantheon Club, and inspiring "every true republican" to plot. When police closed the Pantheon Club, they "resume[d] the work interrupted by 9 Thermidor" by conspiring for a revolution "whose final result would be equal distribution of knowledge and goods." They had the support of thousands, but, like the Jacobins before them, were betrayed.[18]

This is a history of a narrow, coherent, far-seeing elite. Sweeping aside the activism of Picard peasants, Parisian sans-culottes, independent militants like Babeuf, and millions like them who fought for liberty in ways large and small, Buonarroti depicted the French Revolution as a Jacobin achievement. Robespierre and his followers, he argued, understood what was necessary and fought for it on two fronts, opposing an aristocracy of "egoism" and educating the masses about rights they would not otherwise have recognized.[19]

The old conspirator's account of the plot in which he shared is equally narrow. By describing the Equals as descendants of the Jacobins, he denied the originality of the former and vastly inflated the radicalism of the latter but succeeded in positioning his cohort among the revolutionary greats. By claiming that the Equals singlehandedly mobilized democratic opposition after 1795, he obscured their disarray and isolation. By dismissing the remarkable range of democratic opinion that flourished in the revolution's final years, he insisted that the Equals alone could have saved the republic and, even then, only through insurrection.

In many ways, Buonarroti agreed with what the directors had claimed in 1796. Like them, he depicted the Equals as Jacobins reborn who defined the alpha and omega of democratic activism, and who might have toppled the government were it not for Grisel's betrayal. If these claims were true, then so, too, were the Directory's. For if the Equals had fifteen thousand eager followers, as Buonarroti said, the panic that followed Babeuf's arrest was neither overreach nor purge, but the rational response of a regime under existential threat. If every "true republican" was conspiring against the Directory, then the executives were right in 1796 to condemn democrats' skepticism about the plot as subversive and, in later years, to denounce left-wing electoral challengers as seditious.

In sum, Buonarroti agreed with the vanished directors that the republic's abject end was caused not by the government's violations of constitution and revolutionary principle but by the nation's inability to reconcile. Refusing the reform, renewal, and accommodation counseled by thinkers like

Thomas Paine, J.-N. Pache, and, above all, P.-A. Antonelle, Buonarroti agreed with the directors that the republic would not be sustained by sound institutions and popular democracy, but could only be redeemed by elites.

Unsurprisingly, Buonarroti's account of the trial was an afterthought. Because he cast the Equals as the sole moving force of opposition or critique from the moment of the Directory's inauguration, there was no need to explain how the trial bestowed celebrity. Because he denied other currents of democratic thought, there was no need to explain how the Equals redefined themselves before the high court, casting off their status as revolutionary opponents of property to become peaceful defenders of civil liberties and popular democracy. *The Conspiracy* reduced the complex process that unfolded in and beyond Vendôme, and its prolonged aftermath, to a simple decision by the defendants to deny their conspiracy in court in order to save everyone.

When he turned to the doctrine of perfect equality, Buonarroti quickly summarized Babeuf's central idea. "The mass of people have never reached the degree of instruction or independence necessary to exercise political rights essential for their liberty, conservation, and happiness," because private property permits "the clever and fortunate" to plunder them. A just society would preserve all members' well-being by compensating for the advantages of the "clever and fortunate" and eradicating the inequality that accumulates from generation to generation. It would do so by replacing private property with "community of goods and labor," to banish oppression forever.[20]

This was an overview of the *Statement of Babeuf's Doctrine* that the Equals had published on handbills shortly before their arrest, and which Buonarroti reprinted at the end of his book. Original and gloss were sketches of principle, stripped of the rich allusions to revolutionary conditions with which Babeuf defended them in his *People's Tribune* and before the high court. When Buonarroti elaborated on that principle, he did so without looking to Babeuf and the revolutionary past. Instead, he conjured up an idealized future with a claim that this was what the conspirators themselves had defined.

The Equals expected cities to vanish, he said, leaving a nation of small villages where sound country ways replaced urban corruption. Almost every feature of daily life would change. Citizens would be trained for particular jobs, according to talents, inclinations, gender, and the nation's needs. Simplicity in housing, clothing, and furnishings would foster a collective sense of equality, and imposing architecture would be reserved to public buildings. Boys would be armed and trained for national defense, girls readied for motherhood and domestic life. Everyone would gather regularly for the instruction, festivals, entertainment, and worship that would "give solid foundation to liberty and steadily improve customs, rendering the French happy, united, beloved, respected, and invincible."[21]

This account did not just extend Babeuf's writing about what was to come but fundamentally reshaped his thought. Babeuf had gone well beyond the utopian dream of equality by formulating a concrete plan to realize it, informed by revolutionary experience. Buonarroti began with Babeuf's practical aspirations and returned to the utopia of a perfect world. Babeuf envisioned redistribution that would serve people, rural and urban alike, using storehouses to share resources between city and countryside, civilian and soldier, as the Jacobins had done in 1793–94. Buonarroti rejected the industrialization and urbanization he had witnessed in his own lifetime for a preindustrial idyll like the one the philosopher Rousseau had counseled decades before the Revolution.[22]

Most troubling, Buonarroti repudiated the popular democracy that Babeuf held so dear. Although *The Conspiracy* pays lip service to political equality, it assigns a great many overseers to the people. A small body of militants would supervise legislators, Buonarroti promised; magistrates would instill love of "common good" in the debased citizenry, and "ancients" would insure that the people made wise political decisions. Security, defense, and subsistence would be supervised by a "long chain" of magistrates who implemented orders descending from on high, rather than by citizens organized to remake the nation from below, as Babeuf once imagined. A cult of the Supreme Being would keep everyone in line by threatening judgment of "thoughts and . . . secret actions that the law cannot reach." *The Conspiracy* even denied the free speech Babeuf thought indispensable to protect against abuses of power. "No one," Buonarroti intoned, "may express opinions contrary to the sacred principles of equality and popular sovereignty."[23]

Despite Buonarroti's promise of universal liberation, it is difficult to see how that was to arrive. His *Conspiracy* leaves no room for popular initiative and gives no hint that citizens' supervisors might require citizens' supervision. Instead, it describes an egalitarian future that marches in step with Buonarroti's history of the revolutionary past by celebrating heroic leaders who know better what the people needs than does the people itself.

The parting of ways between Babeuf and Buonarroti was rooted in their different experiences of the world and particular philosophical inclinations. As a poor man, a political outsider, and a careful reader of the classical republican Mably, Babeuf had a robust suspicion of "humanity's enduring penchant for domination." His conviction that the people could overcome domination was nourished in the revolution's early years by collective action that won extraordinary concessions from the powerful. As crowds ebbed and citizens retreated, Babeuf looked more favorably on revolutionary elites. He identified himself as one of Mably's sentinels and justified revolutionary government as "fiendishly clever." But that last statement came late and at a particularly hard moment in his life, making it difficult to know how much he would have approved the far-reaching elite Buonarroti imagined decades later.[24]

As a former administrator, lifelong Jacobin, and partisan of an Enlightenment suspiciousness of popular ignorance, Buonarroti feared ordinary citizens' vulnerability to deceit far more than he worried about the ambitions of the powerful. Having outlived Babeuf by decades, he witnessed deepening repression and popular apathy that can only have confirmed his conviction that a narrow elite must drive change. In this, Buonarroti once more aligned himself with political thinkers to his right, dismissing, along with Boissy d'Anglas and the high court prosecutors, the conviction of men like Babeuf and Antonelle that political liberty and social equality are necessarily joined.[25]

Buonarroti's *Conspiracy* was an equivocal achievement. It guaranteed the enduring memory of Gracchus Babeuf, but in terms the subject might have been hard pressed to recognize. And it reinscribed inequality like that which Babeuf had confronted in his own lifetime. For just as Buonarroti once joined fellow insider Antonelle in persuading Babeuf to disavow the Equals' conspiracy on a national stage, so his book buried the radicalizing experience of a poor man and popular militant beneath a revolution imagined by philosophers and carried out by a political elite. Indeed, its original title—*The Conspiracy for Equality, known as Babeuf's*—speaks volumes. Buonarroti described the conspiracy as he wished it had been, appending Babeuf as a remembered martyr to the cause.

Buonarroti's *Conspiracy* was published in Brussels in 1828, published again in France in 1830, translated into English, and published yet again in 1836. That was just the beginning. It was published in four abridged French editions over the next three decades, translated and published in German, Russian, Chinese, and in another full French edition in the next century. At least four more editions of the book appeared in the first twenty years of the twenty-first century.[26]

Readers accepted the book then, and often now, as a faithful account. "Until its appearance," an old democrat marveled, "I believed the conspiracy to have been, like so much else, a figment of the Directory's imagination." The activist Bronterre O'Brien explained his decision to translate it into English by calling it "the most luminous and correct estimate to be found in any language of the leading men and events of the great French Revolution." The *Quarterly Review* of 1831 thought the book "trustworthy in all its statements," adding that "[Buonarroti] is perfectly explicit . . . about the object at which he aimed and the means by which [the conspiracy] was to be realized."[27]

It was remarkable trust to accord the man who admitted organizing the charade of innocence before the high court and created secret societies that withheld their true aims from their own members. But Buonarroti's framing of *The Conspiracy* inspired confidence. He affirmed the directors' claims, produced a history that agreed with contemporaries in depicting the revolution as the work of elites, and offered documents from the past to sustain his account. Finally, he promised that the evidence he published was enhanced by his own memory and by private notes long hidden. To read *The Conspiracy* was to be in on a momentous secret.

The importance of that secret endured. *The Conspiracy* was among the first histories to celebrate radical republican aspirations to a generation raised on the exaltation of revolutionary liberalism. Its account of the Equals' aims and methods, even in corrupted form, inspired argument and emulation across the nineteenth century. Most significantly, Buonarroti sent word of this first attempt to bring communism into being to the most important modern theorists of the idea: Karl Marx and Friedrich Engels. With that, he wove Babeuf into debates that would endure to the end of the next century.[28]

Buonarroti returned to France after the Revolution of 1830 and was welcomed by activists as a militant theorist, living link to the great Revolution of 1789, and the charmer he had always been. When he died in 1837, at the age of seventy-seven, fifteen hundred democrats attended the funeral in Paris, where a speaker promised that future generations would celebrate this last revolutionary.[29]

The prediction was borne out. As surging industrialization encouraged workers in the 1840s to combat the vicious inequities plaguing them, many embraced communism. Known as "neo-Babouvists," they understood—as Babeuf and Buonarroti had not—that industrialization might improve their material conditions but were embittered by their exploitation and deprivation amid growing plenty. Like Babeuf, Buonarroti, Germain, and Darthé in 1796, the neo-Babouvists of the 1840s hoped to revive a democratic republic and replace private property with community of goods. They promoted those ideas in workers' organizations, published them in newspapers, and joined public debate, feeding the political effervescence that would generate a new revolution and produce a new republic in 1848.[30]

This was the Paris to which Karl Marx came in 1843, a city bubbling with left-wing talk, worker activism, and lively camaraderie. As he researched the French Revolution for a book he would never write, coordinated with editors of working-class papers, and attended political meetings, Marx absorbed French radicalism past and present. He met Friedrich Engels for the first time and, during his eighteen months in the French capital, experienced an intellectual radicalization that fostered notions of communism he would spend the rest of his life working out.[31]

As Marx watched French workers eating, drinking, and talking together, he came to believe that "the brotherhood of man is no mere phrase with them, but a fact of life." To explore that brotherhood and address the material conditions associated with it, Marx married philosophical reflection to the historical study of economy and society. He would come to argue that capitalism creates alienation by transforming labor, which ought to be an expression of self, into repetitive acts performed for wages, and by dividing workers with the myth that competition is more natural than cooperation. Communism, he believed, could heal sicknesses of self and society by abolishing class exploitation and market exchange, guaranteeing rights and freedom to all.[32]

It is tempting to identify Babeuf and Buonarroti as the source of these ideas. After all, Marx met French neo-Babouvists and their German counterparts during his transformative time in Paris, and he and Engels would soon praise the conspiracy of Equals for "giving rise to the communist idea." They even considered translating *The Conspiracy* into German and publishing it. But admiration is not emulation. The relationship of the founding fathers of modern socialism to their revolutionary forebears is less direct.[33]

Marx formulated a very different notion of revolution than Buonarroti had advertised, rejecting elites' seizure of state power and gift of truth to backward masses. He envisioned, instead, a proletariat that transforms itself through political struggle. "Revolution is necessary," he and Engels argued, "not only because the ruling class cannot be overthrown in any other way, but also because the class overthrowing it can only in a revolution succeed in ridding itself of all the muck of ages and become fitted to found society anew."[34]

If Marx was closer to Babeuf in the rejection of a revolutionary elite, he remained fundamentally distinct from the tribune in his conception of the historical nature of class struggle. By 1795, Babeuf believed it possible to eliminate poverty and preserve the republic by channeling what remained of revolutionary energy into a fight for democracy and against private property. He thought the people had all it needed and must exploit that before the moment passed, for, he warned, there was no knowing when another opportunity might arise. Marx, in contrast, thought Babeuf's failure inevitable because communist revolution could not succeed without a mature proletariat. For that, decades of industrialization and class formation would be necessary. Babeuf may have pointed the way toward the future, Marx and Engels concluded, but he could do no more than that.

Nonetheless, Marx and Engels's claim that the conspiracy of Equals "gave rise to the communist idea" excited decades of reflection. Historians, political theorists, and activists returned regularly to the conspiracy, debating the practical and philosophical origins of Babeuf's communism, the social structures he faced, how he defined class and revolutionary leadership. All too often, they took Buonarroti's book as gospel, confusing the ideas of the chronicler for those of his subject. More troubling still, they missed the particularity of Babeuf's role in the French Revolution. By making his story exclusively one of communist conspiracy, they missed all that the tribune's life revealed about popular revolution and how republics live and die.[35]

Conclusion

Gracchus Babeuf was both unique and exemplary. Introspective, articulate, and determined, he could not have achieved all that he did without the French Revolution. He might have ensured modest comforts to his family and perhaps indulged more utopian ideas like those he shared with the academician Dubois de Fosseux, but it is difficult to imagine this poor provincial rising far through the rigid hierarchies of the Old Regime. The French Revolution liberated him, like millions of others, by encouraging new thinking, offering new opportunity, and giving new respectability to men and women long marginalized by the hazards of birth. As excitement blossomed among citizens liberated to remake themselves and their world, Babeuf fought alongside provincials for fairer taxation and access to land, served in public office, helped guarantee food to his fellow citizens, published pamphlets and newspapers, formulated radical notions of social and political equality.

But the change that Babeuf and the rest of the nation witnessed after 1789 was as frightening as it was exciting. Men and woman who had monopolized land, wealth, and honor for centuries were threatened by redistribution. Citizens who hoped for moderate reform were angered by their fellows' demands for greater change. In a nation uncertain about how to administer new rights and negotiate new conflicts amid breathtaking upheaval, there were bitter disputes and violence. As Buonarroti asked the high court in 1797, "can we imagine that the many errors, biases, and barbaric institutions that overwhelm . . . most men could be attacked without agitation, clamor, resistance?" The opposition between enthusiasm and fear became a confrontation between change and resistance, radicalizing and polarizing the revolution. By 1795, it was not at all clear how France was to move forward.[1]

The Directory, it was hoped, would stabilize the republic by ending the revolution. Its architects might have done so by restoring the democratic constitution they had adopted and immediately suspended in 1793. A restored democratic constitution might have consolidated liberty and equality by redirecting citizens from insurgency to peaceful political engagement, giving them a material stake in the nation by guaranteeing food and work, and enhancing public life through broad suffrage, universal education, civic associations, and a lively press. But, by 1795, fear had gained the upper hand. So Boissy d'Anglas and his colleagues swept away the existing constitution to create one more to their liking. Rather than integrating the people securely into republican political life and rebuilding collectively, these legislators imposed a narrow regime that marginalized citizens at its outset and continued to do so with growing force.

The new constitution initially seemed to win peace by reserving power to a cautious elite. But denying representation sowed discontent and, ultimately, radicalization. Without suffrage or firm rights of free speech, assembly, and petition, citizens who lacked money and status had no way to make their opinions known. Without free primary education, the requirement of literacy for suffrage created formidable obstacles to voting. Without the guarantee of a right to subsistence, popular demands for work and affordable food could be disregarded even when starvation threatened. Against that background, the closing of the Pantheon Club in spring 1796 was the last straw for the radicals who organized themselves as conspiratorial Equals. By withdrawing a vitally important arena of public discussion, the Directory drove its most determined critics underground. On that, at least, the documents of the day and Buonarroti agree.

Even then, the regime might have healed the breach it had opened by more honestly assessing the danger these isolated militants posed and by respecting its own promise never to "criminalize the opinions of the misguided . . . [or] allow lists drawn up by a few conspirators to become lists of proscription." Instead, the regime inflated the nation's threat, using that excuse to harry old democrats and condemn allies who raised questions. By attacking such people, the Directory consolidated them and offered the Equals new opportunity.[2]

If the Directory's origins and its pursuit of the Equals underscore elites' determination to preserve wealth and political power for themselves, the high court trial in Vendôme highlights the malleability of resistance. Undeniably, Babeuf's high court denial of conspiracy and the dream of perfect equality cost him dearly. But the redefinition that Antonelle and Buonarroti proposed in Vendôme—the Equals as peaceful advocates for free speech, free assembly, and universal education against a narrowly exclusive regime—renewed moderate democrats' pride in republican egalitarianism and encouraged their search for new ways to foster liberalization.

Rejecting conspiracy, direct democracy, and communism, the democrats of 1798 and 1799 encouraged modest political engagement by creating constitutional circles, attempting to broaden suffrage, promoting formal and informal means of education, and advocating for modest social welfare. Had they faced a regime prepared to abide by rule of law, they might have evolved into the kind of political party Antonelle imagined, one capable of sharing power, liberalizing politics, and enhancing equity not just to stabilize the republic but to strengthen it. Such innovation might have foreclosed the violence that wasted so many lives across the nineteenth century. It might have saved still more by sharing out property and power with greater equity, to enhance the social, political, and intellectual conditions of all sorts of working people and foster the sense of belonging that would, as P.-A. Antonelle and Tom Paine promised, nourish their commitment to the republic.

But the directors and their reactionary allies were too enamored of their own power, too determined to safeguard their wealth, too fearful of the people, and too horrified by a past they had been unable to control to build on the French Revolution's promise. Depicting much of that revolution as an awful mistake, they used the conspiracy of Equals to insist that popular democracy did not strengthen but threatened the republic.

The pitiful end that came in 1799, when directors and deputies abandoned the republic, is unsurprising given all that preceded. The French

Revolution established one of the modern world's first republics and its first popular democracy, but it also proved how easily both may be shattered. In just four years, the Directory violated its constitution time and time again, building steadily from abridging civil liberties to interfering in elections and, finally, staging coups. The last of those coups, 18 Brumaire, was the French Revolution's final tragedy, which stands as potent reminder of the fragile nature of all republics. They depend on laws and institutions that are, paradoxically, both stable and flexible. They require governors who operate honestly and with an eye to the public good. And they demand an informed, engaged citizenry. As Babeuf's beloved Mably and other classical republicans like him had long argued, republics cannot survive without perpetual vigilance. But however difficult they may be to sustain, no other form of governance has shown such potential to serve so many, so fairly.

Historians have argued that France's first republic fell in 1799 because the nation was unable to overcome the experience of the Terror or because its European wars posed insurmountable challenges. The trial of the Equals and its effects, which rippled geographically outward from Vendôme and temporally forward from 1797, suggest that the republic failed because directors, legislators, and their reactionary allies were determined to reverse the Revolution's empowerment of millions of new citizens.[3]

Babeuf's melancholy farewell was prescient. "Dying for my homeland . . . would be easier if I did not [foresee] the destruction of liberty and the prohibition of everything true republicans hold dear." And yet, like the Directory's pursuit of the Equals, its devastation of the republic illuminates the enduring versatility of resistance. Buonarroti's *Conspiracy* may have reshaped the French Revolution and the conspiracy of Equals to reflect his vision of history and society. But his book also succeeded in preserving aims that others reconfigured to defend liberty, equality, and fraternity against regimes determined to restrict the franchise, aggressively defend property rights, and encourage capitalism regardless of the cost to those whose labor produces its wealth.[4]

Might the conspiracy of Equals have succeeded under different circumstances? Might the Equals have managed to create a world of perfect equality? That is difficult to believe. Babeuf's economic radicalism was far beyond what most of his contemporaries were likely to have embraced. That is not to suggest, however, that his vision was pointless or his radicalism nihilistic. Fostered by exclusion and repression, his ideas defined new horizons of change. If those horizons exceeded the flexibility, negotiation, and compromise that complex societies require, Babeuf and the rest of the Equals fostered new aspirations for equity and encouraged new struggle to win it.

The tribune believed he had nothing to bequeath because he could not imagine how generations to come would bear the oppression he saw approaching. But by fusing his experience of poverty, exclusion, and militancy with hard-won education to imagine a more equitable world, he galvanized others and lent singular voice to a chorus that continues to demand liberation from grinding poverty, political exclusion, and the disdain of difference. With millions of others, he experienced the transformation of consciousness that Marx and Engels would speak of decades later, throwing off the "muck of ages" to demand a society that nourishes and respects all its members.

ABBREVIATIONS

AHRF   *Annales historiques de la Révolution française*

AN   Archives nationales

BN   Bibliothèque nationale

Débats   *Débats du procès instruit par la haute cour de justice, contre Drouet, Baboeuf et autres* (Paris: Baudouin, 1797)

JDHL   *Journal des hommes libres de tous les pays, ou le Républicain* ([Paris]: [R. Vatar], [1793–98])

JHC   *Journal de la Haute-Cour de justice; ou l'Écho des hommes libres, vrais et sensibles*, par Hésine (facsimile [Paris: Edhis, 1966])

JLP   *Journal de la liberté de la presse* ([Paris]; L'Imprimerie Guffroy, [1794])

PS   Haute Cour de Justice, *Copie des pièces saisies dans le local que Babœuf occupoit lors de son arrestation* (Paris: Imprimerie nationale, Nivôse an V [1796–1797]), 2 vols.

TDP   *Le Tribun du peuple, ou le Défenseur des droits de l'homme*; en continuation du *Journal de la liberté de la presse*, par Gracchus Babeuf ([Paris]: [1794–96])

Introduction

1. Report by Dossonville (21 Floréal V), AN, F7 4278, dossier 4; Directoire Executif, *Le Directoire Executif aux Citoyens de Paris* (Imprimerie du Directoire Executif, an IV); R. B. Rose, *Gracchus Babeuf: The First Revolutionary Communist* (Stanford: Stanford University Press, 1978), 271–72; *L'ami des lois* (23 Floréal IV); *Le Rédacteur* (22 Floréal IV).

2. Karl Marx and Friedrich Engels, *The Holy Family*, chap. 6, 3c, "Critical Battle against the French Revolution," https://www.marxists.org/archive/marx/works/1845/holy-family/ch06_3_c.htm; Jean Bruhat, "La Révolution française et la formation de la pensée de Marx," *AHRF* 38, no. 184 (1966): 125–70, at 160.

3. It is difficult to do justice to the riches of Babeuf scholarship in a single note. Key accounts of the conspiracy, its ideas, and its impact include the following: Georges Lefebvre, "Les origines du communisme de Babeuf," in *Études sur la Révolution Française* (Paris: Presses universitaires de France, 1954), 305–14; Claude Mazauric, *Babeuf et la Conspiration pour l'Egalité* (Paris: Éditions sociales, 1962); Maurice Dommanget, *Sur Babeuf et la conjuration des égaux* (Paris: Maspero, 1970); *Babeuf et les problèmes du Babouvisme: Colloque international de Stockholm* (Paris: Éditions sociales, 1963); Alain Maillard, Claude Mazauric, and Eric Walter, eds., *Présence de Babeuf: Lumières, Révolution, Communisme* (Paris: Publications de la Sorbonne, 1994); Jean-Marc Schiappa, *Gracchus Babeuf avec les Egaux* (Paris: Publications de la Sorbonne, 1991). Foremost biographies are Rose, *Gracchus Babeuf*; and V. M. Daline, *Gracchus Babeuf à la veille et pendant la Révolution française, 1785–1794*, trans. (from Russian) Jean Champenois (Moscow: Éditions du progrès, 1987). For debates about totalitarianism and liberation, see J. L. Talmon, *The Origins of Totalitarian Democracy* (New York: Praeger, 1960); Herbert Marcuse, "Thoughts on the Defense of Gracchus Babeuf," in John Anthony Scott, ed., *The Defense of Gracchus Babeuf before the High Court of Vendôme* (New York: Schocken Books, 1972). The most notable example of explaining away evidence that contradicts Buonarroti is Armando Saitta, "Autour de la conjuration de Babeuf: Discussion sur le communisme (1796)," *AHRF* 32, no. 162 (October–December 1960): 426–35. Saitta responds to Buonarroti's claim that Antonelle was a conspirator

by arguing that Antonelle publicly criticized Babeuf only to give him opportunity to elaborate on "perfect equality."

4. For an overview of histories of a corrupt Directory, see C. H. Church, "In Search of the Directory," in J. F. Bosher, ed., *French Government and Society, 1500–1850* (London: Athlone Press, 1975). The most striking celebration of the Directory is that of François Furet, who argued that Thermidor marked "society's recovery of its independence [from ideology] . . . whether in everyday life, in mores and habits, or in the expressions of passions and interests." One might reply that Thermidor liberated only those with wealth and power. The poor continued to experience the impress of ideology on their lives, often in ways deadlier after Thermidor than before. François Furet, "The Revolution Is Over," in *Interpreting the French Revolution*, trans. Elborg Forster (Cambridge: Cambridge University Press, 1981), 74. For different ways of framing the Directory as restoration of order, see James Livesey, *Making Democracy in the French Revolution* (Cambridge, MA: Harvard University Press, 2001); Andrew Jainchill, *Reimagining Politics after the Terror: The Republican Origins of French Liberalism* (Ithaca, NY: Cornell University Press, 2008). More explicitly critical accounts of the Directory include: Pierre Serna, *La République des girouettes (1789–1815 . . . et au-delà)* (Seyssel, France: Éditions Champ Vallon, 2005); Marc Belissa and Yannick Bosc, *Le Directoire: La république sans la démocratie* (Paris: La fabrique éditions, 2018).

5. For an overview of the decades-long debate on the origins of the French Revolution, see William Doyle, *Origins of the French Revolution*, 2d ed. (Oxford: Oxford University Press, 1988). Twentieth-century studies of mobilization include the following: George Rudé, *The Crowd in the French Revolution* (Oxford: Clarendon Press, 1959); Albert Soboul, *The Sans-Culottes*, trans. Remy Inglis Hall (Princeton, NJ: Princeton University Press, 1980); P. M. Jones, *The Peasantry in the French Revoution* (Cambridge: Cambridge University Press, 1988); Dominique Godineau, *The Women of Paris and Their French Revolution*, trans. Katherine Streip (Berkeley: University of California Press, 1998); Lynn Hunt, *Politics, Culture, and Class in the French Revolution* (Berkeley: University of California Press, 1984); Suzanne Desan, *Reclaiming the Sacred: Lay Religion and Popular Politics in Revolutionary France* (Ithaca, NY: Cornell University Press, 1990); Laura Mason, *Singing the French Revolution: Popular Culture and Politics, 1787–1799* (Ithaca, NY: Cornell University Press, 1990). Debate on the Terror is ongoing. However, critical interventions that explicitly link it to twentieth-century revolution are Arno Mayer, *The Furies: Violence and Terror in the French and Russian Revolutions* (Princeton, NJ: Princeton University Press, 2000) and the related forum in *French Historical Studies* 24 no. 4 (2001): 549–600.

6. Babeuf to Dubois de Fosseux (1 June 1786) in V. Daline, A. Saitta, and A. Soboul, eds., *Oeuvres de Babeuf*, vol. 1: *Babeuf avant la Révolution* (Paris: Bibliothèque nationale, 1977), 114; Victor Dalin, "Les idées sociales de Babeuf à la veille de la Révo-

lution," in *Babeuf et les problèmes du babouvisme: Colloque international de Stockholm* (Paris: Éditions sociales, 1963), 55–72; Philippe Riviale, *Babeuf, Oeuvres* (Paris: L'Harmattan, 2016), 1:246–47; [P.-A. Antonelle], *Observations sur le droit de cité* (Paris: chez Vatar, l'an III [1795]) 4.

Chapter 1. Must There Be Distinctions among Men? (1760–92)

1. Pierre Goubert, "Les techniques agricoles dans les pays picards au XVIIe et XVIIIe siècle," *Revue d'histoire économique et sociale* 35, no. 1 (1957): 24–40; Albert Demangeon, *La Picardie et les régions voisines, Artois, Cambrésis, Beauvaisis* (Paris: Librairie Guénégaud, 1973), 266–76; Steven Kaplan, *The Bakers of Paris and the Bread Question, 1700–1775* (Durham, NC: Duke University Press, 1996), 48–49, 89, 92; V. M. Dalin, *Gracchus Babeuf à la veille et pendant la grande Révolution française: 1785–1794* (Moscow: Éditions du progrès, 1987), 66–70.

2. Jean Lestocquoy, *Histoire de la Picardie et du Boulonnais* (Paris: Presses universitaires de France, 1970), 97–103; Pierre Goubert, *Cent mille provinciaux au XVIIe siècle: Beauvais et le Beauvaisis de 1600 à 1730* (Paris: Flammarion, 1968), 365–78; Pierre Goubert, *The French Peasantry in the Seventeenth Century*, trans. Ian Patterson (New York: Cambridge University Press, 1989), 110–13.

3. Dalin, *Gracchus Babeuf*, 74, 52–61; Goubert, *French Peasantry*, 82–94, 97–109; P. M. Jones, *The Peasantry in the French Revolution* (New York: Cambridge University Press, 1988), 8–10, 34–59, 79; Bryant Ragan, "Fiscal Impositions and Rural Political Activism in the French Revolution," in Bryant Ragan and Elizabeth Williams, eds., *Re-creating Authority in Revolutionary France* (New Brunswick, NJ: Rutgers University Press, 1992), 39.

4. Dalin, *Gracchus Babeuf*, 33–35; Victor Advielle, *Histoire de Gracchus Babeuf et du babouvisme* (1884; reprint, Geneva: Slatkine, 1978), 1:1–2; R. B. Rose, *Gracchus Babeuf: The First Revolutionary Communist* (Stanford: Stanford University Press, 1978), 7–10.

5. Dalin, *Gracchus Babeuf*, 36.

6. Dalin, *Gracchus Babeuf*, 37; Maurice Dommanget, "Tempérament et formation de Babeuf," in *Babeuf et les problèmes du babouvisme: Colloque international de Stockholm* (Paris: Éditions sociales, 1963), 23.

7. TDP 29 (22 Vendémiaire III), 285 (misprinted on page as 185); Dalin, *Gracchus Babeuf*, 85.

8. Rose, *Gracchus Babeuf*, 13; Dalin, *Gracchus Babeuf*, 42–43; Philippe Riviale, ed., *Gracchus Babeuf: Oeuvres* (Paris: L'Harmattan, 2016), 1:278–79.

9. Antoine Pelletier, "Babeuf feudiste," *AHRF* 179, no. 1 (1965): 29–65, at 57; Rose, *Gracchus Babeuf*, 17–19.

10. Advielle, *Histoire*, 1:20.

11. Florence Gauthier and Guy-Robert Ikni, "Le mouvement paysan en Picardie: Meneurs, pratiques, maturation et signification historique d'un programme," in Jean Nicolas, ed., *Mouvements populaires et conscience sociale: XVIe–XIXe siècles: Actes du colloque de Paris, 24–26 mai 1984* (Paris: Maloine, 1985); Olwen Hufton, *The Poor of Eighteenth-Century France, 1750–1789* (Oxford: Oxford University Press, 1974); Alan Forrest, *The French Revolution and the Poor* (Oxford: Blackwell, 1981); Kathryn Norberg, "Poverty," in Alan Charles Kors, ed., *Encyclopedia of the Enlightenment* (Oxford: Oxford University Press, 2003).

12. Babeuf to Dubois de Fosseux (1 June 1786) in V. Daline, A. Saitta, and A. Soboul, eds., *Oeuvres de Babeuf*, vol. 1: *Babeuf avant la Révolution* (Paris: Bibliothèque nationale, 1977), 114 (for entire letter, see 79–118); Victor Dalin, "Les idées sociales de Babeuf à la veille de la Révolution," in *Babeuf et les problèmes du babouvisme*, 65–70.

13. Claude Mazauric, ed., *Gracchus Babeuf: Écrits* (Paris: Messidor/Éditions sociales, 1988), 134–35.

14. Marcel Reinhard, ed., *Correspondance de Babeuf avec l'Académie d'Arras, 1785–88* (Paris: Presses universitaires de France, 1961), 66–71; Nicolas Collignon, *Avant-coureur du changement du monde entier par l'aisance, la bonne éducation, et la prospérité générale de tous les hommes. Prospectus d'un mémoire patriotique* (London: n.p., 1786).

15. Collignon, *Avant-coureur*, 49, 26.

16. Mazauric, ed., *Babeuf: Écrits*, 169–70, 171.

17. Advielle, *Histoire*, 2:209; Stéphanie Roza, *Comment l'utopie est devenue un programme politique: Du roman à la Révolution* (Paris: Classiques Garnier, 2015), 231.

18. Reinhard, ed., *Correspondance de Babeuf*, 146–47; Rose, *Gracchus Babeuf*, 25–28.

19. Dalin, *Gracchus Babeuf*, 114–29; Rose, *Gracchus Babeuf*, 43–51.

20. François-Noel Babeuf, "Discours préliminaire," *Cadastre perpetuel* ("à Paris chez les auteurs," 1789), xix–xxx, xlvi.

21. Dalin, *Gracchus Babeuf*, 129–30.

22. Advielle, *Histoire*, 1:55.

23. Michael Kwass, *Contraband: Louis Mandrin and the Making of a Global Underground* (Cambridge, MA: Harvard University Press, 2014), 243–46; Rose, *Gracchus Babeuf*, 58.

24. Rose, *Gracchus Babeuf*, 65–79; Ragan, "Fiscal Impositions"; Dalin, *Gracchus Babeuf*, 223.

25. Dalin, *Gracchus Babeuf*, 226, 132, 143; Robert Legrand, *Babeuf et ses compagnons de route* (Paris: Société des études robespierristes, 1981), 65–70; Rose, *Gracchus Babeuf*, 48, 79–80.

26. Gracchus Babeuf, "Lueurs philosophiques," in Riviale, *Babeuf: Oeuvres*, 1:227–440; Keith Michael Baker, "A Script for a French Revolution: The Politicial Consciousness of the Abbé Mably," in *Inventing the French Revolution* (New York: Cambridge

University Press, 1990); Johnson Kent Wright, *A Classical Republican in Eighteenth-century France: The Political Thought of Mably* (Stanford: Stanford University Press, 1997); V. M. Dalin, "Babeuf's Social Ideas on the Eve of the Revolution," *Soviet Studies in History* 1, no. 3 (1962): 57–72.

27. Riviale, *Babeuf: Oeuvres*, 1:286–93, 258–59; Rose, *Gracchus Babeuf*, 100–101; Mazauric, *Babeuf: Écrits*, 236–37.

28. Rose, *Gracchus Babeuf*, 105–7; Ian Birchall, "Babeuf and the Oppression of Women," *British Journal for Eighteenth-century Studies* 20 (1997): 63–75; "Lettre de Babeuf au Comité de recherches," in Mazauric, *Babeuf: Écrits*, 214–19; "Lettre à Coupé sur la nouvelle législature" (20 August 1791), in Maurice Dommanget, ed., *Babeuf: Pages choisies* (Paris: A. Colin, 1935), 103–21; Riviale, *Babeuf: Oeuvres*, 1:304–5.

29. Michael Fitzsimmons, *The Night the Old Regime Ended: August 4, 1789 and the French Revolution* (University Park: Penn State University Press, 2003); Bernard Bodinier, "L'accès à la propriété: Une manière d'éviter les révoltes?" *Cahiers d'histoire: Revue d'histoire critique* 94–95 (2005), http://journals.openedition.org/chrhc/1210; Hannah Callaway, "Revolutionizing Property: The Confiscation of Émigré Wealth in Paris and the Problem of Property in the French Revolution," PhD diss., Harvard University, 2015; Rafe Blaufarb, *The Great Demarcation: The French Revolution and the Invention of Modern Property* (New York: Oxford University Press, 2016).

30. R. B. Rose, "The 'Red Scare' of the 1790s: The French Revolution and the 'Agrarian Law,' " *Past and Present* 103, no. 1 (May 1984): 113–30; Peter Jones, "The 'Agrarian Law': Schemes for Land Redistribution during the French Revolution," *Past and Present* 133, no. 1 (November 1991): 96–133.

31. Riviale, *Babeuf: Oeuvres*, 1:240–41, 246–47.

32. Riviale, *Babeuf: Oeuvres*, 1:270.

33. "Seconde lettre de F. N. Cam. Babeuf, citoyen, à J. M. Coupé, législateur" (10 Sept 1791), in Dommanget, *Pages choisies*, 124.

34. Dommanget, *Pages choisies*, 121–30.

35. Laura Mason and Tracey Rizzo, comps., *The French Revolution: A Document Collection* (Boston: Houghton Mifflin, 1999), 153; Timothy Tackett, *When the King Took Flight* (Cambridge, MA: Harvard University Press, 2003), 97–118, 124–37.

36. Rose, *Gracchus Babeuf*, 111–15.

37. Rose, *Gracchus Babeuf*, 118–24.

38. Rose, *Gracchus Babeuf*, 124–26.

Chapter 2. Hope and Despair (1793–95)

1. *Le publiciste de la République française, par Marat l'ami du peuple* (16 March 1793); *Le père Duchesne* (5 May 1793).

2. Albert Soboul, *The Sans-Culottes: The Popular Movement and Revolutionary Government, 1793–1794*, trans. Remy Inglis Hall (Princeton, NJ: Princeton University Press, 1980), 98. This classic account has been challenged and nuanced by R. B. Rose, *The Making of the Sans-Culottes: Democratic Ideas and Institutions in Paris, 1789–1792* (Manchester, UK: Manchester University Press, 1983); Richard Andrews, "Social Structures, Political Elites and Ideology in Revolutionary Paris, 1792–94," *Journal of Social History* 19, no. 1 (Fall 1985): 71–112; Haim Burstin, *L'invention du sans-culottes: Regards sur Paris révolutionnaire* (Paris: O. Jacob, 2005); Morris Slavin, "The Enragés and the French Revolution" and "Jean Varlet as Defender of Democracy," in *The Left and the French Revolution* (Atlantic Highlands, NJ: Humanities Press, 1995). See also Citoyen Varlet, *Déclaration solennelle des droits de l'homme dans l'état social* (Paris, 1793; reprint, Paris: EDHIS, 1967).

3. David Andress, *The Terror: The Merciless War for Freedom in Revolutionary France* (New York: Farrar, Straus & Giroux, 2005), 149–70.

4. R. B. Rose, *Gracchus Babeuf: The First Revolutionary Communist* (Stanford: Stanford University Press, 1978), 130–31.

5. Steven L. Kaplan, *The Famine Plot Persuasion in Eighteenth-century France* (Philadelphia: American Philosophical Society, 1982), 62–63; Steven L. Kaplan, *The Stakes of Regulation: Perspectives on Bread, Politics and Political Economy Forty Years Later* (London: Anthem Press, 2015), 15–18.

6. Cynthia A. Bouton, *The Flour War: Gender, Class, and Community in Late Ancien Régime French Society* (University Park: Penn State University Press, 1993); Florence Gauthier, "De Mably à Robespierre: De la critique de l'économique à la critique du politique," in Florence Gauthier and Guy-Robert Ikni, eds., *La Guerre du Blé au XVIIIe siècle* (Paris: Éditions de la Passion, 1988).

7. Manuela Albertone, "Physiocracy," in Alan Charles Kors, ed., *Encyclopedia of the Enlightenment* (Oxford: Oxford University Press, 2003); Simone Meyssonnier, *La balance et l'horloge: La genèse de la pensée libérale en France au xviiie siècle* (Paris: Éditions de la Passion, 1989); Loic Charles and Arnaud Orain, "François Véron de Forbonnais and the Invention of Antiphysiocracy," in Steven Kaplan and Sophus Reinert, eds., *The Economic Turn: Recasting Political Economy in Enlightenment Europe* (New York: Anthem Press, 2019); Jean-Pierre Gross, *Égalitarisme jacobin et droits de l'homme (1793–1794)* (Paris: Éditions Kimé, 2016), 27.

8. Gauthier, "De Mably à Robespierre," 272–73; Julie Ferrand, "Mably and the Liberalisation of the Grain Trade: An Economically and Socially Inefficient Policy," *European Journal of the History of Economic Thought* 20, no. 6 (2013): 882–905.

9. George Rudé, *The Crowd in the French Revolution* (New York: Oxford University Press, 1967); Rebecca Spang, *Stuff and Money in the Time of the French Revolution* (Cambridge, MA: Harvard University Press, 2017); Katie Jarvis, *Politics in the Marketplace: Work, Gender, and Citizenship in Revolutionary France* (New York: Oxford University Press, 2019).

10. Sans-culottes in Soboul, *Sans-culottes*, 53–54; Roux in William Sewell, "The Sans-Culotte Rhetoric of Subsistence," in K. M. Baker and Colin Lucas, eds., *The French Revolution and the Creation of Modern Political Culture*, vol. 4: *The Terror* (Oxford: Pergamon Press, 1994), 255. See also Gauthier, "De Mably à Robespierre"; Florence Gauthier, *Triomphe et mort du droit naturel en Révolution, 1789–1795–1802* (Paris: Presses universitaires de France, 1992); Gross, *Égalitarisme jacobin*, 163; Spang, *Stuff and Money*; Jarvis, *Politics in the Marketplace*.

11. Quoted in Gross, *Égalitarisme jacobin*, 30, also 31–34; Marcel Dorigny, "Les Girondins et le droit de propriété," *Bulletin d'histoire économique et sociale de la Révolution française* (1980–81): 15–31; Albert Mathiez, *La vie chère et le mouvement social sous la Terreur* (Paris: Payot, 1927), 1:149; Peter McPhee, *Robespierre: A Revolutionary Life* (New Haven: Yale University Press, 2013), 146, 150.

12. Maximilien Robespierre, "Draft Declaration of the Rights of Man and Citizen" (24 April 1793), in Slavoj Žižek, ed., *Robespierre: Virtue and Terror* (New York: Verso, 2017), 66–72; *Archives parlementaires de 1787 à 1860: Ser. 1 (1787–99)* (Paris: CNRS, 1969), 63:197–200; Rose, *Gracchus Babeuf*, 141; Gauthier, "De Mably à Robespierre," 285; Rudé, *Crowd*, 113–19; Mathiez, *Vie chère*, 157–81.

13. Maurice Dommanget, ed., *Babeuf: Pages choisies* (Paris: A. Colin, 1935), 142–47; V. M. Dalin, *Gracchus Babeuf à la veille et pendant la grande Révolution française, 1785–1794* (Moscow: Éditions du progrès, 1987), 427–29; Rose, *Gracchus Babeuf*, 140–42.

14. Rose, *Gracchus Babeuf*, 140–49.

15. Andress, *The Terror*, 164–77; Charles Walton, "*Les graines de la discorde*: Print, Public Spirit, and Free Market Politics in the French Revolution," in Charles Walton, ed., *Into Print: Limits and Legacies of the Enlightenment: Essays in Honor of Robert Darnton* (University Park: Penn State University Press, 2011).

16. Dalin, *Gracchus Babeuf*, 435; Robert Legrand, *Babeuf et ses compagnons de route* (Paris: Société des études robespierristes, 1981), 133–34; Rose, *Gracchus Babeuf*, 144.

17. Pierre-Henri Billy, "Des prénoms révolutionnaires en France," *AHRF* 322, no. 4 (October–December 2000): 39–60; P.-F.-N. Fabre d'Eglantine, *Rapport fait à la Convention nationale . . . au nom de la Commission chargée de la confection du calendrier* (Paris: Imprimerie nationale, [l'an II de la république]).

18. Gauthier, "De Mably à Robespierre"; Gauthier, *Triomphe et mort du droit naturel*; Gross, *Égalitarisme jacobin*.

19. Gross surveys aspirations to egalitarianism which, while imperfectly realized, were significant. See *Égalitarisme jacobin*. See also Alan Forrest, *The French Revolution and the Poor* (Oxford: Blackwell, 1981); Colin Jones, *The Charitable Imperative: Hospitals and Nursing in Ancien Regime and Revolutionary France* (London: Routledge, 1989); Suzanne Desan, *The Family on Trial in Revolutionary France* (Berkeley: University of California Press, 2004); Jean-Pierre Gross, *Fair Shares for All* (New York: Cambridge University Press, 1996), 88–89.

20. Gross, *Fair Shares*, 127.

21. Maximilien Robespierre, "Discours sur la propriété" (24 April 1793), in A. Vermorel, ed., *Oeuvres de Robespierre* (Paris: F. Cornol, 1866), 268–76; Gross, *Fair Shares*, 93; Jean-Pierre Hirsch, "Terror and Property," in Baker and Lucas, eds., *French Revolution*, vol. 4: *The Terror*; R. B. Rose, "The 'Red Scare' of the 1790s: The French Revolution and the 'Agrarian Law,' " *Past and Present* 103, no. 1 (May 1984): 113–30.

22. *Archives parlementaires* 73:411–18; Law on Suspects in Laura Mason and Tracey Rizzo, comps., *The French Revolution: A Document Collection* (Boston: Houghton Mifflin, 1999), 230–32.

23. Dalin, *Gracchus Babeuf*, 484–85.

24. Rose, *Gracchus Babeuf*, 150–54.

25. *Archives parlementaires* 73:411–18; Andress, *The Terror*, 205–9, 289–90.

26. Andress, *The Terror*, 250, 210–51; *Moyse Bayle, au Peuple Souverain et à la Convention Nationale*, 8 pp. ([Paris]: Imprimerie de R. Vatar, n.d.); *Moyse Bayle, au Peuple Souverain et à la Convention Nationale*, 17 pp. ([Paris]: Imprimerie de R. Vatar, n.d.).

27. Gross, *Fair Shares*, 101–21.

28. Law of 22 Prairial II in Mason and Rizzo, *French Revolution*, 241–43; Patrice Higonnet, *Goodness beyond Virtue: Jacobins during the French Revolution* (Cambridge, MA: Harvard University Press, 1998), 52; David Jordan, *The Revolutionary Career of Maximilien Robespierre* (Chicago: University of Chicago Press, 1985), 204; for attacks on Hébertists and Dantonists, see R. R. Palmer, *Twelve Who Ruled: The Year of the Terror in the French Revolution* (Princeton, NJ: Princeton University Press, 2017), 291–304.

29. Martyn Lyons, "The 9 Thermidor: Motives and Effects," *European Studies Review* 5, no. 2 (April 1975): 123–46; Andress, *The Terror*, 334–44; Hugh Gough, *The Terror in the French Revolution*, 2d ed (New York: Palgrave Macmillan, 2010), 98–101.

30. Lyons, "The 9 Thermidor"; Françoise Brunel, *Thermidor: La chute de Robespierre* (Brussels: Complexe, 1989); Bronislaw Baczko, *Ending the Terror: The French Revolution after Robespierre*, trans. Michel Petheram (New York: Cambridge University Press, 1994); Sergio Luzzatto, *L'Automne de la Révolution: Luttes et cultures politiques dans la France thermidorienne*, trans. Simone Carpentari Messina (Paris: Champion, 2001); Laura Mason, "Thermidor and the Myth of Rupture," in David Andress, ed., *Oxford Handbook of the French Revolution* (Oxford: Oxford University Press, 2015).

31. *TDP* 27 (22 Vendémiaire III), 229.

32. *JLP* 1 (17 Fructidor II), 7; 18 (6 Vendémiaire II), 2.

33. *JLP* 7 (28 Fructidor II), 3–7; 20 (9 Vendémiaire III), 3–7; Kåre D. Tønnesson, *La défaite des sans-culottes: Mouvement populaire et réaction bourgeoise en l'an III* (Paris: Presses universitaires, 1959), 56–74; Mason, "Thermidor and the Myth of Rupture."

34. *Bulletin de littérature, des sciences et des arts* 20 (Paris: Imprimerie F. Hocquet, n.d. [l'an III]); Charles-Pierre Ducancel, *L'intérieur des comités révolutionnaires ou les*

Aristides modernes (Paris: chez Barba, l'an III); Luzzatto, *L'automne de la Révolution*, 75–123; Laura Mason, "The Culture of Reaction: Demobilizing the People after Thermidor," *French Historical Studies* 39, no. 3 (August 2016): 445–70; Hugh Gough, *The Newspaper Press in the French Revolution* (London: Routledge, 1988), 118–23. See also Baczko, *Ending the Terror*; Ronen Steinberg, *The Afterlives of the Terror: Facing the Legacies of Mass Violence in Postrevolutionary France* (Ithaca, NY: Cornell University Press, 2019).

35. Mette Harder, "Reacting to Revolution—The Political Career(s) of J.-L. Tallien," in David Andress, ed., *Experiencing the French Revolution* (Oxford: Voltaire Foundation, 2013); Mason, "The Culture of Reaction."

36. *L'Orateur du peuple* (9 Vendémiaire III); Rose, *Gracchus Babeuf*, 162–65.

37. *TDP* 23 (14 Vendémiaire III), 3.

38. *TDP* 27 (22 Vendémiaire III), 219, 211; Gabriel Bonnot de Mably, *Des droits et devoirs du citoyen dans les circonstances présentes* (Kell, 1789), 60.

39. Rose, *Gracchus Babeuf*, 164–65.

40. Joachim Vilate, *Causes secretes de la Révolution du 9 au 10 Thermidor* (Paris: n.p., l'an III); Baczko, *Ending the Terror*, 153, 157; *Procès criminel des membres du comité révolutionnaire de Nantes* (Paris: "chez la citoyenne Toubon," l'an III), 6.

41. Gracchus Babeuf, *Du système de dépopulation, ou la vie et les crimes du Carrier* (Paris: Imprimerie Franklin, [1794]), 13–23, 32–33, 35.

42. Tønnesson, *Défaite des sans-culottes*, 87–94, 111; Raymond Monnier, "Le tournant de Brumaire: Dépopulariser la révolution parisienne," in Michel Vovelle, ed., *Le tournant de l'an III: Réaction et Terreur blanche dans la France révolutionnaire* (Paris: Éditions du CTHS, 1997); François Hincker, "Comment sortir de la terreur économique?" in Vovelle, ed., *Le tournant de l'an III*; Kåre Tønnesson, "La mort politique de la sans-culotterie parisienne," in Roger Dupuy and Marcel Morabito, eds., *1795: Pour une République sans Révolution* (Rennes: Presses universitaires de Rennes, 1996).

43. *TDP* 28 (28 Frimaire III), 237.

44. *TDP* 29 (1–19 Nivôse III), 263, 266; Kare Tønnesson, "L'an III dans la formation du babouvisme," *AHRF* 162 (October–December 1960): 411–25.

45. Rose, *Gracchus Babeuf*, 180.

46. *TDP* 31 (9 Pluviôse III), 312, 315, 317.

47. Richard Cobb, "L'arrestation de Babeuf à Paris le 20 pluviôse an III," *AHRF* 33 (1961): 393–94.

Chapter 3. Re-imagining Revolution

1. Georges Lefebvre, *Les thermidoriens* (Paris: A. Colin, 1937), 105; Kåre D. Tønnesson, *La défaite des sans-culottes: Mouvement populaire et réaction bourgeois en l'an III* (Oslo: Presses universitaires, 1959), 119–36; Richard Cobb, *The Police and the*

People: French Popular Protest 1789–1820 (Oxford: Clarendon Press, 1970), 158–60; Richard Cobb, *Death in Paris, 1795–1801* (New York: Oxford University Press, 1978).

2. *Le réveil du peuple*, in Laura Mason, *Singing the French Revolution* (Ithaca, NY: Cornell University Press, 1996), 134–35; François Gendron, *The Gilded Youth of Thermidor* (Montreal: McGill-Queen's University Press, 1993), 30–82.

3. Gendron, *Gilded Youth*, 110–18; George Rude, *The Crowd in the French Revolution* (Oxford: Oxford University Press, 1977), 147–52.

4. Albert Mathiez, "Les journées de Prairial an III," in *La réaction thermidorienne*, introd. Yannick Bosc and Florence Gauthier (Paris: La fabrique éditions, 2010); Bronislaw Baczko, *Ending the Terror: The French Revolution after Robespierre*, trans. Michel Petheram (New York: Cambridge University Press, 1994), 239.

5. Tønnesson, *Défaite*, 306–44; Haim Burstin, "Échos faubouriens des journées de Prairial," *AHRF* 304 (1996): 373–85; Raymonde Monnier, "L'Étendu d'un désastre: Prairial et la révolution populaire," *AHRF* 304 (1996): 387–400; Morris Slavin, "L'épuration de prairial an III dans la section des Droits de l'homme," *AHRF* 304 (1996): 283–304; Françoise Brunel, "Pourquoi ces 'six' parmi les 'derniers montagnards'?" *AHRF* 304 (1996): 401–13.

6. Cobb, *The Police and the People*, 131–50; Colin Lucas, "The First Directory and the Rule of Law," *French Historical Studies* 10, no. 2 (Autumn 1977): 231–60; Stephen Clay, "Le massacre du fort Saint-Jean, une épisode de la Terreur blanche à Marseille," in Michel Vovelle, ed., *Le tournant de l'an III: Réaction et Terreur blanche dans la France révolutionnaire* (Paris: Éditions du CTHS, 1997).

7. Robert Legrand, *Babeuf et ses compagnons de route* (Paris: Société des études robespierristes, 1981), 182.

8. Jean-Claude Fichaux, *Les prisons d'Arras et les hommes* (Bouvignies: Nord Avril, 2010), 38–70; Legrand, *Babeuf et ses compagnons*, 188–90; R. B. Rose, *Gracchus Babeuf: The First Revolutionary Communist* (Stanford: Stanford University Press, 1978), 186–88; Victor Advielle, *Histoire de Gracchus Babeuf et du babouvisme* (1884; reprint, Geneva: Slatkine, 1978), 1:149; Louis Jacob, "Correspondance avec Babeuf," *AHRF* 11, no. 63 (May-June 1934): 253–59.

9. Maurice Dommanget, "Un leader babouviste méconnu: Charles Germain," in *Sur Babeuf et la conjuration des égaux* (Paris: François Maspero, 1970), 303–23.

10. Interrogatoire de Germain devant Gérard (30 Floréal IV), AN, W559, dossier "Germain & Guilhem," no. 14.

11. Advielle, *Histoire de Gracchus Babeuf*, 1:164–65; Germain to Babeuf (13 Messidor III), AN, Fonds Dommanget 14, AS 287.

12. Germain (16 Messidor III), AN, Fonds Dommanget 14, AS 287; Legrand, *Babeuf et ses compagnons*, 378; Dommanget, *Sur Babeuf*, 309–10. Babeuf's original letter has not been found, but Germain's reply suggests that it favored agrarian law. See Rose, *Gracchus Babeuf*, 189–90.

13. Gracchus Babeuf to Charles Germain (10 Thermidor an III), in Maurice Dommanget, ed., *Babeuf: Pages choisies* (Paris: A. Colin, 1935), 208–11, 213 (for entire letter, see 207–23).

14. Stéphanie Roza, *Comment l'utopie est devenue un programme politique: Du roman à la Révolution* (Paris: Classiques Garnier, 2015); Jean-Louis Lecercle, "Introduction," in Gabriel Bonnot de Mably, *Des droits et des devoirs du citoyen* (Paris: Librairie Marcel Didier, 1972).

15. Dommanget, *Sur Babeuf*, 312; Dommanget, *Pages choisies*, 217–18, 219.

16. Dommanget, *Sur Babeuf*, 314; Legrand, *Babeuf et ses compagnons*, 379–80; Germain to Babeuf (27 and 28 Thermidor III), AN, Fonds Dommanget 14, AS 287.

17. Germain to Babeuf (14 Messidor III), AN, Fonds Dommanget 14, AS 287. Although Babeuf did not use the word "democracy," he gestured to that notion in his discussion of "patrician" and "plebeian" factions in the National Convention, *TDP* 29 (19 Nivôse III), 263–65; John Dunn, *Democracy: A History* (New York: Atlantic Monthly Press, 2006), 123–30.

18. Andrew Jainchill, *Reimagining Politics after the Terror: The Republican Origins of French Liberalism* (Ithaca, NY: Cornell University Press, 2008), 29.

19. Jainchill, *Reimagining Politics*, 50–51; Christine LeBozec, "Boissy d'Anglas et la constitution de l'an III," in Roger Dupuy and Marcel Morabito, eds., *1795: Pour une République sans Révolution* (Rennes: Presses universitaires de Rennes, 1996); Marcel Morabito, "Les nouveautés constitutionnelles de l'an III," in Dupuy and Morabito, eds., *1795*; Yannick Bosc, "Boissy d'Anglas et le rejet de la Déclaration de 1793," in Roger Bourderon, ed., *L'an I et l'apprentissage de la démocratie* (Saint Denis: Éditions PSD, 1995); Guy Braibant, "La Déclaration des droits de l'an III," in Gérard Conac and Jean-Pierre Machelon, eds., *La constitution de l'an III: Boissy d'Anglas et la naissance du libéralisme constitutionnel* (Paris: Presses universitaires de France, 1999); François Luchaire, "Boissy d'Anglas et la Constitution de l'an III," in Conac and Machelon, eds., *La constitution de l'an III*; Françoise Brunel, "Aux origines d'un parti de l'ordre: Les propositions de la constitution de l'an III," in Jean Nicolas, ed., *Mouvements populaires et conscience sociale, XVIe–XIXe siècles* (Paris: Maloine, 1985).

20. Germain to Babeuf (16 Messidor III), AN, Fonds Dommanget 14, AS 287.

21. Germain to Babeuf (18 [*sic*], 19, 20 Fructidor III), AN, Fonds Dommanget 14, AS 287; Babeuf to Germain (18 Fructidor III), Dommanget, *Pages choisies*, 222.

22. Germain in Legrand, *Babeuf et ses compagnons*, 334, 184; Jacob, "Correspondance avec Babeuf," 11; AN, Fonds Dommanget 14, AS 287.

23. On Lebon, see Ronen Steinberg, *The Afterlives of the Terror: Facing the Legacies of Mass Violence in Postrevolutionary France* (Ithaca, NY: Cornell University Press, 2019).

24. Filippo Buonarroti, *La conspiration pour l'égalité, dite de Babeuf* (Paris: Éditions sociales, 1957), 1:61.

25. Émile to Gracchus Babeuf (30 Messidor III/28 July 1795), in Legrand, *Babeuf et ses compagnons*, 194–95; Advielle, *Histoire de Gracchus Babeuf*, 2:69.

26. Gendron, *Gilded Youth*, 166–78.

27. P.-F. Réal, *Essai sur les journées des treize et quatorze Vendémiaire* (Paris: [n.p.], "l'an IV" [1795]).

Chapter 4. The Plot against the Government

1. *Journal des patriotes de '89* (18 Brumaire IV).

2. Marc Belissa and Yannick Bosc, *Le Directoire: La république sans la démocratie* (Paris: La fabrique éditions, 2018), 38–39; François-Antoine Boissy d'Anglas, "Discours préliminaire au projet de constitution," in *Choix de rapports, opinions, et discours prononcés à la Tribune nationale*, vol. 15: 1794–95 (Paris: Eymery, 1821), 109–58.

3. Laure Junot d'Abrantès, *Histoire des salons de Paris: Tableaux et portraits du grand monde sous Louis XVI, le Directoire, le Consulat et l'Empire, la Restauration et le règne de Louis-Philippe* (Paris: Chez Ladvocat, 1837–38), 3:229; Steven Kale, *French Salons: High Society and Political Sociability from the Old Regime to the Revolution of 1848* (Baltimore: Johns Hopkins University Press, 2004), 69–75; Rebecca Spang, *The Invention of the Restaurant: Paris and Modern Gastronomic Culture* (Cambridge, MA: Harvard University Press, 2000), 138–45; Louis Sébastien Mercier, *Paris pendant la révolution ou, Le nouveau Paris* (Paris: Poulet-Malassis, 1862), 1:383–87.

4. Max Fajn, *The Journal des hommes libres de tous les pays, 1792–1800* (The Hague: Mouton, 1975), 55–60; Hugh Gough, *The Newspaper Press in the French Revolution* (London: Routledge, 1988), 125–34.

5. *Patriotes de '89* (12 Brumaire IV); *J. de l'opposition* 7 [n.d.]; Laura Mason, "Après la conjuration: Le Directoire, la presse, et l'Affaire des Égaux," *AHRF* 354 (December 2008): 77–103.

6. Pierre Serna, "Réal ou la république réaliste," in Michel Vovelle, ed., *Le Tournant de l'an III: Réaction et Terreur blanche dans la France révolutionnaire* (Paris: Éditions du CTHS, 1997); *Patriotes de '89* (18 Brumaire IV).

7. [P.-A. Antonelle], *Observations sur le droit de cité* (Paris: chez Vatar, l'an III), 4; Pierre Serna, *Antonelle: Aristocrate révolutionnaire, 1747–1817* (Paris: Éditions du Félin, 1997), 259–60.

8. Antonelle in Serna, *Antonelle*, 263–64; Minchul Kim, "Pierre-Antoine Antonelle and Representative Democracy in the French Revolution," *History of European Ideas* 44, no. 3 (2018): 344–69; Yannick Bosc, *La terreur des droits de l'homme: Le républicanisme de Thomas Paine et le moment thermidorien* (Paris: Éditions Kimé, 2016); P. F. T., "Sur l'utilité pour les patriotes de connaître la constitution et les lois," *JDHL* (4 Frimaire IV); Isser Woloch, *Jacobin Legacy: The Democratic Move-*

ment under the Directory (Princeton, NJ: Princeton University Press, 1970), 19–25; Louis Bigard, *Le comte Réal, ancien Jacobin* (Paris: Imprimerie Firmin-Didot, 1937), 91; Ch. Picquenard, "La société du Panthéon et le parti patriote à Paris," *Révolution française* 33 (1897): 318–48; Philippe Raynaud, "Preface," in Benjamin Constant, *De la force du gouvernement actuel de la France et de la nécessité de s'y rallier* (Paris: Flammarion, 1988), 8–16; Albert Mathiez, *Le Directoire* (Paris: Armand Colin, 1934), 141.

9. *JDHL* (14 Brumaire IV).

10. Kåre D. Tønnesson, *La défaite des sans-culottes: Mouvement populaire et réaction bourgeoise en l'an III* (Oslo: Presses universitaires, 1959); Richard Cobb, *The Police and the People: French Popular Protest, 1789–1820* (Oxford: Clarendon Press, 1970); Raymonde Monnier, "L'Étendu d'un désastre: Prairial et la révolution populaire," *AHRF* 304 (1996): 387–400, at 391; François Brunel, "Pourquoi ces 'six' parmi les 'derniers Montagnards'?" *AHRF* 304 (1996): 401–13; Haim Burstin, "Echos faubouriens des journées de Prairial," *AHRF* 304 (1996): 373–85; Martyn Lyons, *France under the Directory* (New York: Cambridge University Press, 1975), 68–83; George Lefebvre, *The Thermidorians and the Directory*, trans. Robert Baldick (New York: Random House, 1964), 219–31.

11. *TDP* 34 (15 Brumaire IV), 6, 17, 51.

12. *JDHL* (17 Brumaire IV); Réal in *Patriotes de '89*, quoted in Picquenard, "La société du Panthéon," 332. See also Woloch, *Jacobin Legacy*, 23–24; *Orateur plébéien*, quoted in Natalie Lambrichs, *La liberté de la presse en l'an IV, les journaux républicains* (Paris: Presses universitaires de France, 1976), 75.

13. *TDP* 35 (9 Frimaire IV), 82; 36 [20 Frimaire IV], 115.

14. *TDP* 35 (9 Frimaire IV), 86–87. For comparison with agrarian law, see: R. B. Rose, "The 'Red Scare' of the 1790s: The French Revolution and the Agrarian Law," *Past and Present* 103, no. 1 (May 1984): 113–30; Peter Jones, "The Agrarian Law: Schemes for Land Redistribution during the French Revolution," *Past and Present* 133, no. 1 (November 1991): 96–133.

15. *TDP* 35 (9 Frimaire IV), 101.

16. Babeuf identified the quote from Morelly as a text by Diderot. *TDP* 35 (9 Frimaire IV), 93, 105.

17. *TDP* 35 (9 Frimaire IV), 92–99.

18. [Marc-Guillaume Alexis Vadier], *À Gracchus Babeuf, Tribun du Peuple* (Paris, 30 Pluviôse an IV), AN, W563; P.-A. Antonelle, *L'orateur plebéien* 9 (16 Frimaire IV); *Patriotes de '89* (14 Ventôse IV).

19. For circulation rates, Fajn, *Journal des hommes libres*, 52. Using numbers from *L'éclair*, a royalist newspaper likely to underestimate the republican press, Fajn claims that republican papers had about 4,000 readers: roughly 500–600 apiece for *La Sentinelle, L'ami des lois*, and *Patriotes de '89*, and 2,200–2,500 for *JDHL*. The figures don't add up, because Fajn also acknowledges Babeuf's 590 subscribers.

20. Desplace to Babeuf (1 Ventôse IV), AN, F7 4278, dossier 2; *Débats*, 3:610; R. B. Rose, *Gracchus Babeuf: The First Revolutionary Communist* (Stanford: Stanford University Press, 1978), 214, 219–20; Woloch, *Jacobin Legacy*, 32–46; Isser Woloch, "The Revival of Jacobinism in Metz during the Directory," *Journal of Modern History* 38, no. 1 (March 1966): 13–37; Huningue to Babeuf (25 Ventôse IV), AN, F7 4278; Desplaces to Babeuf (1 Ventôse IV), AN, F7 4278.

21. *TDP* 35 [9 Frimaire IV], 56–61; 36 [20 Frimaire IV], 114, 122–23; 38 [n.d.], 165–73; 40 [n.d.], 233–36.

22. Boissy d'Anglas, "Discours préliminaire," 119.

23. Bureau d'esprit public à Ministre de l'Intérieur (22 Brumaire IV), AN, F7 3448; F.-A. Aulard, *Paris pendant la réaction thermidorienne et sous le directoire* (Paris: [n.p.], 1898–1902), 2:459.

24. *TDP* 36 [20 Frimaire IV], 126; Rose, *Gracchus Babeuf*, 220–21.

25. *JDHL* (2 Ventôse IV).

26. Mathiez, *Directoire*, 141–43; Picquenard, "La société du Panthéon et le parti patriote à Paris"; Rose, *Gracchus Babeuf*, 222–25; *TDP* 38 [n.d.], 162–63; *TDP* 40 [5 Ventôse IV], 240.

27. Aulard, *Paris pendant la réaction*, 3:14; *JDHL* (13 Ventôse IV).

28. [Félix Lepelletier], *Soldat arrete et lis*, in Filippo Buonarroti, *La conspiration pour l'égalité dite de Babeuf* (Paris: Éditions sociales, 1957), 2:78–79; *Opinion sur nos deux constitutions, soumise au jugement de ceux qui décrétèrent, présentèrent à la France, et jurèrent l'une et l'autre* (Paris, 23 Germinal IV); *Analyse de la doctrine de Babeuf, Tribun du Peuple, proscrit par le Directoire exécutif, pour avoir dit la vérité* [n.d.], AN, W564.

29. Aulard, *Paris pendant la réaction*, 3:59.

30. Aulard, *Paris pendant la réaction*, 3:116–17, 164–65; "Au citoyen DuMoulin" from Toulouse (8 Germinal IV), AN, F7 4278, dossier 4; denunciation to public prosecutor of Châlons (24 Germinal IV), AN, AF III 42.

31. *Patriotes de '89* (14 Ventôse IV); *Le messager du soir* (17 Ventôse IV).

32. *Courier républicain* (25 Germinal IV), in Aulard, *Paris pendant la réaction*, 3:111. See also *Journal de Marseille* (9 Floréal IV); Aulard, *Paris pendant la réaction*, 3:131–32; letter from Solignac in *Patriotes de '89* (21 Ventôse IV).

33. *Bulletin des Lois* 40 (27 Germinal IV).

34. Rose, *Gracchus Babeuf*, 256–58; Jean Tulard, "Le recrutement de la Légion de police de Paris sous la Convention thermidorienne et le Directoire," *AHRF* 36, no. 175 (1964): 38–64; "Loi qui assimile la légion de police aux autres troupes de la république, et la met à la disposition du Directoire exécutif. Du 5 Floréal [IV]," in *Collection générale des lois et des actes du corps législatif et du Directoire exécutif . . . Floréal et Prairial an IV* (Paris: Baudouin, [1796]), 48.

35. Aulard, *Paris pendant la réaction*, 3:165.

36. Grisel to Lazare Carnot (15 Floréal IV), Conseil des Cinq-Cents, *Messages du Directoire Exécutif, et pièces envoyées par lui au Conseil des Cinq-Cents, relativement au représentant du peuple DROUET* (Paris: Imprimerie nationale, Floréal an IV), AN, AF III 43, 157/4.

37. Rose, *Gracchus Babeuf*, 270–71; *Débats*, 3:398–99.

38. "Rapport fait par Dossonville" (21 Floréal IV), AN, F7 4278.

39. *Le Directoire Executif aux Citoyens de Paris* ([Paris], Imprimerie du Directoire, an IV).

Chapter 5. Fear and Polarization

1. Interrogations of Filippo Buonarroti (21 Floréal IV), Augustin Darthé (22 Floréal IV), Charles Germain (30 Floréal IV), AN, W559; "Drouet au Conseil des Cinq-Cents," (25 Floréal IV), AN, W566; Haute Cour de Justice, *Copie de l'Instruction personnelle au représentant du peuple DROUET* (Paris: de l'Imprimerie nationale, Frimaire an V).

2. Interrogation of Babeuf (21 Floréal IV), AN, W559.

3. Babeuf to the Executive Directory (23 Floréal IV), *PS*, 2:235–39.

4. *Le censeur des journaux* (23 Floréal IV); *L'ami des lois* (23 Floréal IV); F.-A. Aulard, *Paris pendant la réaction thermidorienne et sous le directoire* (Paris: [n.p.], 1898–1902), 3:189–90. Reports on popular unrest in AN, F7 4276.

5. Martyn Lyons, *France under the Directory* (Cambridge: Cambridge University Press, 1975), 175–88; Rebecca Spang, *Stuff and Money in the Time of the French Revolution* (Cambridge, MA: Harvard University Press, 2015), 210–46; Marc Belissa and Yannick Bosc, *Le Directoire: La république sans la démocratie* (Paris: La fabrique éditions, 2018), 101–34. Cases were dismissed against journalist Richer-Sérisy for his part in the Vendémiaire insurrection of 1795 and several men charged with responsibility for the September massacres of 1792. For discussion of acquittals, especially in relation to arrest and likely prosecution of Babeuf, see *La Sentinelle* (26 Floréal IV); *L'ami des lois* (28 Floréal IV); *Courier républicain* (28 Floréal IV); *JDHL* (28 Floréal IV); *Gazette nationale, ou Le Moniteur universel* (30 Floréal IV); *Le messager du soir* (30 Floréal IV). See also below, chapter 7, note 10; chapter 13, note 2.

6. AN, AF III 42, 152/7, 152/11; Richard Cobb, "Notes sur la répression contre le personnel sans-culotte de 1795 à 1801," *AHRF* 26, no. 134 (January–March 1954): 23–49; AN, AF III 42, 152/22; F7 4276, pieces 2–125.

7. *Le Rédacteur* (24 Floréal IV).

8. *Le Directoire Executif aux Citoyens de Paris* (n.p., an IV); *PS*, 1:238–42, 80–86. Texts reprinted in *L'historien* (27 Floréal IV); *Le censeur des journaux* (27 Floréal IV); *Messager du soir*, which reduced its font size to accommodate the full text (29 Floréal IV); Conseil des Cinq-Cents, *Messages du Directoire Exécutif, et pièces*

envoyées par lui au Conseil des Cinq-Cents, relativement au représentant du peuple DROUET (Paris: Imprimerie nationale, Floréal an IV), AN, AF III 43 157/4; *L'historien* (24 Floréal IV).

9. See, for example, Hugh Gough, *The Newspaper Press in the French Revolution* (London: Routledge, 1988); Jeremy Popkin, *Revolutionary News: The Press in France, 1789–1799* (Durham, NC: Duke University Press, 1990); Robert Darnton and Daniel Roche, eds., *Revolution in Print: The Press in France, 1775–1800* (Berkeley: University of California Press, 1989). On press after Thermidor, see Nathalie Lambrichs, *La liberté de la presse en l'an IV: Les journaux républicains* (Paris: Presses universitaires de France, 1976); Jeremy Popkin, *The Right-Wing Press in France, 1792–1800* (Chapel Hill: University of North Carolina Press, 1980); Laura Mason, "Après la conjuration: Le Directoire, la presse, et l'Affaire des Egaux," *AHRF* 354 (December 2008): 77–103.

10. *Messager du soir* (23 Floréal IV); *Censeur des journaux* (23 Floréal IV). See also *Courier républicain* (23 Floréal IV).

11. *Messager du soir* (8 Prairial IV); *Censeur des journaux* (11 Prairial IV). See also *Le nécessaire, ou Journal du département de la Côte-d'Or* (5, 10, 25 Prairial IV); *L'anti-terroriste, ou Journal des principes; suite au journal du département de Haute-Garonne* (4, 6, 9, 13 Prairial IV); *Journal politique et littéraire de Rouen, et du département de la Seine inférieure* (13, 14 Prairial IV); *Journal de Lyon, par Pelzin* (6, 10, 14 Prairial IV).

12. *Rédacteur* (5 Prairial IV), also (2, 4, 7, 8, 11, 14 Prairial IV); Pincra to Directors (22 Floréal IV), AN, F7 4276, pieces 301–400; Isser Woloch, "The Revival of Jacobinism in Metz during the Directory," *Journal of Modern History* 38, no. 1 (March 1966), 13–37; Durand of Ste. Ménéhoult (22 Floréal IV), AN, F7 4276, pieces 501–600; *Fayolle, député de la Drôme . . . , au Ministre de la police générale* (Paris, 29 Prairial IV).

13. Isser Woloch, *Jacobin Legacy: The Democratic Movement under the Directory* (Princeton, NJ: Princeton University Press, 1970), 49, 55–56; Jean-René Suratteau, "Les Babouvistes, le Péril Rouge et le Directoire (1796–1798)," in *Babeuf et les problèmes du babouvisme: Colloque international de Stockholm* (Paris: Éditions sociales, 1963); Albert Mathiez, *Le Directoire* (Paris, 1934), 219–22; Jean Marc Schiappa, *Les babouvistes: Aspects de l'implantation de la Conjuration babouviste* (Saint-Quentin, 2003); Mason, "Après la conjuration," 77–103. Archival sources for the crackdown are extensive. For the Directory's statements, correspondence with provincial administrators, and warrants for arrest, see AN, AF III 42–43. For declarations and denunciations against possible accomplices, see AN, F7 4276. See also *Arrêté du département de la Marne* (28 Floréal IV), AN, C396; Naverrere to Directory (26 Floréal IV), AN, W563; "Papiers se rapportant au complot babouviste," AN, F7 4278, dossier 4; Maugerets, de la Gironde, à M. de la police générale (29 Floréal IV), AN, F7 7145; Lapeyre au Ministre de la Police Générale (22 Floréal IV), AN, W563, dossier 76.

14. *Journal des patriotes de '89* (8 Prairial IV); *JDHL* (24, 25, 26 Floréal IV); *L'ami du peuple* (28 Floréal IV). See also *Patriotes de '89* (23, 27, 30 Floréal IV); *L'ami du peuple* (25, 26 Floréal IV); *L'ami des lois* (23, 24 Floréal IV); *Journal de Toulouse* (29 Floréal IV).

15. *JDHL* (23 Floréal IV); *L'ami des lois* (23 Floréal IV). See also *Patriotes de '89* (23, 26, 28 Floréal IV); *JDHL* (25, 26 Floréal IV); *L'ami des lois* (24, 28 Floréal IV); *L'ami du peuple* (25, 28 Floréal IV); *La sentinelle* (26 Floréal IV); *Journal de Toulouse* (26, 29 Floréal IV).

16. "Drouet au Conseil des Cinq-Cents," AN, W566, liasse 10.

17. *Patriotes de '89* (23 Floréal IV). See also *Patriotes de '89* (25 Floréal, 11 Prairial IV); *L'ami des lois* (28 Floréal IV); *JDHL* (25, 28 Floréal, 13 Prairial IV).

18. *L'historien* (28 Floréal IV). See also *Censeur des journaux* (25, 26, 27 Floréal IV); *Messager du soir* (26 Floréal IV).

19. *L'anti-terroriste, ou Journal des principes* (13 Prairial IV). See also *L'anti-terroriste* (6, 9 Prairial IV); *Messager du soir* (3, 4 Prairial IV); *Censeur des journaux* (8 Prairial IV); *Journal politique et littéraire de Rouen, et . . . de la Seine inférieure* (6, 30 Prairial IV); *Journal de Lyon, par Pelzin* (23 Prairial IV).

20. *Patriotes de '89* (11 Prairial IV); *JDHL* (17 Prairial IV).

21. "Ex Fumo Lucem," *L'historien* (17 Prairial IV). See also *L'historien* (23, 24, 25, 27, 28 Floréal, 8, 11, 14 Prairial IV).

22. *Journal de Lyon* (29 Floréal, 6 Prairial IV); *Messager du soir* (23 Floréal, 14 Prairial IV); *L'anti-terroriste* (29 Floréal IV); *Le nécessaire* (5 Prairial IV); *Journal politique et littéraire de Rouen* (13, 14 Prairial IV); *Courier républicain* (2 Prairial IV); *Censeur des journaux* (23 Floréal; 8, 11 Prairial IV).

23. On fear, see Marisa Linton, *Choosing Terror: Virtue, Friendship, and Authenticity in the French Revolution* (New York: Oxford University Press, 2013); Timothy Tackett, *The Coming of the Terror in the French Revolution* (Cambridge, MA: Harvard University Press, 2015). On conspiracy, see Peter Campbell, Thomas Kaiser, and Marisa Linton, eds., *Conspiracy in the French Revolution* (Manchester, UK: Manchester University Press, 2007).

24. On assumptions about ties between the Directory and *Le Rédacteur*, see *Journal de Marseilles* (16, 19 Messidor IV); *Le Rédacteur* (26, 29 Floréal IV).

25. *Le Rédacteur* (3 Prairial IV).

26. *Le Rédacteur* (28 Floréal, 26 Prairial IV); *JDHL* (7, 10, 12 Prairial IV); Max Fajn, *The Journal des hommes libres de tous les pays, 1792–1800* (The Hague: Mouton, 1975), 66; Henri Welschinger, *Le journaliste Lebois et l'Ami du peuple (an III–an VIII)* (Paris: Imprimerie A. Quantin, [1885]), BN, NUMM-5450456; Woloch, *Jacobin Legacy*, 50; *Le ministre de la police générale de la république, aux administrations centrales et municipales, et aux commissaires du pouvoir exécutif près les Tribunaux criminels et civils* [n.p., n.d.] [7 Prairial IV], AN, F7 7146; Ministre de la police générale au ministre de la justice (19 Prairial IV), AN, BB3 21 no. 155;

Conseil des Cinq-Cents, *Mémoire justificatif de Drouet, . . . en réponse à la dénonciation faite contre lui par le Directoire exécutif . . . lu dans le séance du 28 prairial* (Paris: Imprimerie nationale, an IV), AN, AF III 43 157/3.

27. *Patriotes de '89* (1, 6, 11 Prairial IV). On Méhée, see Louis-Gabriel Michaud, *Biographie universelle ancienne et moderne* (Leipzig: F. A. Brockhaus, 1854[–1865]), whose thumbnail sketch begins by calling him "one of the most contemptible men produced by our revolutions." See also Alfred Cobban, "The Great Mystification of Méhée de la Touche," *Historical Research* 41, no. 103 (May 1968): 100–106.

28. "Mémoire justificatif de Drouet," in Haute-Cour de Justice, *Copie de l'instruction personnelle au representant du people Drouet* (Paris: Imprimerie nationale, Frimaire V), 200–201, 203, 33–35, 211–12. For Drouet's complete statement, see 183–95.

29. Although Thibaudeau was the only right-wing deputy to publish an opinion on the case, his opinions aligned closely with those of reactionary journalists, so he is likely to have spoken for like-minded legislators as well. A. C. Thibaudeau, *Discours prononcé par . . ., le 2 messidor* (Paris: chez Maret, an IV), 14, 21–23, 8, 6, 37; BN 8-Le43–3890.

30. David Andress, *The Terror: The Merciless War for Freedom in Revolutionary France* (New York: Farrar, Straus & Giroux, 2005), 164–77; Marisa Linton, " 'Do You Believe That We're Conspirators?' Conspiracies Real and Imagined in Jacobin Politics, 1793–94," in Campbell, Kaiser, and Linton, eds., *Conspiracy in the French Revolution;* Hugh Gough, *The Terror in the French Revolution,* 2d ed. (New York: Palgrave Macmillan, 2010), 60–64. See also Article 8 of Law of 22 Prairial II, in Laura Mason and Tracey Rizzo, comps., *The French Revolution: A Document Collection* (Boston: Houghton Mifflin, 1999), 242.

31. F. Lamarque, *Discours prononcé au Conseil des Cinq-Cents . . . S'il y a lieu à examen de la conduite du représentant Drouet* (Paris: Imprimerie R. Vatar, an IV), 14, 26, 9.

32. *Constitution du 5 Fructidor an III,* articles 111–16; Robert Legrand, *Babeuf et ses compagnons de route* (Paris: Société des études robespierristes, 1981), 317; *Journal de Marseille* (3 Thermidor V). For the decree that all accused would be tried by the high court, see *Conseil des Anciens* (24 Messidor IV), AN, AF III 42, 153/82.

33. *JDHL* (3 Fructidor IV); *L'ami du peuple* (5 Fructidor IV).

34. Claude Mazauric, "Carnot et les Babouvistes," in J.-P. Charnay, ed., *Lazare Carnot ou le savant-citoyen* (Paris: Presses de l'Université Paris-Sorbonne, 1990).

35. *L'ami des lois* (26 Messidor IV); *JDHL* (29 Messidor IV); *Patriotes de '89* (20 Messidor IV).

Chapter 6. The Case for Conspiracy

1. Jean Vassort, *Une société provinciale face à son devenir: Le Vendômois aux XVIIIe et XIXe siècles* (Paris: Publications de la Sorbonne, 1995); Paul Wagret, *Histoire de Vendôme et du Vendômois* (Toulouse: Privat, 1984).

2. Jean Vassort, "Le Vendômois à l'époque du procès de Babeuf," *Bulletin de la société archéologique, scientifique et littéraire du Vendômois* (1999): 38–42.

3. R. Bouis, "Du choix de Vendôme pour siège de la haute cour," *AHRF* 53, no. 245 (July–September 1981): 454–59; Claude Bonin and Jean-Claude Pasquier, "Du choix de Vendôme pour l'établissement de la haute cour de justice," *Bulletin de la société archéologique, scientifique et littéraire du Vendômois* (1999): 43–44; "Extrait des registres des délibérations du Directoire Exécutif" (28 Thermidor IV), AN, BB3 21 no. 244; Decree of 24 Fructidor IV, AN, W565; Decree of 21 Fructidor IV, AN, C400; "Les administrateurs du Directoire du département de Loir et Cher aux citoyens composant le Directoire exécutif" (29 Thermidor IV), AN, F7 7178 no. 378; "Loi contenant des mesures pour assurer la tranquillité dans la commune de Vendôme" (17 Fructidor IV), AN, W565.

4. Bourdon to Cochon (3ème sans-culotide IV; 17 Vendémiaire V). See also: Bourdon to Cochon (21, 23 Fructidor IV; 21 Vendémiaire, 19 Brumaire, 3, 7, 14, 19, 25 Frimaire, 25, 27, 29 Nivôse, 9 Pluviôse, 23 Germinal V), AN, F7 7178; Wagret, *Histoire de Vendôme*, 152–53.

5. James Logan Godfrey, *Revolutionary Justice: A Study of the Organization, Personnel, and Procedure of the Paris Tribunal, 1793–1795* (Chapel Hill: University of North Carolina Press, 1951); Raymonde Monnier, "Le peuple juge," in Philippe Boucher, ed., *La Révolution de la justice: Des lois du roi au droit moderne* (Paris: De Monza, 1989); Isser Woloch, *The New Regime: Transformations of the French Civic Order, 1789–1820s* (New York: W. W. Norton, 1994), 364–68; Carla Hesse, "La preuve par la lettre: Pratiques juridiques au tribunal révolutionnaire de Paris (1793–1794)," *Annales: Histoire, sciences sociales* 51, no. 3 (May–June 1996): 629–42; Alex Fairfax-Cholmeley, "Creating and Resisting the Terror: The Paris Revolutionary Tribunal, March–June 1793," *French History* 32, no. 2 (2018): 203–25.

6. "Installation de la haute cour de justice" (14 Vendémiaire V), AN, BB3 23.

7. Adolphe-Emile Lair, *Des hautes cours politiques en France et à l'Etranger* (Paris: Ernest Thorin, 1889); A. Esmein, *Éléments de droit constitutionnel Français et comparé* (Paris: Éditions Pantheon-Assas, 2001); Robert Allen, *Les tribunaux criminels sous la Révolution et l'Empire, 1792–1811* (Rennes: Presses universitaires de Rennes, 2005), 113–14; J. D. Jackson, "Two Methods of Proof in Criminal Procedure," *Modern Law Review* 51, no. 5 (September 1988): 549–68; "Yves-Marie Gandon," in Prosper-Jean Levot, *Biographie bretonne* (Geneva: Slatkine Reprints, 1971).

8. Jean François Eugène Robinet, Adolphe Robert, and J. le Chaplain, *Dictionnaire historique et biographique de la Révolution et de l'Empire* (Paris: Librairie historique et biographique de la Révolution et de l'Empire, [1899]); "René Viellart," in Louis-Gabriel Michaud, *Biographie universelle ancienne et moderne* (Leipzig: F. A. Brockhaus, 1854[–1865]); "René Viellart," in Edna LeMay, *Dictionnaire des*

constituants, 1789–1791 (Oxford: Voltaire Foundation, 1991); for Nicolas Bailly, see Gérard Gayot, ed., *Révolution en Ardennes, de l'Argonne au Namurois* (Charleville-Mézières: Terres ardennaises, 1989), 238–39; Bourdon to Cochon (9 Ventôse V), AN, F7 7178.

9. Lair, *Hautes cours politiques*, 130–39; Esmein, *Éléments de droit constitutionnel*, 1059; Interrogatoire de Babeuf devant Gandon, président de la haute cour (4 Brumaire V), AN, W564; *Débats* 1:49–51.

10. Victor Advielle, *Histoire de Gracchus Babeuf et du babouvisme* (1884; reprint, Geneva: Slatkine, 1978), 1:249–51.

11. "Lovely structure" are the words of Philippe Bourdin, "Jean-François Gaultier de Biauzat (1739–1815), Hortensius ou Nouveau Robespierrre?" *AHRF* 307 (January–March 1997): 31–60, at 54. See also Francisque Mège, *Gaultier de Biauzat, Député du Tiers-Etat aux États-Généraux de 1789: Sa Vie et Sa Correspondance* (Clermont-Ferrand: [n.p.], 1890).

12. Bourdin, "Gaultier de Biauzat," 56; Advielle, *Gracchus Babeuf,* 1:250.

13. PS.

14. *Débats*, 3:212; Elizabeth Eisenstein, *The First Professional Revolutionist* (Cambridge, MA: Harvard University Press, 1959), 8–24; George Weil, "Philippe Buonarroti (1761–1837)," *Revue historique* 76 (1901): 241–75.

15. Auguste Joseph Paris, *La Terreur dans le Pas-de-Calais et dans le Nord: Histoire de Joseph Le Bon et des Tribunaux révolutionnaires d'Arras et de Cambrai,* 2d ed. (Arras: Rousseau-Leroy, 1884), 1:105–7, 210–12; *PS*, 1:238; "Augustin Darthé," in Michaud, *Biographie universelle.*

16. "Création d'un directeur insurrecteur," *PS*, 1:169–82. Buonarroti claimed that Babeuf organized the Secret Directory with Félix Lepeletier, Sylvain Maréchal, and P.-A. Antonelle. Historians have accepted this assertion uncritically, although it is contradicted by contemporary evidence in the *Pièces saisies* and Grisel's testimony. Grisel told the high court that the Secret Directory was composed of five men: Babeuf, Buonarroti, Darthé, Germain, and Didier. *Débats*, 2:77. Buonarroti may have thought the men he named as the Secret Directory's founders retained a certain celebrity thirty years on. See Filippo Buonarroti, *La conspiration pour l'égalité* (Paris: Éditions sociales, 1957), 1:98.

17. "Création d'un directeur insurrecteur," *PS*, 1:169–82.

18. *Débats*, 1:80–81; *PS*, 1:198, 205–6; *PS*, 2:153.

19. "Au Directoire du Salut public" (10 Floréal), *PS*, 2:115; "L'agent principal du second arrondissement au Directoire secret du salut public" (6 Floréal IV), *PS*, 2:146; "Au comité secret du salut public" (25 Germinal IV), *PS*, 2:227.

20. "L'agent du quatrième arrondissement au Directoire" (6, 10 Floréal), *PS*, 2:121–23, 117–19; notes from sixth arrondissement (9 Floréal), *PS*, 2:90, 92; on marksmen and cannoneers (9 Floréal, n.d.), *PS*, 2:90, 93, 112, 116; *PS* 1: folders 1–5.

21. "Doit-on obéissance à la constitution de 1795?" in Buonarroti, *Conspiration*, 2:124–29; "Aux départements de la République française," *PS*, 1:216–19, "Les citoyens de Paris, à leurs majestés le Directoire exécutif de France," *PS*, 1:121–23; *TDP* 42 [24 Germinal IV]; *L'éclaireur du peuple*, nos. 6–7; untitled text by Buonarroti, *PS*, 1:88–91; "Aux armées campées devant Paris," *PS*, 1:112–18; *Soldat, arrête encore* [n.p., n.d.], AN, W563, and noted for distribution in *PS*, 1:54; "Réponse à une lettre signée M. V.," in Buonarroti, *Conspiration*, 2:145–54, at 149; *Analyse de la doctrine de Babeuf, Tribun du Peuple, proscrit par le Directoire exécutif, pour avoir dit la vérité* [n.p., n.d.], AN, W564.

22. *PS*, 1:24–26, 55–59, 149–51; *Débats*, 1:102–3.

23. "Le Directoire aux agents," (n.d.), *PS*, 1:55–59.

24. Vingt-troisième pièce, "paraît être de la main de Babeuf," *PS*, 1:67–68; also *PS*, 1:65–66, 80–86, 203–4; *Débats*, 2:105–7; also *Débats*, 1:69–74, 80–86.

25. *JDHL* (26 Floréal IV).

26. Agents' names, *PS*, 1:52; correspondence with Secret Directory, *PS*, 1:244–334; *PS*, 2:86–233.

27. *PS*, 1:283–85.

28. *PS*, 1:256, 244.

29. *PS*, 1:333, 332, 328.

30. *PS*, 2:162, 104–8; *PS*, 1:298–310.

31. Timothy Tackett, *The Coming of the Terror in the French Revolution* (Cambridge, MA: Harvard University Press, 2015), especially 159–65; Marisa Linton, *Choosing Terror: Virtue, Friendship, and Authenticity in the French Revolution* (New York: Oxford University Press, 2013).

32. Jean Tulard, "Le recrutement de la Légion de police de Paris sous la Convention thermidorienne et le Directoire," *AHRF* 36, no. 175 (1964): 38–64; *PS*, 1:32–38.

Chapter 7. The Equals in Vendôme

1. Charles Germain, "Translation de Paris à Vendôme d'une partie des accusés de la prétendue conspiration du 21 floréal," Fonds Babeuf, Société archéologique, scientifique et littéraire du Vendômois; Rémy Fouquet, "A propos du procès de Babeuf: Comment les accusés furent amenés de Paris à Vendôme, *Bulletin de la Société archéologique, scientifique et littéraire du Vendômois* (1954): 42–48; (1955): 13–30.

2. François Rouzet, *Journal de la Haute-Cour de Justice, établie à Vendôme* (2 Brumaire V); Bourdon to Cochon (11 Nivôse V), AN, F7 178. For a full description of the layout of abbey, prison cells, and court, see Jean-Claude Pasquier, "Essai de localization de la Haute Cour de Justice à Vendôme," *Bulletin de la Société archéologique, scientifique et littéraire du Vendômois* (1999): 45–54.

3. Robert Legrand, *Babeuf et ses compagnons de route* (Paris: Société des études robespierristes, 1981), 295–347.

4. For biographical information on Boudin, Bouin, Cordas, Drouin, see Legrand, *Babeuf et ses compagnons*, 301–2, 334–35, 340–41; Maurice Roy to Directory (8 Thermidor IV) and to Minister of Justice (12, 24 Thermidor IV), AN, BB3 21; *Débats*, 3:605–12; subscribers to *Tribun*, AN, F7 4278; interrogation of Fossard (19 Floréal IV), AN, W564; Nayez to Minister of Justice (10 Vendémiaire IV), AN, BB3 21; Richard Cobb, *The Police and the People: French Popular Protest 1789–1820* (Oxford: Clarendon Press, 1970), 165–67.

5. "Pièces contre Jean Baptiste Breton, Jeanne Ansiot, sa femme, La veuve Monnard, Thierry Drouin, filles Lambert et Lapierre," AN, W560, dossier 4954; "Nicole Pognon, femme Martin," in Legrand, *Babeuf et ses compagnons*, 330.

6. Bourdon to Cochon (1 Nivôse, 14 Vendémiaire V), AN, F7 7178.

7. Bourdon to Cochon (7 Vendémiaire, 15 Nivôse V), AN, F7 7178; Daude to Minister of Justice (30 Vendémiaire, 22 Brumaire, 9 Frimaire, 17, 23, 30 Pluviôse V), AN, BB3 20.

8. "Copie des déclarations du citoyen Pillé," in Conseil des Cinq-Cents, *Messages du Directoire Exécutif, et pièces envoyées par lui au Conseil des Cinq-Cents, relativement au représentant du peuple DROUET* (Paris: Imprimerie nationale, Floréal an IV), AN, AF III 43; Pillé au Ministre de la Police Générale (23 Floréal IV), AN, W563; Bourdon to Cochon (25 Frimaire V), AN, F7 7178; Administrative papers (11–14 Nivôse V), dossier Pillé, AN, W564.

9. For prison life before the trial began, see letters from the warden, Daude, AN, BB3 20, F1a 549; letters from police spy Bourdon to minister of police Cochon (29 Vendémiaire, 19 Brumaire, 25 Frimaire, 11, 15 Nivôse V), AN, F7 7178; Dossier Pillé, AN, W564; Hésine, *JHC* (15 Brumaire, 19 Frimaire, 20 Nivôse, 4 Pluviôse V); Rouzet, *Journal de la Haute-Cour de Justice* (17 Vendémiaire V).

10. "Protestation motivée de plusieurs citoyens prévenus de complicité dans la prétendue conspiration du 21 floréal" (25 Fructidor IV), AN, W565. Reactionary editor Richer-Sérizy, who had been charged with rousing the Vendémiaire insurrection, and several men accused of leading the September Massacres had been acquitted by separate juries in the same week that Babeuf and the others were arrested. See above, chapter 5, note 5; also *L'ami du peuple* (26 Floréal, 4 Prairial IV); *Le messager du soir* (30 Floréal IV); *Le moniteur universel* (30 Floréal IV). See also chapter 13, note 2.

11. *JHC* (15 Brumaire V).

12. *JHC* (23 Fructidor IV); Bourdon to Cochon (7, 17, 19 Vendémiaire V), AN, F7 7178; "Haute-cour de justice. Séance du 19 vendémiaire, lundi 10 octobre" and "Suites," Rouzet, *Journal de la Haute-Cour de Justice* (18, 19, 20 Vendémiaire V), Bibliothèque municipale de Vendôme.

13. *JHC* (18 Brumaire V); on Poggi, Elizabeth Eisenstein, *The First Professional Revolutionist* (Cambridge, MA: Harvard University Press, 1959), 26; Bourdon to Cochon (21 Fructidor IV, 21 Vendémiaire, 5 Brumaire, 15 Nivôse V), AN, F7 7178; Cochon to Bourdon (9 Brumaire V), AN, F 7178; defenders in *JDHL* (24, 29

Fructidor IV); Legrand, *Babeuf et ses compagnons*, 274; Archives départementales, Somme F129.

14. Pierre Serna, *Antonelle: Aristocrate révolutionnaire, 1747–1817* (Paris: Éditions du Félin, 1997), 86–91.

15. Quoted in Serna, *Antonelle*, 220. See also 206–8.

16. Serna, *Antonelle*, 241–51; P.-A. Antonelle, *Quelques idées à l'ordre, mais peut-être pas à la couleur du jour* (Paris: Imprimerie R. Vatar, an III [1795]), 91–94.

17. [P.-A. Antonelle], *Observations sur le droit de cité* (Paris: chez Vatar, l'an III [1795]), 4, 9–12; Serna, *Antonelle*, 254–64; Minchul Kim, "Pierre-Antoine Antonelle and Representative Democracy in the French Revolution," *History of European Ideas* 44, no. 3 (2018): 344–69.

18. *JDHL* (17 Brumaire, 2 Germinal IV), quoted in Serna, *Antonelle*, 301n, also 305–10.

19. *JDHL* (12 Prairial, 23, 25 Floréal IV); Babeuf's letter to Hésine in R. Bouis, "Autour de Babeuf," *AHRF* 171 (January–March 1963): 70–96. Although Babeuf told Hésine that Antonelle was part of the conspiracy, and Buonarroti said the same thing long after the marquis's death, no further evidence has ever surfaced. Filippo Buonarroti, *La conspiration pour l'égalité* (Paris: Éditions sociales, 1957), 1:99. Nonetheless, scholars continue to argue that Antonelle was part of the conspiracy. Thus, Armando Saitta explained Antonelle's criticism of Babeuf's doctrine as intended to give the tribune opportunity to better explain *perfect equality*. Armando Saitta, "Autour de la conjuration de Babeuf: Discussion sur le communisme (1796)," *AHRF* 32, no. 162 (October–December 1960): 426–35. See also Serna, *Antonelle*, 312–19. Perhaps Antonelle believed the conspiracy was counter-productive and did not join in. Perhaps Babeuf claimed Antonelle was a fellow conspirator because he believed that would blunt the latter's claims.

20. John Dunn, *Democracy: A History* (New York: Atlantic Monthly Press, 2005), 76; James Kloppenberg, *Toward Democracy: The Struggle for Self-Rule in European and American Thought* (New York: Oxford University Press, 2016), 225–42, 425–33.

21. Pierre Rosanvallon, "Revolutionary Democracy," in Samuel Moyn, ed., *Democracy Past and Future* (New York: Columbia University Press, 2006); Patrice Guennifey, "Democracy," in Edward Berenson, Vincent Duclert, and Christophe Prochasson, eds., *The French Republic: History, Values, Debates* (Ithaca, NY: Cornell University Press, 2011); Marisa Linton, *Choosing Terror: Virtue, Friendship, and Authenticity in the French Revolution* (New York: Oxford University Press, 2013).

22. [P.-A. Antonelle], "Sur la véritable conjuration et sur les prétendus anarchistes," *JDHL* (1, 14 Thermidor V).

23. Pierre-Antoine Antonelle, *Encore un mot sur le grand acte d'accusation* (Vendôme: Imprimerie Cottereau-Pinçon, an V), 1; *JDHL* (30 Messidor, 1, 10, 14, 16 Thermidor, 22 Fructidor IV). Although Antonelle continued to use "plot" and "conspiracy" interchangeably in the body of the articles he published in *JDHL* in year IV, he began to break out meanings between them in titles, labeling essays that attacked the Directory's "plotting" as "la véritable conjuration."

24. [P.-A. Antonelle], *Sur la prétendue conspiration du 21 floréal: Premier appendice de la seconde déclaration du ci-devant Hermite des environs de Paris* (Vendôme, an V), 1–2, 4.

25. Antonelle, *Encore un mot*, 4; [P.-A. Antonelle], "La mi-nuit du ci-devant hermite des environs de Paris," *JDHL* (25, 26 Nivôse V).

26. [P.-A. Antonelle], *Sur la prétendue conspiration du 21 floréal: Troisième déclaration que fait le ci-devant Hermite des environs de Paris, le jour même où les Débats doivent s'ouvrir* (Vendôme, [Ventôse V]), 5.

27. Bouis, "Autour de Babeuf," 79–82.

28. M. R. Bouis, "Le Patriote Pierre-Nicolas Hésine: Ses luttes ardentes en Loir-et-Cher de la veille de la Révolution à la Restauration (1785–1817), à Pontlevoy, Blois et Vendôme," *Bulletin de la Société archéologique, scientifique et littéraire du Vendômois* (1969): 86–101.

29. *JDHL* (4 Fructidor IV); Commissaire Provisoire près l'administration municipale de Canton du Mondoubleau au Citoyen Commissaire près celle de Vendôme (6 Fructidor IV), AN, F7 7178 no. 158; Loi contenant des mesures pour assurer la tranquillité dans la commune de Vendôme (17 Fructidor IV), AN, W565; R. B. Rose, *Gracchus Babeuf: The First Revolutionary Communist* (Stanford: Stanford University Press, 1978), 290; Daude to Minister of Interior (26 Fructidor IV) and unsigned letter from Vendôme to Paris police (14 Frimaire V), AN, F1a 549; Daude (11 Floréal V), AN, BB3 20.

30. Bouis, "Autour de Babeuf," 79–83; *JHC* signed by "femme Hésine" as "propriétaire du journal," 41 (24 Ventôse V).

31. *JHC* (15, 18, 21 Brumaire, 9 Frimaire, 4 Pluviôse V).

32. *JHC* (9 Frimaire, 1 Nivôse V), 3.

33. *JHC* (12 Frimaire V), 1. See also *JHC* (*prospectus*, 23 Fructidor IV, 9 Brumaire, 1, 3, 16, 19 Frimaire, 22 Nivôse, 16, 20 Pluviôse V).

34. *JHC* (18, 21 Brumaire V); *Supplément* (1 Frimaire V); (9 Frimaire V).

35. The paper's limited circulation is suggested by the fact that no complete press run was discovered until the late twentieth century. For examples of excerpting from or sharing with Hésine: *L'ami du peuple* (21 Frimaire, 8 Nivôse, 17 Pluviôse, 7 Ventôse V); *JDHL* (4 Fructidor IV, 6, 11 Ventôse V). For dissemination from Paris to the provinces: the Jacobin *Observateur Démocrate* in Metz and the *Journal du département de la Marne* drew heavily on *JDHL*. Isser Woloch, "The Revival of Jacobinism in Metz during the Directory," *Journal of Modern History* 38, no. 1 (March 1966): 13–37; Georges Clause, "Un journal républicain de l'époque directoriale à Chalons-sur-Marne: 'Le journal du département de la Marne' 1796–1800," *Mémoires de la Société d'agriculture, commerce, sciences et arts du département de la Marne* 90 (1975): 275–313.

Chapter 8. Squaring Off

1. Philippe Rouillac, "Un procès en apparat, décor, mobilier, et costume," *Bulletin de la Société archéologique, scientifique et littéraire du Vendômois* (1999): 55–67; JHC (12, 19 Frimaire, 1 Nivôse V).

2. Rouillac, "Un procès," 66–67.

3. *Débats*, 1:7–14.

4. *Débats*, 1:24.

5. *Débats*, 1:17–25; reference to Agier in *PS*, 1:259–60.

6. *Débats*, 1:51. For entire speech, see 1:25–51.

7. Bourdon (17 Ventôse V), AN, F7 7178; Daude (15 Ventôse V), AN, BB3 20; *Censeur des journaux* (20 Ventôse V).

8. Jean Nicolas Dufort de Cheverny, *Mémoires sur les règnes de Louis XV et Louis XVI et sur la Révolution* (Paris: E. Plon, Nourrit & Cie, 1886), 314.

9. "René Viellart," in Louis-Gabriel Michaud, *Biographie universelle ancienne et moderne* (Leipzig: F. A. Brockhaus, 1854[–1865]); "René Viellart," in Edna LeMay, *Dictionnaire des constituants, 1789–1791* (Oxford: Voltaire Foundation, 1991); Jean-Louis Halpérin, *Le tribunal de cassation et les pouvoirs sous la Révolution, 1790–1799* (Paris: Librairie générale de droit et de jurisprudence, 1987), 146–47.

10. François Antoine Boissy d'Anglas, "Motion d'ordre contre les terroristes et les royalistes" (Paris: Imprimerie nationale, an III), 5–6.

11. François Antoine Boissy d'Anglas, "Discours préliminaire au projet de Constitution . . . 5 messidor an III," in *Choix de rapports, opinions et discours prononcés à la Tribune Nationale depuis 1789 jusqu'à ce jour*, vol. 15: 1794–95 (Paris: Alexis Eymery, 1821), 125.

12. *Débats*, 1:71–72, 74, 86–87, 73, 118–19. For entire speech, see 1:70–121.

13. *Débats*, 1:100.

14. *Débats*, 1:99, 76. See also Dufort de Cheverny, *Mémoires*, 244–46, 315.

15. Méhée to *L'ami des lois* (26 Messidor IV); Merlin to Méhée (7 Fructidor IV), AN, BB3 21.

16. Louis Bigard, *Le comte Réal, ancien Jacobin* (Versailles: Administration de la Revue, 1937); Pierre Serna, "Réal ou la république 'réaliste,' " in Michel Vovelle, ed., *Le tournant de l'an III: Réaction et Terreur blanche dans la France révolutionnaire* (Paris: Éditions du CTHS, 1997); Laura Mason, "The 'Bosom of Proof': Criminal Justice and the Renewal of Oral Culture during the French Revolution," *Journal of Modern History* 76, no. 1 (March 2004): 29–61. See also Pierre-François Réal, *Rapport fait à la Convention nationale, sur l'affreux régime des prisons, et les cruautés exercées par les patriotes par les ordres du scélérat Robespierre* (Paris: Toubon, An II); *Essai sur les journées des treize et quatorze vendémiaire* (Paris: chez l'auteur, l'an IV); *Procès de Barthélemy Tort de Lasonde, accusé de conspiration contre l'État et de complicité avec Dumouriez . . .* (Paris: Réal, an V).

17. *Débats*, 1:154.
18. *Débats*, 1:121–22; *Débats*, 2:59; *L'ami du peuple* (29 Thermidor IV). See also Bourdon to Cochon (6 Ventôse V), AN, F7 7178.

Chapter 9. Witnesses for the Prosecution

1. Adolphe-Emile Lair, *Des hautes cours politiques en France et à l'Etranger* (Paris: Ernest Thorin, 1889), 164.
2. Robert Allen, *Les tribunaux criminels sous la Révolution et l'Empire, 1792–1811* (Rennes: Presses universitaires de Rennes, 2005).
3. *Débats*, 1:125–43; 245, 153.
4. *Débats*, 1:125–28, 382, 238.
5. *Débats*, 1:358–74, 376, 378, 382–84.
6. *Débats*, 1:408–15.
7. *Débats*, 1:420 (for entire speech, 415–20).
8. *Débats*, 1:421–22.
9. *Débats*, 1:423–28.
10. *Débats*, 2:130–32, 65–66; Robert Legrand, *Babeuf et ses compagnons de route* (Paris: Société des études robespierristes, 1981), 217–18.
11. *Débats*, 2:68–71.
12. *Lettre de Franc-Libre, soldat de l'armée circo-parisienne, à son ami La Terreur, soldat de l'armée du Rhin* (Paris: n.p., n.d.), AN, W563; PS, 1:46–48.
13. *Débats*, 2:73–80, 86–91.
14. *Création d'un Directoire insurrecteur*, PS, 1:169–81; *Lettre de Franc Libre*.
15. *Débats*, 2:95–100.
16. *Débats*, 2:92.
17. *Débats*, 2:94.
18. R. Bouis, "Autour de Babeuf," *AHRF* 171 (January–March 1963), 70–96; R. B. Rose, *Gracchus Babeuf: The First Revolutionary Communist* (Stanford: Stanford University Press, 1978), 266–67.
19. *Débats*, 2:90.
20. Legrand, *Babeuf et ses compagnons*, 218; minute of Executive Directory decree (17 Floréal IV), AN, AF III 42.
21. *Débats*, 2:105–15.
22. *Débats*, 2:115.
23. *Débats*, 2:116.
24. *Débats*, 2:137, 151.
25. *Débats*, 2:148.
26. *Débats*, 2:162–63.
27. *Débats*, 2:191–97.

28. *Débats*, 2:118, 154, 270. Jean-Marie-Claude Alexandre Goujon, *Défense du représen-tant du peuple Goujon, député par le département de Seine et Oise, traduit devant la commission militaire, sous le prétexte de l'affaire du 1er prairial* (Paris: Imprimerie de R. Vatar, [n.d.]).

29. *Débats*, 2:374–79, 410–24, 440–56, 460–87; *Pièces contre Jean Baptiste Breton, Jeanne Ansiot, sa femme, La veuve Monnard, Thierry Drouin, filles Lambert et Lapierre*, AN, W560, dossier 4954; *Recueil des actes d'accusation des prévenus dans l'affaire de Drouet . . . Babeuf et consorts* (Vendôme: Imprimerie de la haute cour Morard-Colas, an V), 83–87 .

30. *Débats*, 2:456, 472, 379–85, 414–24, 436–40, 466–90.

31. *Débats*, 2:491.

32. *Débats*, 2:492–96. See also *Copie de la procédure commun à Babeuf et co-accusés prévenus de conspiration* (Vendôme: Imprimerie Morard-Colas, n.d.), 36–41; "Extrait de l'interrogatoire subi par le nommé Jean Baptiste Meunier" (16 Floréal IV), AN, W563, dossier 77; "Interrogatoire subi secrètement par Jean Baptiste Meunier" (22 Floréal IV), AN, F7 4276.

33. *Débats*, 2:497–503.

34. *Débats*, 2:504–7.

35. *Débats*, 3:173–80, 187–88, 191, 195–97, 201–3.

Chapter 10. Reclaiming the Revolution

1. *Débats*, 3:205, 204–8; *PS*, 1:26–27, 29–31, 61, 69–72.

2. *Débats*, 3:122. See also 3:67–74, 79–80, 83–95, 103–40, 142–54. *PS*, 1:38.

3. *Débats*, 3:93; see also Germain, *Débats*, 3:137.

4. *Débats*, 2:290–96, 308–12, 314–23. Babeuf previewed this argument in his third po-lice interrogation, in the spring of 1796, published in *JHC* (18, 21 Brumaire, 1 Fri-maire V).

5. *Débats*, 2:245, 198–208, 243–45.

6. *PS*, 1:139–48.

7. *Débats*, 1:86.

8. Johnson Kent Wright, *A Classical Republican in Eighteenth-century France: The Political Thought of Mably* (Stanford: Stanford University Press, 1997), 73–78.

9. Wright, *Classical Republican*; Jean-Louis Lecercle, "Introduction," in Gabriel Bon-not de Mably, *Des droits et des devoirs du citoyen* (Paris: M. Didier, 1972); Ephraim Harpaz, "Mably et ses contemporains," *Revue des sciences humaines* 79 (July–September 1955): 351–66; Keith Michael Baker, "A Script for a French Revolution: The Politicial Consciousness of the Abbé Mably," in *Inventing the French Revolu-tion* (New York: Cambridge University Press, 1990).

10. *Débats*, 2:222–23.

11. *Débats*, 2:230.

12. *Débats*, 2:230, 233.

13. *Débats*, 2:237–38, 239–40, 243; "Liberté, couvres nous d'honneur / Nous voulons périr tes victimes," Jean-Marie-Claude Alexandre Goujon, *Défense du représentant du peuple Goujon, député par le département de Seine et Oise, traduit devant la commission militaire, sous le prétexte de l'affaire du 1er prairial* (Paris: Imprimerie R. Vatar, [n.d.]).

14. *PS*, 1:169–83.

15. *Débats*, 2:251.

16. *Débats*, 2:253–58.

17. *Débats*, 2:274, 276, 274–79.

18. *Débats*, 2:284.

19. Daude (4, 30 Ventôse, 1, 20 Germinal V), AN, BB3 20; Bourdon to Cochon (15, 28, 30 Ventôse V), AN, F7 7178.

20. *Débats*, 2:301.

21. William Sewell, "Historical Events as Transformations of Structures: Inventing Revolution at the Bastille," *Theory and Society* 25, no. 6 (December 1996): 841–81; Colin Lucas, "Revolutionary Violence, the People and the Terror," in K. M. Baker and Colin Lucas, eds., *The French Revolution and the Creation of Modern Political Culture*, vol. 4: *The Terror* (Oxford: Pergamon Press, 1994); Colin Lucas, "Talking about Urban Popular Violence in 1789," in Alan Forrest and Peter Jones, eds., *Reshaping France: Town, Country and Region during the French Revolution* (Manchester, UK: Manchester University Press, 1991).

22. Jean-Clément Martin, *Violence et Révolution: Essai sur la naissance d'un mythe national* (Paris: Seuil, 2006), 271–304; Marc Deleplace, "Le discours sur 'l'anarchie' en l'an III: entre 'terreur' et 'contre-révolution,' " in Michel Vovelle, ed., *Le tournant de l'an III: Réaction et Terreur blanche dans la France révolutionnaire* (Paris: Éditions du CTHS, 1997); Raymond Monnier, "Le tournant de Brumaire: Dépopulariser la révolution parisienne," in Vovelle, ed., *Tournant de l'an III*; Colin Lucas, "Les thermidoriens et les violences de l'an III," in Roger Dupuy and Marcel Morabito, eds., *1795: Pour une République sans Révolution* (Rennes: Presses universitaires de Rennes, 1996); Yannick Bosc, "Boissy d'Anglas et le rejet de la Déclaration de 1793," in Roger Bourderon, ed., *L'an I et l'apprentissage de la démocratie* (Saint Denis: Éditions PSD, 1995).

23. *Débats*, 2:301, 306, 301–8.

24. *Débats*, 3:209; *PS*, 1:88–91.

25. *Débats*, 3:212, 217, 218, 219, 221, 222 (full speech, 211–26).

26. *Débats*, 3:226.

27. *Débats*, 3:238–39.

28. *Débats*, 3:170, 297–98.

29. *Débats*, 3:538.

30. Nayez, *Débats*, 3:9–30; Crépin, *Débats*, 3:406–15; Fossard, *Débats*, 3:611, 605–12; Agier, *Débats*, 1:24.

31. *Débats*, 3:587–96.

32. Richard Cobb, *The Police and the People: French Popular Protest 1789–1820* (Oxford: Clarendon Press, 1970), 166–67.

Chapter 11. Perfect Equality

1. Bourdon to Cochon (21 Nivôse V), AN, F7 7178.

2. Daude (Ventôse–Germinal V), AN, BB3 20.

3. R. B. Rose, *Gracchus Babeuf: The First Revolutionary Communist* (Stanford: Stanford University Press, 1978), 318; Daude (30 Nivôse; 1, 23 Pluviôse V), AN, BB3 20; Bourdon to Cochon (25 Nivôse V), AN, F7 7178.

4. Daude (15 Floréal V), AN, BB3 20; Régis Bouis, "Saisie d'au moins dix lettres d'accusés dont trois de Germain, le 29 germinal an V," in Société archéologique, scientifique et littéraire du Vendômois, *À l'occasion du Bicentenaire de la Révolution française* (Blois: Imprimerie Rollin, 1991); Bourdon (25, 26, 28, 29 Germinal, 1 Floréal V), AN, F7 7178; *Courier républicain* (5, 8 Floréal V); *Censeur des journaux* (6 Floréal V); *Le Thé* (8 Floréal V); *Le messager du soir* (26 Ventôse V).

5. *Débats*, 4:4–5, 9–11.

6. *Débats*, 4:58.

7. John Dunn, *Democracy: A History* (New York: Atlantic Monthly Press, 2005); Pierre Rosanvallon, "Revolutionary Democracy," in Samuel Moyn, ed., *Democracy Past and Future* (New York: Columbia University Press, 2006); Patrice Guennifey, "Democracy," in Edward Berenson, Vincent Duclert, and Christophe Prochasson, eds., *The French Republic: History, Values, Debates* (Ithaca, NY: Cornell University Press, 2011).

8. For moderate opinion: Jean-Sylvain Bailly, *Adresse aux habitants de Paris* (15 October 1789), in Sigismond Lacroix, ed., *Actes de la Commune de Paris* (Paris: Cerf, 1899–1942), 2:307–10. For more radical perspectives: Slavoj Žižek, ed., *Robespierre: Virtue and Terror* (New York: Verso, 2017); Albert Soboul, *The Sans-Culottes: The Popular Movement and Revolutionary Government, 1793–1794*, trans. Remy Inglis Hall (Princeton, NJ: Princeton University Press, 1980), 95–105.

9. Kare Tønnesson, "La démocratie directe sous la Révolution française: Le cas des districts et sections de Paris," in Colin Lucas, ed., *The French Revolution and the Creation of Modern Political Culture*, vol. 2: *The Political Culture of the French Revolution* (New York: Pergamon Press, 1988).

10. *Débats*, 4:59–60.

11. *Débats*, 4:50, 64; summary argument, 3–64.

12. *Débats*, 4:76, 80; summary against Buonarroti, 4:76–83.

13. *Débats*, 4:70; summary against Babeuf, 65–75; 4:86; summary against Germain, 83–93.

14. *Débats*, 1:317.

15. *Débats*, 4:98–99; summary against Darthé, 93–99.
16. *Débats*, 4:133–45, 116.
17. *Débats*, 4:125–27, 101–3.
18. *Débats*, 4:359, 361.
19. *Débats*, 4:246–47, 253–62 (full speech, 241–305).
20. Victor Advielle, *Histoire de Gracchus Babeuf et du babouvisme* (1884; reprint, Geneva: Slatkine, 1978), 2:24–27.
21. Advielle, *Babeuf*, 2:29–30.
22. See, for example, *Analyse de la doctrine de Babeuf* [n.p., n.d.], AN, W564, which asserts that "there is oppression when some exhaust themselves by laboring and lack everything, while others swim in abundance while doing nothing. No one may legitimately appropriate the goods of the earth or of industry exclusively for himself." Claude Mazauric, *Babeuf et la Conspiration pour l'Egalite* (Paris: Éditions sociales, 1962), 115–43; *Débats*, 1:118, 2:233–36, 3:485–86, 4:174–75.
23. Rose, *Gracchus Babeuf*, 318–19; Daude (30 Ventôse, 1 Germinal V), AN, BB3 20.
24. Advielle, *Babeuf*, 2:32–33.
25. Advielle, *Babeuf*, 2:39, 41–42.
26. Advielle, *Babeuf*, 2:44, 48–49, 52, 58–59.
27. Advielle, *Babeuf*, 2:43, 52.
28. Daude (17 Floréal V), AN, BB3 20; Advielle, *Babeuf*, 2:320, 322.

Chapter 12. Speaking to the Nation

1. Laura Mason, "The 'Bosom of Proof': Criminal Justice and the Renewal of Oral Culture during the French Revolution," *Journal of Modern History* 76, no. 1 (March 2004): 29–61; Robert Allen, *Les tribunaux criminels sous la Révolution et l'Empire* (Rennes: Presses universitaires de Rennes, 2005).
2. *JDHL* (10 Ventôse V); defendants' complaints and accusations, *JDHL* (6, 7, 17, 18 Ventôse V); *JHC* (6, 8, 10, 12, 14, 15 Ventôse V); *L'ami du peuple* (7, 9 Ventôse V).
3. *JHC* (20, 22 Ventôse V). The *High Court Journal* was not alone in summarizing so prejudicially. The *Editor* was similarly brief, backing the Directory by saying that Harger affirmed that the line was drawn by Babeuf and suppressing entirely the discussion about his reading of the phrase. *Rédacteur* (24 Ventôse V).
4. *JHC* (27, 28 Ventôse, 8, 10 Germinal V). See also *La Sentinelle* (9 Germinal V); *JDHL* (17, 18, 26, 27 Ventôse V); *Supplément* (26 Ventôse); (10, 24 Germinal V); *L'ami du peuple* (25 Germinal V).
5. *L'ami du peuple* (9 Ventôse V; also 7 Ventôse, 6, 14 Floréal V); *JHC* (12, 14 Germinal V) *JDHL* (1, 6 Ventôse V). For Darthé: *JHC* (18 Ventôse, 24 Floréal V); *L'ami du peuple* (17, 29 Brumaire, 14 Frimaire V); *JDHL* (19–20 Frimaire V).
6. *JHC* (15 Ventôse, 26 Pluviôse, 14 Germinal V); *L'ami du peuple* (1 Ventôse V); *JDHL* (6 Ventôse V).

7. *L'ami du peuple* (3 Germinal V); *JDHL* (14, 19 Germinal V).

8. *L'ami du peuple* (12 Floréal V; also 11 Floréal V); *JDHL* (2, 18, 19 Germinal V); *JHC* (2, 4, 18 Germinal V). Reports of Lamberté's speech highlighted the same issues: *L'ami du peuple* (2 Floréal V); *JHC* (4 Floréal V). For Cazin, see *JHC* (18 Germinal V); for Moroy, *L'ami du peuple* (23 Germinal V). See also P.-A. Antonelle, *L'hermite et le détenu: Les questions du ci-devant hermite des environs de Paris; et les réponses du détenu à Vendôme; soliloque d'un nouveau genre*, which was published as a pamphlet by l'Imprimerie de L'Ami du peuple and serialized through at least five issues of *L'ami du peuple* (7, 8, 11, 15, 18 Germinal V).

9. *L'ami du peuple* (5 Ventôse, 4, 5 Floréal V); Amédée Lepeletier, *Défense de Félix Lepeletier par . . . adressée aux jurés et juges de la haute-cour, séante à Vendôme* (Paris: [n.p.], l'an V); *JHC* (2 Floréal V); celebration of Antonelle as a conspirator: *JDHL* (29 Germinal V).

10. Jean-Nicolas Pache, *Sur les factions et les partis, les conspirations et les conjurations; et sur celles à l'ordre du jour* (Paris: Impr. R. Vatar, an V), dated "à Thim-le-Moutier, 21 Floréal l'an V" on the last page. On political parties see Isser Woloch, "A Revolution in Political Culture," in Peter McPhee, ed., *A Companion to the French Revolution* (Chichester: Wiley-Blackwell, 2013), 447–50.

11. Pache, *Sur les factions*, 5–6, 7, 13–14.

12. *JDHL* (18 Floréal V); *JHC* (20 Floréal V); *L'ami du peuple* (2, 3, 4, 15 Prairial V).

13. *Débats*, 4:362; Victor Advielle, *Histoire de Gracchus Babeuf et du babouvisme* (1884; reprint, Geneva: Slatkine, 1978), vol. 2.

14. Pache, *Sur les factions*, 19.

15. *JHC* (4 Germinal V); *JDHL* (4 Germinal V); *L'ami du peuple* (6 Germinal V).

16. P.-A. Antonelle, *Sur la prétendue conspiration de 21 floréal: Mon examen de conscience; ou le détenu à Vendosme, interrogé par le ci-devant hermite* (Vendôme: Imprimerie Cottereau-Pinçon, an V), 14–15.

17. Isser Woloch, *Jacobin Legacy: The Democratic Movement under the Directory* (Princeton, NJ: Princeton University Press, 1970), 56–79.

18. Hervé Leuwers, *Un juriste en politique: Merlin de Douai (1754–1838)* (Arras: Artois Presses Université, 1996); Henri Welschinger, *Le journaliste Lebois et l'Ami du Peuple (an III–an VIII)* (Paris: Imprimerie A. Quantin, [1885]), BN, NUMM 5450456; Woloch, *Jacobin Legacy*, 50.

19. *JDHL* (7 Prairial V); subscription list to *Tribun du peuple*, AN, F7 4278; *Journal des patriotes de '89* (7 Prairial IV); Max Fajn, *The Journal des hommes libres de tous les pays, 1792–1800* (The Hague: Mouton, 1975), 66–74; Woloch, *Jacobin Legacy*, 52–53.

20. *Débats*, 1:195–97; *JHC* (6 Pluviôse V); Commissaire Provisoire du Pouvoir Exécutif près l'administration municipale de Canton du Mondoubleau (6 Fructidor IV), AN, F7 7178 no. 158; Daude to Minister of Interior (26 Fructidor IV), AN, F Iᵃ 549; Hatry, Général Commandant en chef de la 17e division militaire au Ministre de la

Guerre (17 Frimaire V), AN, F7 7178 no. 287; M. R. Bouis, "Le Patriote Pierre-Nicolas Hésine: Ses luttes ardentes en Loir-et-Cher de la veille de la Révolution à la Restauration," pt. 3, *Bulletin de la Société archéologique, scientifique et littéraire du Vendômois* (1971): 45–65; Conseil des Cinq-Cents, *Rapport fait par Bontoux . . . chargée d'examiner la pétition du citoyen Pierre-Nicolas Hezine . . .* (Paris: Imprimerie nationale, an V).

21. Consider the case of militant Charles Jaubert, arrested for dismissing the conspiracy as a "fable," Woloch, *Jacobin Legacy*, 55. On the democratic press after Thermidor, see Hugh Gough, *The Newspaper Press in the French Revolution* (London: Routledge, 1988), 118–59; Fajn, *The Journal des hommes libres*, 39–112. On provincial violence, see Richard Cobb, *The Police and the People* (Oxford: Clarendon Press, 1970), 131–50.

22. *L'ami des lois* (8 Floréal V); Jeremy Popkin, "The Directory and the Republican Press: The Case of the *Ami des lois*," *History of European Ideas* 10 (1989): 429–42. Poultier made his declaration after the *Débats du procès* wrongly attributed a complaint about conduct of the trial to the assistant prosecutor, Bailly. Although the *Débats* later corrected the misprint and *Le Rédacteur* (20 Floréal V) called Poultier's attention to the erratum, he did not change his tune.

23. *La sentinelle* (18 Ventôse V).

24. Woloch, *Jacobin Legacy*, 51–63; Philippe Bourdin, "Jean-François Gaultier de Biauzat (1739–1815): Hortensius ou Nouveau Robespierrre?" *AHRF* 307 (January–March 1997): 31–60; letters between Camp, Merlin, and Gauthier-Biauzat (14–21 Germinal V), AN, BB3 21 no. 417; *Le Censeur des journaux* (23 Germinal V); Les administrateurs municipaux du canton de Vendôme à Cochon (29 Germinal V), AN, F7 7178 no. 227; Régis Bouis, "Saisie d'au moins dix lettres d'accusés dont trois de Germain, le 29 germinal an V," in Société archéologique, scientifique et littéraire du Vendômois, *À l'occasion du Bicentenaire de la Révolution française* (Blois: Imprimerie Rollin, 1991).

25. *Courier républicain* (18, 20 Ventôse, 11 Germinal V); *Censeur des journaux* (15 Ventôse V). See also: *Censeur des journaux* (6, 11 Germinal V); *Le messager du soir* (26 Ventôse V).

26. Malcolm Crook, *Elections in the French Revolution: An Apprenticeship in Democracy* (New York: Cambridge University Press, 1996), 127; Martyn Lyons, *France under the Directory* (New York: Cambridge University Press, 1975); Howard Brown, *Ending the French Revolution* (Charlottesville: University of Virginia Press, 2006); Marc Belissa and Yannick Bosc, *Le Directoire: La république sans la démocratie* (Paris: La fabrique éditions, 2018).

27. *Journal de Perlet* (2 Ventôse V); *Journal de Marseille* (19 Ventôse V); Crook, *Elections*, 141–47; Harvey Mitchell, *The Underground War against Revolutionary France* (Oxford: Clarendon Press, 1965), 140–61; "Emmanuel Pastoret . . . aux habitants de la Var," in *L'historien* (25 Ventôse V). See also: *L'anti-Terroriste* (12 Ventôse V); *Courier républicain* (2 Germinal V).

NOTES TO PAGES 186–191

28. Marc Deleplace, *L'anarchie de Mably à Proudhon, 1750–1850: Histoire d'une appropriation polémique* (Lyon: ENS éditions, 2000); *Journal de Perlet* (12 Pluviôse V); *L'historien* (27 Nivôse V).

29. *Messager du soir* (11, 12 Ventôse V); *L'historien* (25 Ventôse V); *Journal de Perlet* (18 Ventôse V). See also *Journal de Marseille* (19 Ventôse V); *Censeur des journaux* (1, 6 Germinal V); *Courier républicain* (6 Germinal V); Jean-René Suratteau, "Les élections de l'an V aux Conseils du Directoire," *AHRF* 30, no. 154 (October–December 1958): 21–63; Crook, *Elections*, 138–46.

30. *JDHL* (15 Pluviôse–6 Germinal V).

31. F.-A. Aulard, *Paris pendant la réaction thermidorienne et sous le directoire* (Paris: [n.p.], 1898–1902), 3:777, 4:9.

32. *Messager du soir* (17 Germinal V), quoted in Jeremy Popkin, *The Right-wing Press in France, 1792–1800* (Chapel Hill: University of North Carolina Press, 1980), 84.

33. On right-wing tilt after primary assemblies, see *Messager du soir* (3 Germinal V); *Courier républicain* (3 Germinal V); *Censeur des journaux* (4 Germinal V).

34. Ninety percent of the incoming men (182 deputies) were identified as reactionary or royalist. Suratteau, "Les élections de l'an V," 54–55.

35. *L'ami des lois* (12 Floréal V).

36. Jeremy Popkin, "Les Journaux républicains, 1795–1799," *Revue d'histoire moderne et contemporaine* 31 (1984): 143–57.

Chapter 13. Trial's End

1. Isser Woloch, *The New Regime* (New York: W. W. Norton, 1994), 356–64; Robert Allen, *Les tribunaux criminels sous la Révolution et l'Empire* (Rennes: Presses universitaires de Rennes, 2005), 41–43, 45–49, 52–53.

2. On acquittals of those charged with leading the September Massacres and exciting the Vendémiaire insurrection see *L'ami du peuple* (26 Floréal, 4 Prairial IV); *Le messager du soir* (30 Floréal IV); *Le moniteur universel* (30 Floréal IV). On royalist conspiracy of La Villeurnoy and Brottier, see Harvey Mitchell, *The Underground War against Revolutionary France* (Oxford: Clarendon Press, 1965), 108–17; *Débats du procès instruit par le Conseil de guerre permanent de la XVIIe division militaire . . . contre les prévenus Brottier, Berthelot la Villeurnoy, Dunan, Poly et autres* (Paris: chez Baudouin, 1797). See also above, chapter 5, note 5; chapter 7, note 10.

3. For judges' unilateral power in formulating questions, see Allen, *Les tribunaux criminels*, 141–46.

4. *Résumé du président de la haute cour de justice à la suite du débat dans l'affaire du représentant du peuple Drouet, de Baboeuf et autres, accusés de conspiration contre la sûreté intérieure de la République. Séances des 2, 3 et 4 prairial* (Paris: chez Baudouin, 1797), 67, 69. (Text bound at the end of *Débats*, vol. 4.)

5. *Résumé du president*, 82.

6. *Résumé du president*, 92, 94, 97.

7. Jean Nicolas Dufort de Cheverny, *Mémoires sur les règnes de Louis XV et Louis XVI et sur la Révolution* (Paris: E. Plon, Nourrit & Cie, 1886), 334–36; Daude to Minister of Justice (6, 7 Prairial V), AN, BB3 20.

8. *JHC* (9 Prairial V); *L'ami des lois* (11 Prairial V); *Journal de Toulouse, ou l'Observateur* (18 Prairial V); *Résumé du president*, 116–34.

9. Daude to Minister of Justice (7 Prairial V), AN, BB3 20; *L'ami du peuple* (9 Prairial V); *L'ami des lois* (11 Prairial V); *JHC* (7 Prairial V).

10. Dufort de Cheverny, *Mémoires*, 336; *JDHL* (10, 11, 12 Prairial V); *L'ami des lois* (13 Prairial V).

11. *Messager du soir* (10, 11 Prairial V). See also *Censeur des journaux* (14 Prairial V).

12. *Courier républicain* (14 Prairial V); *Messager du soir* (11 Prairial V). See also *Courier républicain* (11 Prairial V); *Messager du soir* (10 Prairial V), *Censeur des journaux* (14 Prairial V), *Le Thé* (20 Prairial V).

13. *Messager du soir* (10 Prairial V).

14. "Au rédacteur," *L'anti-terroriste, ou Journal des principes* (2 Messidor V). *L'ami des lois* reported an "aristocrate" saying: "We could have condemned them legally, and we did them the honor of murdering them!" (15 Prairial V); *Messager du soir* (10 Prairial V); *Courier républicain* (19 Prairial V); *Le Thé* (20 Prairial V).

15. *L'ami du peuple* (11, 13, 25 Prairial V); *JDHL* (12, 24 Prairial V); *L'ami des lois* (11 Prairial V), reprinted by *L'ami des principes, ou Journal du républicain impartial et juste* (Angers) (12 Prairial V). See also *L'ami des lois* (13, 14, 15 Prairial V). For discussion of Topino-LeBrun's visual commentary on events in Vendôme through *The Death of Caius Gracchus*, see James Henry Rubin, "Painting and Politics II: J.-L. David's Patriotism, or the Conspiracy of Gracchus Babeuf and the Legacy of Topino-Lebrun," *Art Bulletin* 58, no. 4 (December 1976): 547–68; Philippe Bordes, "Les Arts après la Terreur: Topino-Lebrun, Hennequin, et la peinture politique sous le Directoire," *Revue du Louvre* 29 (1979): 199–212.

16. *Journal de Toulouse* (16 Prairial V); *JDHL* (13 Prairial V).

17. *L'ami du peuple* (23 Prairial V); Jeremy Popkin, "The Directory and the Republican Press: The Case of *L'ami des lois*," *History of European Ideas* 10, no. 4 (1989): 429–42.

18. *JDHL* (14, 15, 16 Prairial V).

19. *JDHL* (14 Prairial V); *L'ami du peuple* (20 Prairial V).

20. *JDHL* (24 Prairial V).

Chapter 14. The Republic Imperiled

1. R. Bouis, "Autour de Babeuf," *AHRF* 171 (January–March 1963): 93–94. Forty-seven defendants were present for the trial: in addition to five exiles and the two men condemned to death, Vadier, Amar, and Cochet were imprisoned on other charges.

On return: Taffoureau to Executive Directory (25 Prairial V), AN, F7 4276; Breton and wife to Executive Directory (29 Messidor V), AN, BB3 22; Minister of Justice, report to Executive Directory (2 Thermidor V), AN, AF III 42; François Lamarque, *Rapport . . . sur la pétition de plusieurs citoyens acquittés par la haute cour de justice . . .* (Paris: [n.p.], an VI [1797]).

2. Daude (23 Prairial V), AN, F1a 549. See also reports for 11 Prairial V, AN, F1a 549; reports for 15, 17, 21 Prairial V, AN, BB3 20; J. N. Dufort de Cheverny, *Mémoires sur les règnes de Louis XV et Louis XVI et sur la Révolution* (Paris: E. Plon, Nourrit & Cie, 1886), 2:267.

3. Paul Robiquet, "Les déportés Babouvistes au Fort National," *La Révolution française* 62 (January–June 1912): 481–509, at 500.

4. Robert Legrand, *Babeuf et ses compagnons de route* (Paris: Société des études robespierristes, 1983), 299, 333–34; Robiquet, "Les déportés Babouvistes"; Jean Dautry, "L'incarcération à Cherbourg de Buonarroti et de ses compagnons," *AHRF* 33, no. 163 (January–March 1961): 74–87.

5. Jean-René Suratteau, "Les Babouvistes, le Péril Rouge et le Directoire (1796–1798)," in *Babeuf et les problèmes du babouvisme: Colloque international de Stockholm* (Paris: Éditions sociales, 1963), 159; Georges Duruy, ed., *Mémoires du Barras* (Paris: [n.p.], 1895), 394–414; Jacques de Dampierre, ed., *Mémoires de Barthélemy* (Paris: [n.p.], 1914), 208; Albert Meynier, *Les coups d'état du Directoire*, vol. 1: *Le dix-huit fructidor an V* (Paris: Presses universitaires de France, 1927), 16–17; Georges Lefebvre, *The French Revolution*, trans. Elizabeth Moss Evanson (New York: Columbia University Press, 1962), 2:304; Denis Woronoff, *La République bourgeoise de Thermidor à Brumaire* (Paris: Seuil, 1972); M. J. Sydenham, *The French Revolution* (New York: Capricorn Books, 1966); Albert Mathiez, *Le directoire* (Paris: A. Colin, 1934); W. R. Fryer, *Republic or Restoration in France?* (Manchester, UK: Manchester University Press, 1965), 234–36; Colin Lucas, "The First Directory and the Rule of Law," *French Historical Studies* 10 (1977): 231–60; Jean Dautry, "Les démocrates parisiens avant et après le coup d'état du 18 fructidor an V," *AHRF* 22, no. 118 (April–June 1950): 141–51, at 142; *Courier républicain* (9, 28 Messidor V) and *Nouvelles politiques* (21 Messidor V) in F.-A. Aulard, *Paris pendant la réaction thermidorienne et sous le directoire* (Paris: [n.p.], 1898–1902), 4:193, 212–13, 205–6.

6. Honoré Riouffe, *Discours lu au Cercle Constitutionnel le neuf messidor . . .* (Paris: Imprimerie nationale, [an V]), 4–5; *JDHL* (20 Messidor V); Béatrice Jasinski, "Constant et le Cercle constitutionnel," in Dominique Verrey and Anne-Lise Delacrétaz, eds., *Benjamin Constant et la Révolution française, 1789–1799* (Geneva: Librairie Droz, 1989), 119; Gérard Gengembre, "Le Cercle constitutionnel: Un laboratoire du libéralisme?" in Verrey and Delacrétaz, eds., *Benjamin Constant*. On Réal, see Léonce Pingaud, *Jean de Bry (1760–1835)* (Paris: Plon, 1909), 63. For Antonelle, Eugène Asse, "Benjamin Constant et le Directoire," *Revue de la Révolution* 15 (May–August 1889): 337–56 and 433–53, at 439.

7. Isser Woloch, *Jacobin Legacy: The Democratic Movement under the Directory* (Princeton, NJ: Princeton University Press, 1970), 65–70; *Courier républicain* (9 Messidor V), quoted in Aulard, *Paris pendant la réaction thermidorienne*, 4:193; Pierre Serna, *Antonelle: Aristocrate révolutionnaire, 1747–1817* (Paris: Éditions Félin, 1997), 347; *Gazette nationale, ou le Moniteur universelle* (10 Thermidor V); Decree of 7 Thermidor V, Meynier, *Coups d'état du Directoire*, 1:48–49.

8. *Moniteur universelle* (10 Thermidor V); Woloch, *Jacobin Legacy*, 70–75; Aulard, *Paris pendant la réaction*, 4:277–80, 308, 310, 313–14; Charles Ballot, *Le coup d'Etat du 18 Fructidor an V* (Paris: Société de l'histoire de la Révolution française, 1906), 77–78, 93–94, 108–9, 111–16, 118–19, 125–27, 130–31; Meynier, *Coups d'état du Directoire*, 1:80–81; excerpt from *Moniteur* (23 July 1797), in Lewis Goldsmith, ed., *Recueil des manifestes, proclamations, discours decrets, etc. de Napoléon Buonaparte . . .* (London: [n.p.], 1810), 31–32.

9. *Démocrate constitutionnel* 2 [n.d.]; Dautry, "Démocrates parisiens," 141–51; *JDHL* (9 Fructidor V); Pierre Serna, "Comment être démocrat et constitutionnel en 1797?" *AHRF* 308, no. 1 (1997): 199–219; Serna, *Antonelle*, 345–52.

10. M. J. Sydenham, *The First French Republic, 1792–1804* (Berkeley: University of California Press, 1973), 125–34; Fryer, *Republic or Restoration*, 201–11.

11. Meynier, *Coups d'état du Directoire*, 1:167–70, 178; "Loi du 19 fructidor an 5," in Aulard, *Paris pendant la réaction*, 4:317–23; Sydenham, *French Revolution*, 151; Woloch, *Jacobin Legacy*, 83–84. Harvey Mitchell and W. R. Fryer question the seriousness of any threat of a royalist coup against the Directory, although Mitchell argues that the directors who staged the Fructidor coup genuinely believed in that danger. See Harvey Mitchell, *The Underground War against Revolutionary France* (Oxford: Clarendon Press, 1965); Fryer, *Republic or Restoration*.

12. Antonelle quoted in Dautry, "Démocrates Parisiens"; provincial journalists in Hugh Gough, "National Politics and the Provincial Jacobin Press during the Directory," *History of European Ideas* 10, no. 4 (1989): 443–54; Benjamin Constant, *Discours prononcé au Cercle constitutionnel pour la plantation de l'arbre de la liberté* (Paris: Imprimerie de la Veuve Galletti, an V); Bernard Gainot, "Benjamin Constant et le Cercle Constitutionnel de 1797: La modération impossible," *AHRF* 357 (July–September 2009): 103–18.

13. Louis Marie Larévellière-Lépeaux, *Réflexions sur le culte, . . . et sur les fêtes nationales* (Paris: H.J. Jansen, an V), 35; James Livesey, *Making Democracy in the French Revolution* (Cambridge, MA: Harvard University Press, 2001), 205–18; "Affaires de l'Intérieur," *La Décade philosophique, littéraire, et politique* 15 (30 Pluviôse VI); François Lamarque, *Rapport fait . . . sur la pétition de plusieurs citoyens acquittés par la haute cour de justice . . .* (Paris: Impr. nationale, an VI).

14. Germain au Directoire exécutif (10 Vendémiaire VI), AN, BB3 21 no. 434; *Petition des . . . condamnés à la déportation . . .* (Paris: Imp. Lamberté, [an VII]), AN, BB3 21 no. 431.

15. The most comprehensive work on constitutional circles is Isser Woloch's *Jacobin Legacy*, on which the following pages rely. See especially 86–99, 116–47, 242–63. For revival of Salmists, *L'Ami des Lois*, in Aulard, *Paris pendant la réaction*, 4:344; Woloch, *Jacobin Legacy*, 76–95. For Antonelle, Jacques Godechot, "Le Directoire vu de Londres," *AHRF* 22, no. 117 (January–March 1950): 6; *Résumé des travaux du Cercle Constitutionnel de la rue du Bacq . . .* (Paris: Imprimerie de la rue de l'Université, [an VI]); M.-J. Satur, *Les Préjugés constitutionnels* (Paris: [n.p.], an VI), 68; Français de Nantes, *Coup-d'oeil rapide sur les moeurs, les lois, les contributions, les secours publics, les sociétés politiques . . .* (Grenoble: P. Cadou & David, ainé, an VI), 5–7 .

16. Aulard, *Paris pendant la réaction*, 4:370; Godechot, "Le Directoire vu de Londres"; *Résumé des travaux du Cercle Constitutionnel de la rue du Bacq . . .*; Woloch, *Jacobin Legacy*, 62, 128, 242–63. The rue du Bac circle, to which Vatar, Eon, and Gaultier belonged, was in the faubourg Saint-Germain. On its elite character, see David Garrioch, *The Making of Revolutionary Paris* (Berkeley: University of California Press, 2002), 317; *Le Tribun du peuple et l'ami des défenseurs de la patrie*, par des associés Prevost et Donnier (22 Fructidor V–11 Nivôse VI).

17. F. E. Lenglet, *De la propriété et de ses rapports avec les droits et avec la dette du citoyen* (Paris: Moutardier, an VI), 59–60; Woloch, *Jacobin Legacy*, 180–85, 154.

18. "Le Directoire exécutif au citoyens de Paris," *Moniteur universel* (19 Fructidor V); Meynier, *Coups d'état du Directoire*, 1:177; Jean-René Suratteau, *Les Elections de l'an VI et le 'Coup d'Etat du 22 Floréal'* (Paris: Les Belles Lettres, 1971), 78–79; Woloch, *Jacobin Legacy*, 62–63; Elizabeth Eisenstein, *The First Professional Revolutionist: Filippo Michele Buonarroti* (Cambridge, MA: Harvard University Press, 1959), 31; Council of Ancients in *Moniteur universel* (1–2 Pluviôse VI).

19. Hugh Gough, *The Newspaper Press in the French Revolution* (London: Routledge, 1988), 141–42, 150–51; *Moniteur* (23 Pluviôse VI); Suratteau, *Elections de l'an VI*, 93; Woloch, *Jacobin Legacy*, 89–92, 123–25, 232–37, 278–79; Meynier, *Coups d'état du Directoire*, 1:56, 177.

20. "Proclamation du directoire exécutif, relative aux élections. Du 28 pluviôse" and "Proclamation du directoire exécutif, aux français, relative aux assemblées primaires de l'an VI. Du 9 ventôse," in *Messages, Arrêtés, et Proclamations du Directoire Exécutif* (Paris: Baudouin, n.d.), 4:375–81, 420–28; Meynier, *Coups d'état du Directoire*, 2:56.

21. Constant, *Discours au Cercle constitutionnel*, 7–8, 10; Woloch, *Jacobin Legacy*, 347.

22. Woloch, *Jacobin Legacy*, 283–85; Suratteau, "Les Babouvistes, le Péril Rouge et le Directoire (1796–1798)," 170–71; Suratteau, *Elections de l'an VI*, 263–91, 186; "Le directoire exécutif aux électeurs de l'an 6," *Moniteur* (4 Germinal VI).

23. Woloch, *Jacobin Legacy*, 288–98, 324.

24. *Tentatives de réaliser le systeme de Babeuf par la voie des élections*, AN, AF III 100.

25. Quoted by Woloch, *Jacobin Legacy*, 332; on Oratoire, 311–43.

26. Woloch, *Jacobin Legacy*, 310; Sydenham, *French Revolution*, 173; Suratteau, *Elections de l'an VI*, 320–25, 407; P.-J.-B. Buchez and P. C. Roux, *Histoire parlementaire de la Révolution française* (Paris: Paulin, 1838), 37:473–79.

27. Speeches by Lamarque, Hardy, and Dubois-Dubay, in Buchez and Roux, *Histoire parlementaire*, 37:479–82.

28. Speeches summarized in Meynier, *Coups d'état du Directoire*, 2:73–76. See also [Courtois], *Précis de ce qui s'est passé dans le département de l'Aube pendant la tenue de l'assemblée eléctorale* (Imprimerie Ant. Bailleur, n.d.); [Forest, Meaudre, Duguet], *Sur les élections du département de la Loire, l'an 6* (Imprimerie Baudouin, l'an VI); *Sur les élections* [n.p., n.d.], BN, Lb42 1816; *Comment faire pour avoir un Roi? ou Dialogue entre Mathurin Bonace et le Docteur Rébus* [Imprimerie Befort, [an VI]), AN, AF III 100; Abbert, *Justice rendu à quelques électeurs* (Imprimerie Courvillot, rue Montmartre, n.d. [an VI]), AN, III 100 442/48; [Hennequin], *Découverte d'une conspiration tendante à renverser le Directoire* (Paris: Imprimerie La Chave, n.d.).

29. Marc Belissa and Yannick Bosc, *Le Directoire: La république sans la démocratie* (Paris: La fabrique éditions, 2018), 248–51; Georges Lefebvre, *The Thermidorians and the Directory*, trans. Robert Baldick (New York: Random House, 1964), 428–32.

30. Sydenham, *First French Republic*, 193, citing Meynier, *Coups d'état du Directoire*, 3:199–200; Bernard Gainot, *1799, un nouveau jacobinisme? La démocratie représentative, une alternative à Brumaire* (Paris: Comité des travaux historiques et scientifiques, 2001), 133–34, 59, 235–45, 502; F.-A. Aulard, "Les derniers Jacobins," *La Révolution française* (1894): 385–407; summary of Félix Lepeletier's *Testament des Jacobins* in Meynier, *Coups d'état du Directoire*, 3:27–28; Max Fajn, *The Journal des hommes libres de tous les pays, 1792–1800* (The Hague: Mouton, 1975), 99–111; Henri Welschinger, *Le journaliste Lebois et l'Ami du Peuple (an III–an VIII)* (Paris: Imprimerie A. Quantin, [1885]), BN, NUMM 5450456.

31. *JDHL* (3 Floréal IV); Serna, *Antonelle*, 374–81; Minchul Kim, "Pierre-Antoine Antonelle and Representative Democracy in the French Revolution," *History of European Ideas* 44, no. 3 (2018): 344–69.

32. Antonelle writing as Bonnefoit, "Quelques définitions à l'ordre du moment," *L'Ennemi des oppresseurs de tous les tems* [continuation of *Journal des hommes libres*] (11, 12 Vendémiaire VII).

33. Serna, *Antonelle*, 374–78.

34. On emergence of party politics in America, see Gordon Wood, *The Radicalism of the American Revolution* (New York: Vintage Books, 1991); Rosemarie Zagarri, "The American Revolution and a New National Politics," in Edward G. Gray and Jane Kamensky, eds., *The Oxford Handbook of the American Revolution* (New York: Oxford University Press, 2013), 483–98; Sean Wilentz, *The Politicians and the Egalitarians: The Hidden History of American Politics* (New York: W. W. Norton, 2016).

On French political crisis of 1799, see Sydenham, *First French Republic*, 191–210; Belissa and Bosc, *Directoire*, 253; Victor Bach, *Premier Discours du citoyen Bach à la reunion séant au Manège* . . . (Paris: de l'Imprimerie de Benoist, n.d.).

35. See pamphlets 9925–27, 9958, in Maurice Tourneux, *Bibliographie de l'histoire de Paris pendant la Révolution française* (Paris: Imprimerie nationale, 1890–1913), 2:455–59; Gainot, *1799?* 238–43; Woloch, *Jacobin Legacy*, 383–85; Meynier, *Coups d'état du Directoire*, 3:19–28; Fajn, *The Journal des hommes libres*, 100.

36. Alan Schom, *Napoleon Bonaparte* (Norwalk, CT: Easton Press, 2001), 194–221; Isser Woloch, *Napoleon and His Collaborators: The Making of a Dictatorship* (New York: W. W. Norton, 2002), 3–35.

37. Woloch, *Napoleon and His Collaborators*, 66–80.

Chapter 15. Buonarroti's Gospel

1. Taffoureau to Executive Directory (25 Prairial V), AN, F7 4276; Breton et femme to Executive Directory (29 Messidor V), AN, BB3 22; Minister of Justice to Executive Directory (2 Thermidor V), AN, AF III 42; François Lamarque, *Rapport fait* . . . *sur la pétition de plusieurs citoyens acquittés par la haute cour de justice* . . . (Paris: Impr. nationale, an VI); Pillé to Minister of Police (23 Floréal IV), AN, W563; Robert Legrand, *Babeuf et ses compagnons de route* (Paris, 1981), 336–37.

2. Janette Ponser, in Legrand, *Babeuf et ses compagnons*, 390; Guilhem and wife to Charles Germain (n.d.), AN, F7 4276.

3. Richard Cobb, *The Police and the People* (Oxford: Clarendon Press, 1970), 154–71.

4. Isser Woloch, *Napoleon and His Collaborators* (New York: W. W. Norton, 2002), 66–80; Cordas is mentioned as a representative for the Lombards section, in *PS*, 1:73.

5. Legrand, *Babeuf et ses compagnons*, 318, 373, 255–57; Pierre Baudrier, "Qu'advint-il de Lamberté, Claire Privat et Pignatel?" *Généalogie et Histoire de la Caraibe* 152 (October 2002): 3636, http://www.ghcaraibe.org/bul/ghc152/som152.html; Linda Schneider and Sheila Lee, *Louisiana Newspaper Project, Parish and Chronological Indexes*, LNP Special Collections, LSU Libraries, Baton Rouge, 2003. Thanks to Pierre Baudrier for resurrecting Lamberté by sharing information about his second life in New Orleans. See also F. Larue-Langlois, "Lamberté en Louisiane," *Etudes Babouvistes de l'Association des Amis de Gracchus Babeuf* 4–5 (2007): 76–82.

6. Legrand, *Babeuf et ses compagnons*, 392.

7. Paul Benoît François Bontoux, *Rapport fait par Bontoux* . . . *chargée d'examiner la pétition du citoyen Pierre-Nicolas Hezine* . . . (Paris: [n.p.], 1797); R. Bouis, "P.-N. Hésine, rédacteur du 'Journal de la Haute-Cour ou l'Echo des Hommes vrais et sensibles,' " *AHRF* 32, no. 162 (October–December 1960): 471–87; R. Bouis, "Hésine et les Babouvistes sous l'Empire et la Restauration," *AHRF* 33, no. 163 (January–March 1961): 88–91; R. Bouis, "Le patriote Pierre Nicolas Hésine: Ses luttes ardentes en Loir-et-Cher," *Bulletin de la Société archeologique, scientifique et*

littéraire du Vendômois (1973): 61–74, at 71–72; Isser Woloch, *Jacobin Legacy: The Democratic Movement under the Directory* (Princeton, NJ: Princeton University Press, 1970), 243n.

8. Pierre Serna, *Antonelle aristocrate* (Paris: Éditions du Félin, 1997), 434, 391–441.

9. Louis Bigard, *Le comte Réal, ancien Jacobin* (Paris: Firmin-Didot, 1937), 117; Mathieu-Guillaume-Thérèse Villenave, "Pierre-François Réal," in Louis-Gabriel Michaud, *Biographie universelle ancienne et moderne* (Paris: Michaud Beck, 1811–28); Woloch, *Jacobin Legacy*, 338.

10. Réal (16 Floréal VI), quoted in Bigard, *Le comte Réal*, 115–16. On his role in the Brumaire coup, Alan Schom, *Napoleon Bonaparte* (New York: Harper Collins, 1998), 210–16; Jean Tulard, *Joseph Fouché* (Paris: Fayard, 1998), 111–18, 135–36; Bigard, *Le comte Réal*, 121–72.

11. Bigard, *Le comte Réal*, 129, 134–35; Woloch, *Napoleon and His Collaborators,* 66–80, 211; Jean-Guillaume Locré, *Discussions sur la liberté de la presse, la censure, la propriété littéraire . . .* (Paris: [n.p.], 1819), 50–52.

12. Bigard, *Le comte Réal*, 129; Georges Lefebvre, *Napoleon*, trans. H. F. Stockhold (New York: Columbia University Press, 1969), 2:194.

13. This is Isser Woloch's argument in *Napoleon and His Collaborators*.

14. Arthur Lehning, "Buonarroti and His International Secret Societies," *International Review of Social History* 1 (1956): 112–40; Legrand, *Babeuf et ses compagnons*, 346; Georges Weill, "Philippe Buonarroti (1761–1837)," *Revue historique* 76 (May–August 1901): 241–75, at 258–59; James Billington, *Fire in the Minds of Men: Origins of the Revolutionary Faith* (New Brunswick, NJ: Transaction, 1999), 137; Alexandre Andryane, *Mémoires d'un prisonnier d'état* (Paris: Olivier-Fulgence, 1840).

15. Alessandro Gallante Garonne, "Filippo Buonarroti e Il Convenzionali in esilio (Dalle carte inedite della famiglia Vadier)," *Movimento operaio: Rivista di storia e bibliografia* 5, no. 3 (May–June 1953): 3–65, at 13–22; Sergio Luzzatto, "Un futur au passé: La Révolution dans les Mémoires des Conventionnels," *AHRF* 278 (1989): 455–75.

16. Filippo Buonarroti, *La conspiration pour l'égalité, dite de Babeuf* (Paris: Éditions sociales, 1957), 1:19.

17. Buonarroti names his heroes as Montagnards rather than Jacobins, narrowing the elite further from club members to legislators. Buonarroti, *Conspiration*, 1:41, 44, 46, 51–53.

18. Buonarroti, *Conspiration*, 1:86, 100. On Pantheon Club, Buonarroti, *Conspiration*, 1:75–77; Albert Mathiez, *Le Directoire* (Paris: A. Colin, 1934), 141–59; Ch. Picquenard, "La société du Panthéon et le parti patriote à Paris," *Révolution française* 33 (1897): 318–48.

19. Buonarroti, *Conspiration*, 1:24.

20. Buonarroti, *Conspiration*, 1:79–81.

21. Buonarroti, *Conspiration*, 1:165–67, 189.

22. Marx and Engels argued that Babeuf's reformulation of communism from utopian dream to revolutionary aim was his principal contribution to the history of communism. Karl Marx and Friedrich Engels, *The Holy Family*, chap. 6, 3c, "Critical Battle against the French Revolution," https://www.marxists.org/archive/marx/works/1845/holy-family/ch06_3_c.htm. Stephanie Roza makes Babeuf's turn from utopianism to pragmatic organizing the centerpiece of her book, *Comment l'utopie est devenue un programme politique: Du roman à la Révolution* (Paris: Classiques Garnier, 2015). See also Jean Bruhat, "La Révolution française et la formation de la pensée de Marx," *AHRF* 38, no. 184 (1966): 125–70.

23. Buonarroti, *Conspiration*, 1:192–201, 198, 186, 195–96, 209. For Babeuf's criticism of hierarchical political organizing, see Gracchus Babeuf, *Du systeme de dépopulation, ou la vie et les crimes du Carrier* (Paris: Imprimerie Franklin, [1794]), 17–23.

24. Gracchus Babeuf, "Lueurs philosophiques," in Philippe Riviale, ed., *Gracchus Babeuf: Oeuvres* (Paris: L'Harmattan, 2016), 1:259; *PS*, 2:52.

25. Buonarroti, *Conspiration*, 1:195.

26. Elizabeth Eisenstein, *The First Professional Revolutionist: Filippo Michele Buonarroti* (Cambridge, MA: Harvard University Press, 1959), 65; Pia Onnis, "Filippo Buonarroti, la congiura di Babeuf e al Babouvismo," *Nuova rivista storica* 36–37 (1952–53): 489–514. Twenty-first-century editions include Philippe Buonarroti, *Conspiration pour l'Égalité dite de Babeuf*, with essays by Jean-Marc Schiappa, Stéphanie Roza, Alain Maillard, Jean-Numa Décange (Montreuil: La ville brûle, 2014); Philippe Buonarroti, *Conspiration pour l'Égalité dite de Babeuf*, with introduction by Sabrina Berkane (Paris: La fabrique, 2015); *Vivere eguali: Dialoghi inediti intorno a Filippo Buonarroti*, trans. and introd. Alessandro Galante Garrone, Franco Venturi, and Manuela Albertone (Reggio Emilia: Diabasis, 2009); *Cospirazione per l'eguaglianza detta di Babeuf*, trans. and introd. Gastone Manacorda (Milan: Pantarei, 2011).

27. Marc-Antoine Baudot, *Notes historiques sur la Convention nationale, le Directoire, l'Empire . . .* (Paris: Imprimerie de la Cerf, 1893; Geneva: Slatkine-Megariotis Reprints, 1974), 19; Bronterre O'Brien, "To the Reader," in *Buonarroti's History of Babeuf's Conspiracy for Equality* (London: H. Hetherington, 1836), xiv; "Conspiration pour l'égalité, dite de Babeuf," *Quarterly Review* 45 (April–June 1831).

28. Pamela Pilbeam, "The Insurrectionary Tradition in France 1835–48," *Modern & Contemporary France* 1, no. 3 (1993): 253–64; Pamela Pilbeam, *French Socialists before Marx: Workers, Women and the Social Question in France* (Montreal: McGill-Queen's University Press, 2000), 30–32; Ian Birchall, *The Spectre of Babeuf* (New York: St. Martin's Press, 1997), 86–96; Claude Mazauric, "Buonarroti et l'archaisme révolutionnaire: Re-lecture de la Conspiration pour l'égalité," in *Jacobinisme et révolution* (Paris: Messidor/Éditions sociales, 1984).

29. Eisenstein, *First Professional Revolutionist*, 93–150; Alessandro Galante Garrone, *Philippe Buonarroti et les révolutionnaires du XIXe siècle (1828–1837)*, trans. Anne

and Claude Manceron (Paris: Éditions Champ Libre, 1975), 129–33; Pilbeam, *French Socialists before Marx*, 30–32.

30. Alain Maillard, *La Communauté des Egaux: Le communisme néo-babouviste dans la France des années 1840* (Paris: Kimé, 1999), 152–88.

31. Jonathan Sperber, *Karl Marx: A Nineteenth-Century Life* (New York: W. W. Norton, 2013), 108–52; Antony Burlaud, "La France selon Marx," in Jean-Numa Ducange and Antony Burlaud, eds., *Marx, une passion française* (Paris: Éditions La Découverte, 2018), 15–28.

32. Quoted in Michael Löwy, *The Theory of Revolution in the Young Marx* (Leiden: Brill, 2003), 90. My account of Marx's time in Paris and its impact on his thinking is based on Löwy's reading.

33. Marx and Engels, *The Holy Family*, chap. 6, 3c; Hal Draper, with the assistance of Stephen F. Diamond, *Karl Marx's Theory of Revolution*, vol. 3: *The Dictatorship of the Proletariat* (New York: Monthly Review Press, 1986), 122–23.

34. Marx and Engels, *German Ideology*, quoted in Löwy, *Theory of Revolution*, 112.

35. On Marx, Engels, and the French Revolution, see Marx and Engels, *The Holy Family*, chap. 6, 3c. See also Jean Bruhat, "La Révolution française et la formation de la pensée de Marx," *AHRF* 38, no. 184 (1966): 125–70, at 160; Michael Löwy, "The Poetry of the Past: Marx and the French Revolution," *New Left Review* 1, no. 177 (September–October 1989): 111–24.

Conclusion

1. *Débats*, 3:218.

2. *Rédacteur* (3 Prairial IV).

3. See, for example, James Livesey, *Making Democracy in the French Revolution* (Cambridge, MA: Harvard University Press, 2001), 239–44.

4. JDHL (24 Prairial V).

INDEX

Illustrations are indicated by page numbers in *italics*.